Nine Rules For Driving & Discovering Oahu

9

1. LOOK BEHIND YOU AS YOU GO. Otherwise, you'll be missing half the beauty and *at least* as many photo opportunities.

2. DON'T BE AFRAID OF DEAD ENDS. Dead ends repel crowds, as well as tour buses. Drive to the end of the road.

3. GET OUT OF THE CAR. When you reach that dead end, get out and walk for a few minutes, and you may find a scenic lookout, hidden beach, or bubbling stream that is not in the guidebooks... in addition to blessed solitude —and the real Hawaii.

4. STOP AT ROADSIDE LUNCH WAGONS EVEN IF YOU'RE NOT HUNGRY. Banter with other customers. They are a source of hot local information and advice that will enhance your visit.

5. PICK UP THE FREE VISITOR MAGAZINES. *This Week*, *Spotlight* and *Island Guide* are loaded with coupons and things to do. But be mindful that they benefit their advertisers as well as you. The real Hawaii, the most beautiful and rewarding Hawaii, doesn't cost anything.

6. BUY AN ICE CHEST. Many a potentially wonderful island experience has been cut short by growling stomachs. Don't build your day around the proximity of restaurants. Bring your own. Have a picnic in an unforgettable place.

LIVE LIKE A NATIVE. Get up early and revel in the beauty of the island dawn. Get out of town before the commuters leave and the road crews start tearing up the pavement. Order steamed rice and half a papaya with your morning eggs, instead of hashbrowns. Shop for food in Chinatown, at local farmers' markets and at the Holiday Mart. Listen to the Hawaiian music stations as you explore the island. Buy the daily newspaper to find wonderful keiki (children's) hula contests, local carnivals and church huli-hulis (chicken barbeques), surf contests, Hawaiian song competitions, orchid and anthurium shows, the State Fair.

8. TAKE LOTS OF PICTURES. When you think about it, photographs are miraculous. They are a vivid depiction of a moment in time on a little piece of paper – a veritable pocket-sized memory. No amount of verbal description can ever convey what a photograph can with just one glance. People often regret not taking enough pictures, but rarely do they regret taking too many.

9. LISTEN FOR DIRECTIONS — ISLAND STYLE. On a small island, the terms Mauka and Makai are invaluable— and simple. *Mauka* means toward the mountains. You can remember it this way: the first three letters in both Mauka and Mountain sound the same. *Makai* means toward the sea. *Kai* is a word you will see a lot in Hawaii: it means *sea*.

Published by:

Montgomery Ewing Publishers
1746 Griffith Park Blvd.
Los Angeles CA 90026
USA

Driving & Discovering Oahu was written, designed, photographed, and illustrated by Richard Sullivan
Entire contents © 1993 by Richard Sullivan and Montgomery Ewing Publishers
All rights reserved

Library of Congress
Catalog Number 93-78114

Sullivan, Richard, 1949-
Driving & Discovering Oahu /
Richard Sullivan – 1st edition
ISBN 0-9636828-8-1
1. Oahu (Hawaii) – Description and Travel–
Guidebooks – Photography Books

Coming soon from
Montgomery Ewing Publishers:

Driving & Discovering Maui
Driving & Discovering The Big Island
Driving & Discovering California Hwy. 1 /
Northern California

Driving & Discovering Oahu is dedicated to two extraordinary human beings:

for
Alain-Paul Sevilla

without whose encouragement, patience, and support this book would not exist,

and
Felix Rodriguez Jr.

Although his footprints have disappeared from Hawaii's sands, Felix's spirit will live forever in the hearts and souls of all who loved him.

A volume as packed with information as Driving & Discovering Oahu needs input from scores of sources, most of them human.

Kamaainas from Ka'a'awa to Kawailoa went well out of their way to make sure we included every site on Oahu that they feel says "This is Hawaii". For all those people who shared their secret places, smiling faces, and warm embraces with us, *nui mahalo*.

Special thanks to Denise Takashima, for cherished years of friendship, encouragement and advice.

Heartfelt thanks to:

My Parents, Jeanne & Harry Schwartz
Maya Leland
D. Harry Montgomery
Gordon Kai
Tony Vericella
Gene Yokoi
Larry Clemmons
Donna Sullivan
Rosemary Rodriguez
Jeanne Datz and Hilton Hotels Hawaii
Sandy Wann/Aston Waikiki Sunset
John Clark
Lindy Boyes and the Hawaii Visitors Bureau
B.J. Hughes
Sheila Donnelly
Cliff Weinberg
Jim Wood, Ogilvy & Mather Honolulu
Joyce Matsumoto, Halekulani Hotel
Bennett Hymer, Mutual Publishing, Honolulu
Jip Inglis
David Humphrey
Barbara Hobbs
Rob Solomon
Jerry Hulse, Los Angeles Times
Alfred Lea Beck
Jim Griglak, Los Angeles Magazine
Dan Poynter
Bill Haig
Linda Mitsunaga
Jody and Steve Hayward

TO:
Jacqueline Baladi, for being there all along.
Jean Lorrain and Kevin O'Sullivan, for introducing me to Hawaii the very first time.
Alex Lopez, for showing me the future.

Kodak Fun Saver Camera Photos:
Page 5, #5
Page 6
Page 19, #6

Contents

Driving & Discovering
Oahu

Photographs:

Page 2: Anthuriums shot in studio with direct tungsten lighting and white and colored artcard used as a backdrop. The seams in the paper were hidden behind the flower stems. 4X5 Ektachrome 64 Tungsten film.

Page 3, Top: Waimea Falls, North Shore.
Page 3, Bottom: Aikahi Park, Kailua, Windward Shore.
Page 112: The view from the Kaiwa Ridge Trail, above Lanikai, Windward Shore.
All: Kodachrome 64 film.

Oahu
Just Picture It.

❶

❸

❹

❷

*T*he island of Oahu offers visitors and kamaainas alike some of the most stunning photographic opportunities on this planet. Whether you use a camera that's as simple as the single-use Kodak Fun Saver, a top-of-the-line electronic model, or a sophisticated video camera, the photographic possibilities of a lifetime surround you here.

Oahu's waterscapes are colored in countless hues of blues and greens. Billowing clouds, pushed along by the tradewinds, swiftly race around the skies, colliding silently with lush green mountaintops. Rains falling high atop the sculpted pali —Oahu's sheer corrugated mountainsides— turn each and every crevasse into a waterfall conduit. Ethereal veils of white score these majestic razorback ramparts all along the Windward Coast for as far as the eye can see. Oahu's special combination of wild seascapes, pastoral landscapes, pristine air, brilliantly hued tropical flowers and blossoming trees, gorgeous sunsets and beautiful friendly people provide unlimited photo opportunities.

As you can see, each photo in our destination spreads is assigned a number, and is represented on the maps by a corresponding number —and camera symbols— enabling the photo enthusiast to find the exact spot where the shot was taken. Whether you are a professional shooter or an amateur, a video enthusiast, an artist, a film or TV location scout, or a repeat visitor with a yen for new experiences, ***Driving & Discovering Oahu*** will prove invaluable in helping you locate dozens of beautiful and previously unpublished Oahu locations.

For those serious about improving their landscape and travel photos, an important consideration will be their willingness to go where the scene will be at its best at the appropriate time of day, despite possible inconvenience.

Use the photographs throughout this guide as examples and starting points to create different

versions of these shots for yourself. Perhaps you could shoot one of our midday views at sunrise or sunset, or when the sky is bluer or the water calmer. Thanks to the myriad possibilities presented by Oahu's ever changing weather and lighting conditions, its impossible to "copy" anyone else's photograph.

Film Tips

Negative (print) film is far more forgiving of exposure error than transparency (slide) film. The choice of which to use depends on what your final goal for your photographs is.

Choose negative film if beautiful fine art display prints or snapshots for your album are your goal.

Choose transparency film if you are putting together a slide presentation, or if the publication of your photos is their purpose.

But remember, with transparencies, what you shoot is what you get. If the slide is overexposed –too light– then there's not much you can do to save it. If it turns out dark —underexposed– then it too might be a lost cause.

Two options for salvaging dark slides include having them duplicated lighter (use a professional film lab for best quality), or having "R" prints made, indicating to the lab that you want them printed *lighter* than the dark slide. Make your instructions known by meeting face to face with the lab tech. He or she will tell you what is possible in your case, and what you might expect as a final result. A talented lab technician can work miracles with dark slides. I cringe when I think of how many I threw away before I discovered these methods of retrieval.

Often, especially in scenes with white sand or snow, your camera's light meter can be fooled into giving a wrong exposure. In this case the printed exposure information that comes with

Kodak films is quite often more accurate than your own meter in these situations.

If shooting transparencies, try getting into the habit of **bracketing** your exposures. For example, if your camera's meter, or the exposure chart printed on the film box, indicates that you should shoot a particular photo at F11, then do that. But also shoot the same photo at F13 (one half F stop above) and at F9.5 (one half F stop below) the meter reading. Personally, I shoot *five* different brackets for *each* photo I take on transparency film. If my meter indicates shooting the photo at F11, I do that. But, I also expose the same shot at F13 *and* at F16 (one half F stop and one full F stop smaller than F11), *and* then at F9.5 and F8 (one half F stop and one full F stop larger than F11). That works out to a total of five different exposures just to insure that I end up with a perfectly exposed version of that shot. Its well worth it.

No light meter has yet been devised that can calculate exactly the most visually pleasing exposure. Only when comparing the processed results can you decide which is the best version to your own eye, and its often not the one that is the camera recommended exposure. When the shot is important —and most of the time it is— I bracket widely.

It is not as critical for good results to bracket print film, but if you are serious about getting great pictures, and the finest possible end result, you'll try it. Compare your prints side by side after they come back from being processed, noting which one was the camera's exposure choice. Often you will find that the quality of one of the bracketed exposures will be better than the camera recommended exposure. Bracketing can make all the difference between an acceptable quality and a *great* quality result. If the results from your usual lab are disappointing, ask around to find the best custom color or black and white lab in your vicinity. Take the offending photos and

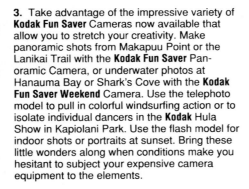

Photographs

1. Cheryl Naluai at the Polynesian Cultural Center.

2. The Iolani Palace is decorated in Hawaii's colors for special occasions.

3. The Hokule'a sails into a dawn sun shower.

4. The Royal Hawaiian Hotel at sunset. Photos 1-4 & 6: **Kodachrome 64**

5. Man meets Dog in the usual way at Sunset Beach. **Kodak Fun Saver Panoramic camera**

6. A rainbow appears over Round Top Drive in the late afternoon.

negatives there and explain the problem. Ask if they could do a better job, You may end up paying more than you're used to, but for those special shots it can really be worth it. A skillful lab can often work what seems like miracles.

As far as fancy photo equipment is concerned, remember: its not the camera that takes great pictures, its the photographer. A good photographer can get great results from the simplest of cameras. As an example, most of the photos in this book were taken with professional Canon camera equipment, but there are a few shots that were taken with **Kodak**'s single use **Fun Saver** cameras, which sell for around $10. Try and guess which ones. You'll find the answer at the bottom of page 2, and we think you'll be surprised. Check out the daily newspapers on Oahu for local sales and specials on **Kodak Fun Saver** Cameras and **Kodak** films. Great prices can be had especially at the Holiday Mart and at Long's Drugs. For creative ideas, check out the book section at photo stores. One personal favorite source for inspiration is the **Communication Arts Photography Annual**, published each year in August. Beautifully printed, and crammed with gorgeous work, it is priced at well under $20 –a real bargain. The **CA Annual** is available at art supply stores.

Here are some final tips for creating your best travel photos, ever:

1. For "people pictures" shot at midday when the harsh sun is overhead, or when the sun is low and beside or behind your subject, activate your flash to fill in the facial shadows. Take one version with flash and one without. Compare the results, and you won't ever be shy about using flash in broad daylight again.

2. Go about your picture taking with a real purpose, as if you have been given a magazine assignment. Plan the kinds of shots you want to take, using **Driving & Discovering Oahu** as your guide, and organize your day so you can

be where you think the picture will be at the time you think is best.

3. Take advantage of the impressive variety of **Kodak Fun Saver** Cameras now available that allow you to stretch your creativity. Make panoramic shots from Makapuu Point or the Lanikai Trail with the **Kodak Fun Saver** Panoramic Camera, or underwater photos at Hanauma Bay or Shark's Cove with the **Kodak Fun Saver Weekend** Camera. Use the telephoto model to pull in colorful windsurfing action or to isolate individual dancers in the **Kodak** Hula Show in Kapiolani Park. Use the flash model for indoor shots or portraits at sunset. Bring these little wonders along when conditions make you hesitant to subject your expensive camera equipment to the elements.

4. In areas where the view is so expansive that you can't fit it all into your frame, take photographs of the vista in sections, and piece them together later, David Hockney style. The example you see on pages 12 & 13 is a 340 degree view taken at stunning Kaiwa Ridge in Lanikai. This time-honored technique has been employed since the beginning of photography, but it took Hockney to widely popularize it as a serious art form. Try also mounting your prints side by side, leaving a small space between, as seen in the *Makapuu* and *Kailua* sections.

5. Keep your fingers away from the lens, and clean the lens often with **Kodak** Lens Cleaning Tissue. This is especially important with inexpensive non-SLR cameras where you do not look through the lens. Salt spray buildup will cloud the lens very quickly. Beware of the rough, damaging lens tissue often found in

bargain lens cleaning kits. *Never put lens cleaning fluid directly on a lens, only on the lens tissue itself.* In a real pinch, the corner of a soft, non-sweaty all-cotton T-shirt can be used if nothing else is available.

6. The rule for choosing film speed is simple: The higher the ISO (also called ASA) number, the greater the film's sensitivity to light, –but the less sensitive it is to subtle differences in color. In the low light of the rainforest you'll need a 400 ISO/ASA film or faster. In the bright sun, anything rated between ISO/ASA 25 and 100 will capture all those stunning island colors beautifully and brilliantly.

7. And finally, here is one classic bit of photo advice that bears repeating: **hold that camera steady while tripping the shutter**. The more inexpensive your camera is, the more critical this advice is. Press the camera gently but firmly against your face, making sure your fingers do not stray in front of the lens, and *hold your breath as you take the shot.* Be sure that nothing moves except your shutter finger.

So now go out and take *lots* of photographs. People often regret not taking enough pictures, but rarely do they regret taking too many.

14 Miles of deserted BEACHES

Because Waikiki is so crowded, and because it gets the lion's share of attention and publicity, many visitors are unaware of how truly beautiful and unspoiled the rest of the island really is.

Driving & Discovering Oahu's purpose is to dispel these misconceptions and open the visitor's eyes as to what awaits just minutes from his hotel room.

No Hawaiian island has more beaches, better beaches, than Oahu.

During the week, even the most popular beach parks will be virtually deserted. But the beaches presented here offer a special opportunity to be alone on long, isolated stretches of sandy Hawaiian seashore, where you will see few, if any, other people.

Mokuleia to Kaena Point
4 1/2 miles / page 94

Mokuleia's beautiful clear turquoise waters perfectly complement Kaena Point State Park's wild and protected seashore. They are linked together on the westernmost part of Oahu's North Shore, and given the isolated nature of their location, personal solitude is almost guaranteed —except on weekends. Because most visitors are interested in the more developed, famous big wave surfing beaches to the northeast, they don't venture much beyond Haleiwa town, leaving the beaches in this district virtually deserted during the week. At 4 1/2 miles in length, and paralleling a dead end road, there is an ocean of room here for you to get lost in your private thoughts.

Kahuku to Turtle Bay
5 miles / page 76

Just north of Malaekahana State Park, the KAMEHAMEHA (83) HWY. begins to veer inland for the four road miles to Turtle Bay. There are no public access roads to the beach within this area, and the resulting isolation has preserved an impressively large chunk of pristine Oahu coastline for those willing to expend the leg power to visit it. Probably thousands of visitors a week pass right by this spectacular, isolated 5 mile length of island seashore paradise, and sadly, unaware of its existence. Even on weekends, you will probably be alone here. Although lacking in safe swimming spots, there are a few, including this lovely miniature lagoon along mile-long Kaihalulu Beach. It is protected from the North Shore's furious breakers even in winter, when this shot was taken. The Turtle Bay Hilton's Kuilima Cove has safe, year-round, lifeguard-protected swimming, and it is open to the public.

Keaau Beach to Kaena Point
7 1/2 miles / pages 108-111

On Oahu's sunny, dry Leeward Shore, all of the beaches are spectacular. Comparatively few visitors venture to the Leeward side, and they're all the poorer for it. Just beyond the world famous winter breakers at Makaha

Beach, the coast quickly becomes depopulated. The black lava shoreline welcomes the white foam of breaking waves, and between these ramparts of ebony rock lie long stretches of wonderful deserted beaches. The further northwest one travels, the more deserted it becomes. The paved road ends at Yokohama Beach, compelling those who wish to continue along the wild and rugged Kaena Point State Park seashore to hike the trail that follows the old dismantled Oahu Railway route. Although almost abandoned during the week, this area is heavily used by fishermen and family groups on weekends.

And these three aren't even the whole story...

Most beaches everywhere on Oahu, except perhaps along the touristy South Shore, will be virtually empty during the week.

Other best bets include some true beauties:

Queen's Beach
(Page 44)
Kokololio Beach
(Page 74)
Malaekahana State Beach
(Page 74)
Kawela Bay
(Page 80)
Kawailoa Beach
(Page 88)

For the definitive last word on Oahu's beaches, their physical conditions and history, check out **John R. K. Clark's The Beaches Of Oahu,** published by University of Hawaii Press.

Available in Hawaii at all Honolulu Bookshops and Waldenbooks locations.

❷

Photographs

1. Mokuleia Army Beach on Oahu's western North Shore is wide, long and sandy, with crystal clear turquoise waters and reefs that attract slipper lobsters and shy but colorful fish.

2. Kaihalulu Beach lies along a five mile stretch of unvisited shoreline between Kahuku and Turtle Bay. This tiny sheltered lagoon offers one of the few places to safely, and comfortably, enter the water along this exposed coast.

3. Moku'auia Beach is one of three on little Goat Island. Situated in a protected bay, the shore bottom is sandy and slopes gradually to deeper waters. We think its Oahu's most perfect deserted beach.

Photo 1: **Kodak Fun Saver** Panoramic Camera.

Photos 2 & 3: **Kodachrome 64**

❸

UNINHABITED

HAWAIIAN
ISLANDS

Deserted Islands...

...are the stuff of legends, Hollywood films and escapist office daydreams. When times get tough, we entertain the possibility of chucking it all to retire to an uninhabited tropical isle so we can just bake away our troubles in the sun.

Of all the magical Hawaiian places enfolded in the arms of goddess Pele, none is more bewitching or magnetic than Windward Oahu's emerald necklace of uninhabited islands. Tantalizingly close, they beckon the curious and adventurous to come and explore. Two of the most beautiful of these, Chinaman's Hat and Goat Island, can in fact be reached by adults on foot at low tide when seas are calm. With the tide table cut from the daily news-paper's weather page as their guide, locals time their journey on foot for when the tide is still going out and conditions are very calm —and predicted to stay that way. If you'd rather be on top of the water than in it, rented kayaks, surfboards, inflatable rafts, chartered boats or hired local fishermen are all employed as modes of transportation for island tripping. If being alone is not a requirement, commercial boat trips are available from Heeia Pier (pg. 60) that run excursions to the Kaneohe Sandbars. Besides those islands included here, many others have been set aside exclusively as bird sanctuaries where the landing of wingless creatures is not allowed. But individuals with ecological or scientific interests may be able to obtain permission to visit from the Division of Fish & Game.

Chinaman's Hat
Pages 66-69

The most distinctively shaped island of this group, Chinaman's Hat is also among the most beguiling. It is close to shore and located away from population centers. Its assets include a little mountain, tidepools, sea caves, and two beaches, one of which is located in a lovely secluded cove facing the open sea and hidden from onshore eyes. Deserted during the week, Chinaman's Hat becomes a magnet for Kualoa Beach Park's visitors on weekends. Sunrises here are unforgettable.

Flat Island
Page 56

Located offshore from popular Kailua Beach Park, little Popia Island, also known as Flat Is-land, gets quite crowded on weekends, when ev-ery flotation device imaginable is used by local kids and grown-ups alike to get there. But during the week, its a safe bet that it will be just you and the sea turtles. There's no beach to speak of, and as its name implies, its as flat as a pancake. But it offers solitude, and wonderful views of the shore, the bay, and its mountainous twin neigh-bors, the Moku Luas.

The Moku Lua Islands
Page 56

Next door to Flat Island, and offshore from Lanikai Beach, lie the jewel-like twin Moku Lua isles. Of the two, only Moku Nui (the one on the left as you face them from shore) is open for landing. Visitors are restricted to the beach area so as not to step on the many seabird nests. This gorgeous island boasts a superb beach, an impressive double-humped moun-tain, and stunning offshore views. Its smaller twin, Moku Iki, lacks a beach, and officially, landing on it is not permitted. Again, there could be dozens of people here on the weekend, but during the week it will most likely be all yours. You'll need to rent a kayak to get here.

Rabbit Island
Page 48

❹

Also known by its Hawaiian name, *Manana Island*, Rabbit Island itself is officially off limits without permission from the Dept. of Fish and Game. But its perfect waves attract surfers who paddle over from Makapuu on their surfboards, and divers come on boats to explore the reefs. Currents in the area are treacherous, so those who get a permit to land must be sure that their mode of transport is reliable and seaworthy. Don't try to kayak-it over here unless you're an expert. Rabbit Island is bone dry, with dramatic high sea cliffs, a long, sandy, shore-facing beach, and a large volcanic crater that is home to thousands of nesting seabirds.

Goat Island
Page 74

Right offshore from Malaekahana Bay State Recreation Area, arguably Oahu's most beautiful beach park, is perhaps the most idyllic of all the uninhabited windward islands. With three lovely beaches on its shores, it too is easily reached by adults on foot, at low tide, in calm seas only, over a reef that stretches from Cooke's Point. It has the most perfect beach of all the little islands... a little ironwood tree shaded, flawless white sand crescent called *Moku'auia*. Located on a shore-facing, protected and picturesque little bay, Moku'auia's welcoming sandy shore bottom slopes gradually into deeper waters. Goat Island is the ideal get away from it all place.

Photographs

1. Chinaman's Hat
2. Moku Nui
3. Chinaman's Hat
4. Goat Island

all photos:
Kodachrome 64

Kaneohe Bay Sandbars
Page 62

When the tide goes out in stunning Kaneohe Bay, dozens of snow-white sandbars emerge from the azure waters as tiny, perfect, temporary little islands. Of all the surrounding island waters featured on this page, enormous Kaneohe Bay's are the most placid and calm...good news for novice kayakers. A couple of commercial outfits run group excursions to visit the sandbars from Heeia Pier, but there are plenty to go around for everybody. The views of the huge turquoise bay, and the pali that ring it, are definitely remarkable.

❸

Most Hawaiian fantasies include a tumbling waterfall, a refreshing pool, and someone special to share them with.

(hidden) *Waterfalls*

Manoa Falls / Page 22

Manoa Falls is a beautiful series of cascades that tumbles down the face of a fern-faced cliff into a clear, *slippery*, chilly pool. On a 5'8" adult the pool depth reaches mid-chest at its deepest point. The trail that leads to the falls is spooky and beautiful with networks of sinuous tree roots lain across the pathway. Manoa Stream is always within gurgling distance of the trail, which is bordered by ginger, giant ferns, brilliant orange blossomed African Tulip trees, and juicy edible mountain apple. What sets Manoa Falls apart from any other fall on Oahu is that its wilderness setting is astonishingly close to Waikiki. Indeed, the falls can be clearly seen from mountain-facing Waikiki high-rise windows, especially after a rain.

Maakua Falls / Page 72

Maakua Falls is at the end of the Maakua Gulch Trail in one of the most isolated places on the island of Oahu. A lovely little cascade is your reward for a difficult 3 hour trek into a magical narrow canyon. One of three trails in the Hauula Trail System, it is deemed difficult because most of the trail is the slippery streambed itself. Obstacles aside, this is one for the adventurous and determined, and for those wanting a true wilderness experience on the island of Oahu. We recommend joining a group hike sponsored by the Sierra Club or the Hawaiian Trail and Mountain Club for this one. Call for their schedules.

Sacred Falls / Page 72

Sacred Falls is located within Sacred Falls State Park about a mile south of Hauula and the Maakua Gulch Trail. One of the most popular Falls on the island, its lovely 87' cascade plunges into a chilly pool surrounded by large flat rocks perfect for drying yourself on or for spreading out a picnic. This trail is a long one, about a four hour round trip.

Maunawili Falls / Page 60

Maunawili is a little known place close to Kailua town, just over the PALI (61) HWY. from Honolulu. Just a 30 minute hike from the start

of the trail, the pool at Maunawili Falls is deep and the lower waterfall, seen here, is about 20' high. There is another cascade above and behind it, but there's no easy way to get to it.

Waimea Falls / Page 84

Waimea Falls is a wonderful cascade within the confines of remarkable Waimea Falls Park (admission charge). The Park presents diving exhibitions from the 45' high brink into the deep pool below. Visitors are invited to swim and enjoy the water also, and there is a *lifeguard on duty*. This is the ideal choice for those who love waterfalls, but hate hiking into them. The Park runs trams that take visitors through its exhibit and garden areas. The property is criss-crossed with lovely, easy to negotiate trails that pass many native and exotic species of plants, which are all marked for easy identification. On full moon nights, **free guided hikes** to Waimea Falls are offered. Call 638-8511 for information.

Waikahulu Falls / Page 30

Not too many major American cities can boast a lovely double waterfall and swimming hole just a few minutes walk from downtown, so chalk up another impressive point for Honolulu. Located on the north side of Foster Botanic Garden, on the opposite, *mauka* side of the H1 FWY, Waikahulu Falls is located in Liliuokalani Garden, a 5 acre natural park on the banks of the Nuuanu Stream. Swimming is allowed, but due to a great deal of upstream runoff, not at all recommended. See photo, right.

Other Falls:

The island of Oahu is webbed with waterfalls large and small. Looking close at the pali, notice that each crevasse is a channel for a waterfall after a rain, and that a number of these ridges cradle waterfalls even when the weather has been dry. Following a stream toward the pali might seem a logical way of finding waterfalls, but due to dense jungle growth, crumbling stream banks and *very slippery conditions*, its a dangerous idea. Your best bet would be the treks that are lead by various hiking and wilderness organizations on Oahu. Feel free to call with specific questions, or about scheduled programs. See the listing on the following page: **Magnificent Hiking Trails.**

Photographs

3.

1. **Manoa Falls**
2. **Waikahulu Falls**
3. **Maunawili Falls**

all photos:
Kodachrome 64

The Kaiwa Trail, Lanikai

Magnificent

O ahu is honeycombed with a great variety of wonderful hiking trails, most of them blazed long ago by the early Hawaiians. Oahu's hiking trails snake through lush rainforest, dip under splashing waterfalls, and traverse the dizzying pali ridges; they amble along pristine deserted seashore, wind over thirsty, cactus-covered bluffs, and over-look thriving Downtown Honolulu through cool upland forests of pine and eucalyptus. Oahu's hiking trails snake past a cornucopia of free edibles on trailside trees, and lead sweaty hikers to mercifully cooling swimming holes.

Professional hiking guides by authors Craig Chisholm, Robert Smith, and others will fill you in as to the particulars. The **Honolulu Bookshops** and **Waldenbooks** have giant Hawaiiana sections overflowing with pertinent mat-erials. **The Department of Forestry and Wildlife (587-0166)** provides color trail maps, *free for the asking*, as well as information-valuable recreation maps for the other islands. The **Hawaii Geographic Society** bookstore carries a wealth of materials and has a very knowledgeable and experienced staff. **The Sierra Club, Hawaiian Trail and Mountain Club, and Hawaii Nature Center** all lead very inexpensive hikes into magical areas that you would never be able to find on your own, —and they'll get you safely back in one piece. If you can't join an organized hike, then plan your hike for a weekend when local

people will be around to help you find your way, or more likely, find your way *out*. Let others —friends, your hotel's front desk— know where you are going and when you plan to be back. If there is a trail sign-in station, use it. It *could* save your life. Do not hike if it has been raining steadily, as trickling streams can quickly turn into raging torrents. If you are caught in the rain, or notice the water level in stream beds rising, get out of the way and up to higher ground, fast.

Following are descriptions of a few of Oahu's most beautiful and enjoyable trails, but it is by no means a complete list. Some

of the island's most rewarding trails are also the easiest to get to:

The Kaiwa Trail

The temptation is great in a guide as varied and detailed as Driving & Discovering Oahu, to with-old information about places the author wants to selfishly keep secret due to their special nature. A prime example is the Kaiwa Trail, also known as the Lanikai Trail. This bogglingly - gorgeous pathway traverses the ridge behind the handsome and private enclave of Lanikai, on the Windward Shore. Only 5 quick-but-steep minutes into it, the views are already magical, and the farther you climb along the

ridge, the more enthralled you will become. The fresh tradewinds blow stiffly through the long grasses, rippling like ocean waves, and the 360 degree views are breathtakingly unforgettable. See the **Kailua-Lanikai** section for more details.

The Hauula Loop Trail

Of the three popular trails that all begin in Hauula, the loop trail is the most enchanting. The trail ascends through crowded forests of ironwood that have lain down thick mats of needles to pad the hiker's footfall. As it climbs, wondrous views along the coast reveal themselves through clearings in the trees, and soon, the forest canopy transforms to perfectly symmetrical fragrant Norfolk Pine. The trail then drops into a humid canyon lush with fern and heavy with tree moss, past a lovely little waterfall, and finally climbs again to follow a ridge at the very pinnacle of the pali and reveal the view pictured here. See the **Punaluu to Hauula** section for more.

Waahila Ridge State Recreation Area.

A secret no longer, only 5 minutes from Waikiki, and perfect for a quick cool early morning trek, Waahila's trails begin past a magical winding park entrance that passes through a sentry of towering Norfolk Pine. The park area has a lot of thoughtfully isolated picnic tables, some of which are sheltered by wooden roofs that are gardens unto themselves, sprouting miniature forests of mosses, ferns and tree seedlings. Waahila's trails provide beautiful views of Waikiki, Diamond Head, and Manoa and Palolo

Hauula Loop Trail

Valleys. See the inside back cover map.

Manoa Falls Trail

Covered in great detail in the **Manoa Falls** section, and within sight of Waikiki hotels, this lovely trail climbs through spookily beautiful rainforest to a wonderful, pencil-thin waterfall and crystal clear pool. Bring your bathing suit —or not.

The Kaena Point Trail

This 5 mile trail begins where the highways end, rounding wild and primitive Kaena Point, following the seashore the whole way. The trail is wide open, so bring sunscreen and body cover. It follows a level but deeply rutted jeep road for most of its length, with lots of footpaths leading off to secret sandy coves and white coral beaches. See the **Mokuleia** and **Kaena Point Leeward Trail** sections.

Kahana Valley State Park

How about a trail for lazy people that's actually a paved road along which friendly, freely wandering horses beg for handouts—a road that takes you within a three minute walk down a dirt path to a cool, clean, clear, refreshing, deep swimming hole, where the sunshine warms your chicken skin, where local Hawaiian and Samoan kids splash and laugh, and where the green mountain called Puu Manamana towers above? See the **Kualoa Park to Kahana Bay** section.

Makapuu Head

Beginning from the tiny parking area at the remarkable Makapuu Lookout, where the South Shore meets the Windward Shore, this series of trails climbs all over the bluff. Astounding views along both coasts enthrall and surprise; abandoned WWII bunkers hide among the rocks, the colors in the waters far, far below blend from cobalt to turquoise to cyan as they reach out to the offshore deserted islands, colorful hanggliders ply the heavens, and a handsome working lighthouse awaits those who have the stamina to reach it. Bring water! See the **Makapuu** section for more.

The list goes on and on: **The Kualoa Gulch Trail** and its double waterfall, the **Maakua Gulch Trail & Falls**, **Pupukea**'s cool upcountry trails on the North Shore, the spider web-like system of footfalls on **Mount Tantalus** –right above busy Downtown Honolulu–, **the Waianae Mountain Trails** on the Leeward Shore with their superlative vistas, the **Maunawili Trail**, just over the Pali HWY., with its double waterfall and deep swimming hole.... Call one of the hiking organizations listed here, and let them take you places you've only dreamed about.... until now.

Makapuu Point

Sierra Club
212 Merchant St., Suite 201
Honolulu HI 96813
538-6616
hikes scheduled on weekends; very low fee.

Hawaii Nature Center
2131 Makiki Heights Drive
Honolulu HI 96822
955-0100

Action Hawaii Adventures
944-6754
commercial; fee

Hawaiian Trail and Mountain Club
734-5515
hikes scheduled on weekends; very low fee.

Hawaii Geographic Society
49 S. Hotel St., Suite 218
Honolulu HI 96813
538-3952
Maps and hiking guides. Store hours are limited; call first.

State Division of Forestry
1151 Punchbowl St., Room 325
Honolulu HI 96813
587-0166
Permits and free hiking maps.

State Parks Division
587-0300
Permits & Information.

Hawaii Audubon Society
212 Merchant St., Suite 320
Honolulu HI 96813
528-1432

Honolulu Dept. of Parks & Recreation
523-4525
Information and camping permits

Photographs

Top: Panoramic mosaic assembled from 3X5 prints: **Kodak Gold 100.**

Bottom: **Kodachrome 64**

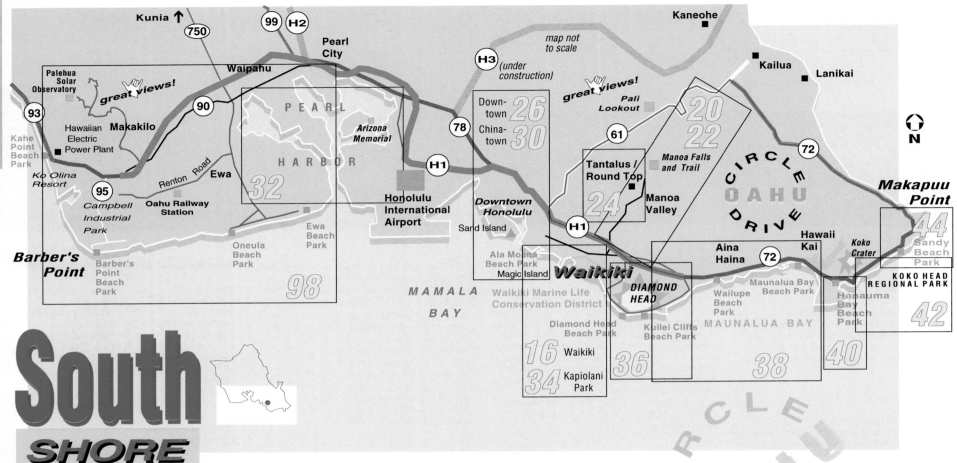

South
SHORE

The South Shore of Oahu is the most diverse of the island's four shores.

The South Shore cradles the lion's share of the state's population and commercial activity, as well as some of its most primeval and pristine landscape. It is a study in extreme contrasts as it stretches from a lonely lighthouse at Barber's Point to a lonely lighthouse at Makapuu Head. Scattered in between are oil refineries, a natural edible seaweed nursery, a lovely old plantation town with a railroad yard full of rolling stock, a strategic and historic naval base, an emergency landing strip for the space shuttle, an international airport, the tenth largest city in the United States, one of the world's most famous and popular resorts, pristine wilderness, numerous waterfalls tumbling into chilly pools, pagodas, temples and historic coral brick churches, the only royal palace on American

soil, an exquisitely beautiful crystalline bay teeming with rainbows of sea life, and a wild, awesome and majestic seashore.

The South Shore has clear calm ocean waters in the wintertime, and ten foot swells during the summer, attracting legions of surfers to Diamond Head and Waikiki. From lookouts along Diamond Head Road, swarms of windsurfers can be seen below, scurrying around, between, and airborne above the waves in a frenzied blur of neon hued sails. Close by, dozens of people show up faithfully each evening to witness a technicolor Hawaiian sunset from the Diamond Head lighthouse lawn.

The South Shore provides the visitor with the choice at any given moment of either being totally alone in a peaceful cocoon of natural

serenity, or happily embroiled in the energy of pulsating resort activity —or any number of choices somewhere in between. The South Shore provides visitors and residents alike with the best of both worlds.

The Circle Drive route follows the coastline from Waikiki, past Diamond Head's lighthouse and windsurfer-watching, through the exclusive residential enclave of Kahala, past no less than 26 beach parks, a justifiably world famous snorkeling mecca, three shopping malls, isolated waterfalls, hidden beach coves, wild and craggy seashore, pastoral farms and ranches, deserted islands, unparalleled scenic vistas, wonderful hiking trails and a cool mountain forest. You *could* zoom past all this in about two hours, but we dare you not to get out of your car at least 20 times along the way.

For those who are pressed for time, there is a superb overview of Oahu's most beautiful sites that can be glanced in in as little as a couple of hours —but you might want to give this route a whole day to enjoy it to the fullest. The pages in this book which the Circle Drive encompasses will be noted with the Circle Drive logo at the top. The route is outlined in red on the right quadrant of the map, above.

The fabulous Circle Drive includes stunning vistas, the island's finest snorkeling, pastoral farms and ranches, towering pali, miles of empty beaches, world class bodysurfing waves, lightning fast windsurfing, hidden waterfalls, cool misty highland rainforest, and Honolulu's Chinatown.

South Shore Beach Parks

Source: City and County of Honolulu

South Shore Beach Parks	Page	Lifeguard	Rest Rooms	Public Telephone	Picnic Tables	Camping	Night Security	Swimming	Snorkeling & Diving	Surfing	Bodysurfing	Windsurfing	Seasonal High Surf
Sandy BP	44							●		●	●		●
Hanuama Bay BP	40	●	●	●	●			●	●				●
Maunalua Bay BP	38		●									●	
Kuliouou BP	38		●	●	●								
Kawaikui BP	38		●	●	●			●					
Wailupe BP	38		●	●	●								
Waialae BP	38		●	●	●			●		●		●	
Kuilei Cliffs BP	36			●	●			●		●	●	●	●
Sans Souci SRA	34	●		●				●	●				
Kapiolani Park	34	●	●	●	●			●	●				
Kuhio BP	16	●	●	●	●			●	●	●			●
Fort DeRussy	16	●	●	●	●			●	●	●			
Magic Island	16		●	●	●			●	●	●	●	●	●
Ala Moana Park	16	●	●	●	●			●		●	●		
Point Panic / Kakaako BP	26		●	●	●					●	●		●
Sand Island SRA			●	●	●	●	●			●	●		●
Keehi Lagoon Park			●	●	●								
Blaisdell Park			●	●	●								
Ewa BP	98		●	●	●			●					●
Oneula BP	98		●					●					●

South Shore Weather

Source: US Dept. of Commerce
National Weather Service Pacific Region
Station: Honolulu

Oahu Weather: 836-0121
Honolulu Weather: 296-1818, X1520
Surf Report: 836-1952 or 296-1818, X1521
Marine Report: 836-3921 or 296-1818, X1522

	Daily High Temperature	Daily Low Temperature	% Of Possible Sunshine	% Of Cloud Cover	Number of Clear Days	Number Partly Cloudy Days	Number of Cloudy Days	Monthly Rainfall In Inches
January	80	65	63%	54%	9.4	13.1	8.6	3.8
February	80	65	65%	56%	7.9	12.2	7.9	2.7
March	81	67	70%	58%	7.2	14.2	9.6	3.5
April	83	69	67%	62%	5.3	14.3	10.4	1.5
May	85	70	69%	60%	6.3	15.2	9.5	1.2
June	86	72	71%	56%	5.9	17.4	6.7	0.5
July	87	73	74%	53%	7.5	18.2	5.3	0.5
August	88	74	75%	53%	7.9	17.0	6.1	0.6
September	88	73	76%	52%	7.8	16.3	5.9	0.6
October	87	72	68%	57%	7.3	15.3	8.4	1.9
November	84	69	61%	57%	7.0	13.9	9.1	3.2
December	81	67	59%	55%	8.5	13.4	9.1	3.4

Waikiki Beach

Everything they said it would be, and much, much more.

To get to the airport from Waikiki, follow the orange line. See map on inside back cover.

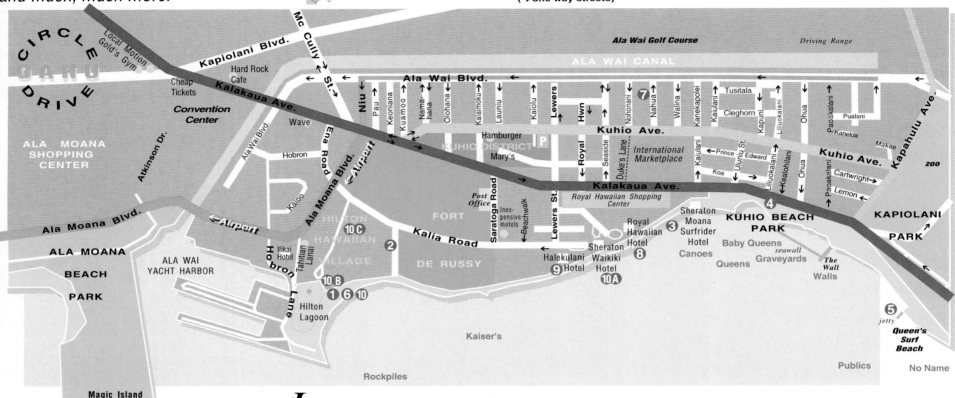

(➔ one way streets)

Map labels: CIRCLE DRIVE OAHU · Local Motion · Gold's Gym · Cheap Tickets · Convention Center · Hard Rock Cafe · Wave · Hobron · Kaioo · Ala Moana Blvd. · Atkinson Dr. · Kapiolani Blvd. · Kalakaua Ave. · Ala Wai Blvd. · Mc Cully St. · Niu · Pau · Keoniana · Kuamoo · Nama-hana · Olohana · Kalaimoku · Launiu · Kaiolu · Lewers · Hwn · Royal · Seaside · Duke's Lane · Nohonani · Nahua · Walina · Kanekapolei · Kaiulani · Tusitala · Cleghorn · Kapuni · Liliuokalani · Ohua · Paoakalani · Pualani · Kaneloa · Makee · Ala Wai Golf Course · Driving Range · ALA WAI CANAL · Kuhio Ave. · KUHIO DISTRICT · Hamburger Mary's · International Marketplace · Prince Edward · Ulunui St. · Koa · Kealohilani · Kapahulu Ave. · ZOO · Ala Moana Blvd. · Airport · Ena Road · Ala Moana Blvd. · Airport · ALA MOANA SHOPPING CENTER · Saratoga Road · Post Office · Inexpensive motels · Beachwalk · Lewers St. · Royal Hawaiian Shopping Center · Kalakaua Ave. · KAPIOLANI PARK · Ilikai Hotel · Tahitian Lanai · Hobron Lane · HILTON HAWAIIAN VILLAGE · Kalia Road · FORT DE RUSSY · Halekulani Hotel · Sheraton Waikiki Hotel · Royal Hawaiian Hotel · Sheraton Moana Surfrider Hotel · KUHIO BEACH PARK · Baby Queens · Canoes · Queens · seawall Graveyards · The Wall Walls · ALA MOANA BEACH PARK · ALA WAI YACHT HARBOR · Hilton Lagoon · Kaiser's · Rockpiles · Magic Island · Islands · Baby Haleiwa · Bombora · Ala Moana Bowls · Publics · No Name · Queen's Surf Beach · jetty · KAPIOLANI PARK

Numbered markers: 7 · 4 · 3 · 8 · 2 · 10 C · 10 B · 1 6 10 · 9 · 10 A · 5

Photographs

1. A star filter was used to create the light points in this early evening Waikiki Beach/ Diamond Head shot taken from the 26th floor of the Hilton Rainbow Tower. The exposure was about 15 seconds on Kodachrome 64 film.

2. Waikiki isn't always jammed with crowds, as this early morning shot shows. It was taken from the Ali'i Tower of the Hilton Hawaiian Village through the park-like landscaping of Fort DeRussy.

Both photos: **Kodachrome 64**

---

*I*n *Driving & Discovering Oahu*'s tour of Waikiki, we're going to go outside the *strict* boundaries of Waikiki a little and begin our journey at **Ala Moana Park**, which encompasses **Ala Moana Beach Park** and **Ainamoana State Recreation Area**, more commonly called **Magic Island**. A favorite place for locals to jog and enjoy the beach, the park includes 76 acres of ocean side trees, lawn, and sand. There's a lot of room to move at Ala Moana Park and the chance to meet and talk with *kamaainas*, as the people who live here are called. The crescent-shaped beach at adjacent 32 acre **Magic Island** is a magnet for **families** and divers because it is protected from waves by a breakwater, and although close to Waikiki, it is isolated from the area's clamor.

Directly across the street from Ala Moana Park is the **Ala Moana Shopping Center (#1450)**, still the world's largest outdoor shopping mall. With 8,000 parking spaces, expect big crowds here. The mall boasts more than 150 shops ranging from the All-American **Disney** store to Japan's **Shirokiya** department store —make sure you check out the fascinating gourmet food department on Shirokiya's 2nd floor. The **Honolulu Book Shop** has a great Hawaiiana section and plenty of local hiking maps, and **Crackseed Center** sells the local delicacy that *keikis* (kids) love, and that mainlanders, well... Let's just say crackseed is an acquired taste.

Traveling *east/diamond head* from Ala Moana Park along Ala Moana Blvd., you will cross the **Ala Wai Canal**, the official boundary of Waikiki. The first street after the canal that the boulevard intersects is HOBRON ST. Make a *right/makai* turn onto it. The street will soon curve to the *left* along the back of the **Ilikai Hotel (#1777)**. At sunset take the exterior glass elevator 30 stories

up for a drink and the unforgettable **view**. Go past the **yacht harbor** —a great place for a sunset stroll. The road then curves to the right, past more boats on the right side, and the **Hilton Lagoon** on the left. The Lagoon's palm planted island hides the pumping equipment that keeps fresh ocean water circulating in this huge natural looking salt water swimming pool. Its a great place to swim for kids and those wary of the ocean. Notice the sheer immensity, by Waikiki standards, of the Hilton's beach.

Backtrack the same way you came in, and *turn right* onto **ALA MOANA BLVD**. The **Waikikian Hotel (#1811)** on the *right/makai* is one of the last of the Hawaiian theme hostelries in Waikiki, the kind of place people in the 50's and 60's associated with Hawaii. It has attractive Polynesian style thatched roof units which border a torch lit pathway. Its **Tahitian Lanai** restaurant is a favorite with kamaainas for breakfast. At the first intersection, **KALIA ROAD**, make a *right turn*. **The Hilton Hawaiian Village (#2005)** on the *right/makai* is ripe for exploration after its amazing makeover, now with beach-facing restaurants, beautiful ocean view super pool, over 60 species of exotic birds including eight South African penguins, and the handsomest shopping complex in Hawaii. Every **Friday at 6:30 p.m.** the Hilton has a terrific **historic show** that includes a torch lighting ceremony, hula, Hawaiian music and a spectacular aerial fireworks display (8 p.m. Summer/Spring or 7:30 p.m. Fall/Winter). Mondays through Thursdays and on Saturdays a delightful **keiki** (children's) **hula show** is performed at 6:30 p.m. *All this entertainment is free.* The Hilton's showplace **Bali-by-the-Sea** is a gorgeously situated restaurant specializing in world class Euro-Island cuisine and superb service. Their bread basket alone is a religious experience. **49 of the Hilton's rooms are especially equipped for the physically challenged, and all 22 lounges, restaurants and showrooms are wheelchair accessible. Wide walkways, sloped and ramped, make touring this property a delight.**

Next to the Hilton is the park-like military property of **Ft. DeRussy**, whose beach is open to the public and is a mecca for girls looking to meet military boys. *Continuing* along KALIA ROAD, notice the little **hotels and motels** near the corner of **KALIA RD. and SARATOGA RD.** Less than a block from the beach, these are among the **least expensive lodgings** in Waikiki. *Continuing* down KALIA RD., we pass **BEACH WALK** where up that little street is another great throwback-to-the-60's hotel, the newly redecorated **Hawaiiana (#260)**, on the ewa side of the street. Its a low-key, friendly, 95 unit place with lush landscaping surrounding its two pools, and it attracts a loyal crowd. Walk in and have a look. The next street you'll pass is **LEWERS ST.**—the noisiest street in Waikiki— where incongruously the quietest and most dignified hotel in Waikiki, the **Halekulani (#2199)**, is located at its terminus. If you are neatly dressed, visit the classy but friendly poolside pavilion, **House Without A Key**, for lunch under the umbrellas and a highly entertaining view of one of the world's best beach parades. All beach traffic at this point is routed along the Halekulani's oceanfront sidewalk, just for your inspection. Older people love coming here for a sunset drink and a romantic moonlit dance to the live Hawaiian music and the elegant hula...not that younger people don't love that stuff too...its just that the atmosphere here, especially at sunset, is a surviving and thriving slice of Hawaii As It Used To Be. But be forewarned –at the Halekulani they make their

own ice cream and pastries right on the premises, so diets may be doomed.

If you are *driving*, because of Waikiki's maze of one-way streets, you'll have to *turn around* at the entrance of the Halekulani, and *backtrack* down KALIA RD. for **2 blocks**, and then make a *right turn* onto **SARATOGA ROAD**. At the next main intersection, make a *right turn* onto **KALAKAUA AVE.**

If *walking*, head *mauka* up **LEWERS ST.**, checking out all the budget restaurants and beach clothing stores, to **KALAKAUA AVE.** To your *right/makai* is the **Royal Hawaiian Shopping Center (#2201)**. Don't ignore the stores on the second and third levels. Some of the best bargains are here, including department store resort clothing close-outs. At the next street, hang a *right* onto **ROYAL HAWAIIAN ST.** to visit the 1927 pink palace, **The Royal Hawaiian Hotel (#2259)**. Have lunch next to the sand at the **Surf Room** and enjoy firsthand the incomparable posing and preening displayed by the beautiful people right there in front of you on Waikiki's infamous **"Watch *Me*" Beach.**

Back on KALAKAUA AVE., the **International Marketplace (#2330)** across the street is filled with repetitive (read: *price competitive*) stores and stalls. The wood-carver near the entrance does really nice work, and will carve to order.

Keep in mind as you wander Waikiki's streets that just about any hotel is worth a look inside, and they all welcome casual visitors with open arms. *They know that today's looky-loos may be tomorrow's guests.* On the *makai* side of KALAKAUA AVE., the splendid porte-cochere of the masterfully restored **Sheraton Moana Surfrider Hotel (#2353)** beckons. Walk around inside the property and marvel at the authentic turn of the century ambience in Waikiki's first and oldest hotel. To the rear, a lovely-wrap around porch overlooking a central court and huge banyan tree beachside is the staging area for **late afternoon Hawaiian entertainment**. This should be a magical spot at any time of day. The Moana Surfrider, not content with just a tour de force restoration, has **made the hotel wheelchair-accessible and redesigned 13 rooms to meet the needs of the physically challenged.**

Next door to the Sheraton Moana Surfrider is the great gathering place, **Kuhio Beach Park**. All kinds of action takes place here, with endless racks of surfboards and other beach equipment for rent, a snackbar, a police station, four legend-

Waikiki

ary "wizard stones", catamaran rides, covered gazebos where nonstop games of cards, chess and checkers are played, sidewalk benches for comfortable people watching, and a large statue of **Duke Kahanamoku**, Hawaii's Olympic swimming champ...and lots and lots of people. Across the street, the twin towered **Hyatt Regency Waikiki (2424)** shelters about **70 shops**, as well as some great public art, and afternoon *pau hana* Hawaiian entertainment at **Harry's Bar**, next to their thundering inner court waterfall. Further down KALAKAUA AVE., is **Gold's Gym**, and the distinctively peak-roofed **St. Augustine's Catholic Church** which holds weekend masses featuring a **Hawaiian or Tongan choir**. Its property houses the **Father Damien Museum**, dedicated to the priest who dedicated his life to working with the lepers of Molokai.

On the eastern boundary of Waikiki, at the corner of KALAKAUA and KAPAHULU AVE., **Denny's** restaurant, up on the second level, has the unbeatable combination of a breezy, bird's eye view, and inexpensive eats. You may have to wait for a railside table.

If you are *walking*, double back along KALAKAUA AVE. for a few blocks, then turn *mauka* on **LILIUOKALANI ST.,** and go 3 very short blocks to **KUHIO AVE.** *Turn left* onto KUHIO AVE.

If you are *driving*, turn left from KALAKAUA AVE. at **Kapiolani Park** onto **KAPAHULU AVE.,** then *turn left* at the first traffic light onto **KUHIO AVE.**

The pink hotel on the corner of **ULUNIU ST.** and **KUHIO AVE.** is the **Royal Grove**, a very popular family owned budget place. Notice **Ruffage** in the same building, a small inexpensive healthfood restaurant/market with superior chili, soups, fruit smoothies and sandwiches —ideal picnic fare. Ruffage becomes a popular **sushi bar** in the evening. The rest of **Kuhio Ave.** abounds with relatively inexpensive places to eat, sleep and shop, generously sprinkled among the pricier and more elegant places, and is just about as lively as **KALA-KAUA AVE.** Toward its end, in the general vicinity of the **Kuhio Theater**, is what is known as the **Kuhio District**, which boasts a concen-trated number of interesting and unusual shops, and

inexpensive restaurants. **Hernando's Hideaway (#2139)** starts attracting crowds of young people, many of them resort workers, in the late afternoon for bargain priced drinks and inexpensive Mexican food. It is hidden well off the street, further back even than **Cafe Guccini (#2139)**, which serves good home made pastas and desserts. **Hamburger Mary's (#2109)**, part of the mainland mini-chain, serves super fresh crisp salads, sandwiches and omelettes. The world famous open air gay disco bar **Hula's** is located directly around the corner, across KALAIMOKU ST. from the **Kuhio Theater (2095 KUHIO AVE.)**. Past the theater where KUHIO AVE. joins KALAKAUA AVE. is little **Waikiki Gateway Park** and its statue of **King David Kalakaua**. See photo, left. Further down KALAKAUA AVE. a few blocks at **#1877** is the **Wave**, the venerable Waikiki disco that still kicks up a ruckus. Across the KALAKAUA AVE. **bridge** is the always popular Honolulu **Hard Rock Cafe** on the *right/mauka* side, and on the *left/makai* side, at the corner of KALAKAUA AVE. and KAPIOLANI BLVD. is **Cheap Tickets**, where you can buy cut rate air tickets either to a **neighbor island**, or around the world. (Remember that the **first** and **last** neighbor island flights of the day are always the **cheapest**.) *Turn left* onto **KAPIOLANI BLVD.**, and on the *right/mauka* side check out the **Local Motion (#1714)** store for the best selection of surf and beach clothes, and have a look around well-equipped **Gold's Gym (#1680)**.

Our final recommendation in Waikiki is to check out the walkway along the **Ala Wai Canal** and **ALA WAI BLVD.** Its a long, uninterrupted, **1.5 mile** expanse of sidewalk where joggers, recreational walkers, and people-watchers can be found at anytime during the day. Near the **MC CULLY ST. bridge**, catamarans enter the water for daily training. Large numbers of Honolulu's citizenry are members of catamaran teams, and you can see them practicing just about any time you pass along the Ala Wai, but especially in the cool of the morning.

Photographs

Left: King David Kalakaua statue in Waikiki Gateway Park.

3. A sign of the times for a favorite Waikiki tradition.

4. A lone surfer girl waits out early morn flat conditions.

5. Sunset-watching from The Wall at the foot of Kapahulu Ave. is a favorite pastime of visitors and kama-ainas alike.

6. A young girl enjoys a dip in a Waikiki hotel swimming pool: Kodak Fun Saver Weekend *Camera.*

7. Late day traffic keeps company with catamarans training on the Ala Wai Canal, as seen from 444 Nahua St.

8. A fantasy sand-castle at the Royal Hawaiian Hotel.

9. Breakfast, exactly as it was served —not setup for the camera— at the Halekulani Hotel's Orchids restaurant. A collapsible reflector was used at camera right as fill.

10. A couple casts late day shadows on the sand. Shot from 26th floor balcony, with 210mm lens.

10A. Surfboards on the Hilton's Beach.

10B. Ala Wai Yacht Harbor at sunset from the Hilton Rainbow Tower: 210mm lens.

10C. Japanese tile rooftop at the Hilton Hawaiian Village Shopping Center : 210mm lens.

All photos except #6: **Kodachrome 64**.

❻
❿

❼
❿ A

❽
❿ B

❾
❿ C

19

Manoa Valley

So close, and yet so far away.

❶

Manoa Valley is a relatively unknown corner of Oahu which you must definitely not miss. Even though it is located within clear sight of Waikiki, incongruously this corner of the city cradles a towering pristine waterfall and one of the best wilderness rainforest experiences on the island. Manoa Valley also shelters an arboretum that even people who normally aren't interested in such things will find fascinating and immensely peaceful; a wonderful old established residential neighborhood; a lovely Chinese graveyard where food is left for the departed; first rate cafes, a vibrant and booming live theater, and the handsome and lively campus of the University of Hawaii. Using the map follow these directions:

In Waikiki, go *mauka* (mauka means "toward the mountains") to ALA WAI BLVD. (it runs along the canal and is a one way street) and *turn left* onto it. Make a *right/mauka* turn at the MC CULLY ST. bridge. Proceed straight ahead on MC CULLY ST., and you will pass over the H1 FWY. Immediately after the overpass *turn right* on METCALF ST. and proceed to UNIVERSITY AVE. *Make a left turn* onto UNIVERSITY AVE. Going uphill, you will see the **University of Hawaii** on your right. Proceed into the valley after passing the University, then either *turn right* at E. MANOA ROAD to

visit the shopping center, cafe, and Chinese cemetery, or *proceed straight ahead* to visit Manoa Falls, the **Lyon Arboretum** and **Paradise Park** (admission charge). After the intersection of E. MANOA ROAD, UNIVERSITY AVE. changes names to become OAHU AVE. OAHU AVE. intersects MANOA ROAD deep in the valley. *Turn left* onto MANOA RD. and proceed to the end. *On the right* you'll see the parking lot for Paradise Park. *Turn left* to visit Lyon Arboretum, or continue straight ahead for just a few yards into a heavily shaded area to park for the hike to **Manoa Falls**. This all sounds complicated, but its very hard to get lost here. If you miss any turns in the valley, just keep heading toward the back left corner of it and you'll end up OK.

The drive up University Ave. and along E. Manoa and Oahu Ave. is interesting due to the many beautiful old homes, the moist, lush greenery, and a strong sense of place and feeling of community. Roughly triangular-shaped, Manoa Valley is a Honolulu city neighborhood, yet it feels physically separate and removed, enclosed on two of its three sides by high mountain ridges. From *mauka*-facing high rise vantage points in Waikiki, Manoa can often be seen shrouded in rainy mists, even as Waikiki Beach has a perfectly sunny day. The

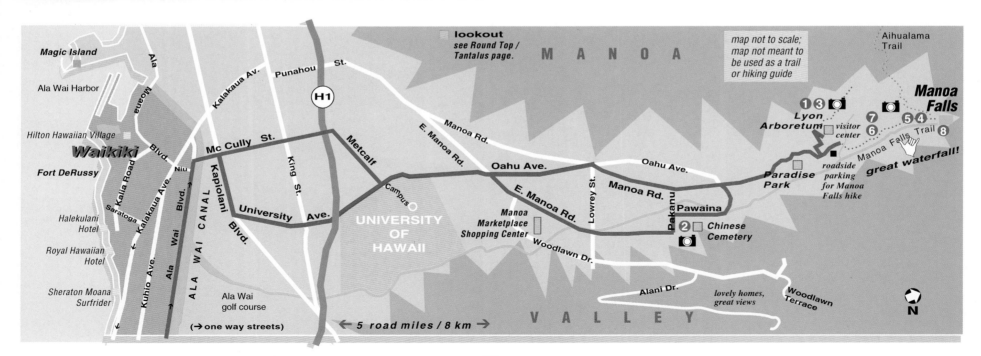

valley has its own shopping center, the **Manoa Marketplace**, where locals gather at the **Manoa Cafe** for a great cup of coffee and delicious baked goods. Little stores along E.MANOA RD. sell the freshest of local produce, including the famous Manoa lettuce, Kula tomatoes and Maui onions. **The Manoa Valley Theater**, located behind the shopping center, mounts a constant stream of sold out productions. Bulletin boards at the Manoa Marketplace and other locations in the area, as well as free copies of the **Manoa Valley Times**, available at businesses locally, can fill the visitor in as to what is happening short term. Continue down E. MANOA ROAD past the shopping center to the **Chinese cemetery** and drive under the red arch and up to the large tree at the back, for an impressive view of the fore-valley and Waikiki. The traditional arch at the entrance welcomes family members bearing gifts of food, fruits and cakes for their departed loved ones.

A drive up WOODLAWN DR. and the sidestreets to the right, like ALANI and PATY will reveal magical old neighborhoods clinging to the steep ridge, where gurgling streams and little waterfalls rush past the bedroom windows and little lanais of the fascinating mix of homes.

Drive along MANOA RD. and OAHU AVE. to view the fine old homes. Park your car and walk and relax, taking a close look at the gardens and the little side streets. A good concentration of homes and streets is in the triangular area where Manoa Road and E. Manoa Road intersect.

The **Lyon Arboretum (988-3177)** is a wide open garden of Eden that is backed right up to the protecting and nourishing flanks of the Koolau Mountains. Its collection includes vast numbers of plants, both rare and endangered. Many varieties of exotic palms sway in the trades that funnel up from the sea, the tendrils of breathtakingly beautiful blooming orchids clinging like spider webs to their trunks. The bizarre and captivating collection includes the alien looking black Bat flower from Thailand, and for chocoholics, it may come as a surprise to see their obsession's natural form — the cocoa pod looks like a big purple football hanging from its tree. Mosquito repellent helps if you plan to explore the arboretum's inner reaches. The gift shop sells plant related items and books. As a delicious way to raise funds, exotic preserves and jams like lilikoi and mango have been put up by Arboretum members for sale here. They make a good souvenir. A small donation is requested to tour the beautiful grounds.

The crowning glory of Manoa Valley is dream-like

Manoa Falls (seen below and on the back cover), the eerily beautiful rain forest trail that leads there, and the clear, cooling pool at its base that lies in wait to refresh sweaty hikers who make the journey. To learn all about Manoa Falls, see page 22.

❺

❹

TheBus
848-5555
Ask driver for directions if unsure.

From Waikiki:
Board bus #4 Nuuanu-Dowsett on the mauka side of Kuhio Ave. and take it to the University of Hawaii Campus. On University Ave., transfer to the #6 Ala Moana-Woodlawn, which will take you past the Manoa Marketplace, within a few blocks of the Chinese Cemetery, and up into the gorgeous Woodlawn residential area. Ride TheBus to the terminus for a nice tour, then alight on the way back at whatever sites interest you.

Return:
Board bus #6 Ala Moana-Pauoa to the corner of University Ave. and Metcalf St. At the same bus stop, transfer to the #4 University-Waikiki.

Photographs

1. The Koolau Mountains cradle the Lyon Arboretum's vast collection of plants and trees at the back of Manoa Valley.

2. The red arch at the Chinese cemetery welcomes visitors who wish to view the headstones and gifts left by loved ones of the departed.

3. Orchids grow in the trees outside the Lyon Arboretum's Visitor Center.

4. Manoa Falls tumbles into a clear, cold pool that welcomes the tired hot bodies of hikers after the 45 minute trek.

5. Neon-bright blossoms of the shaving brush tree at Lyon.

All: **Kodachrome 64**

❷

聯以感情緬懷逝者

❸

Manoa Falls

*A*t the end of MANOA RD. just past the Paradise Park parking lot on the *right,* and the entrance to the Lyon Arboretum further on and to the *left,* is a heavily shaded area of dead end road. You may park alongside it, but do not leave anything visible in the car, or be seen placing anything in the trunk. Make all your preparations for the hike to Manoa Falls before reaching this point. If you don't feel comfortable leaving your car here, park it in the Lyon Arboretum lot, go into the gift shop and pay $2, then walk back down to Manoa Road.

Be sure to bring water. Brief rain showers can be expected almost daily in the afternoon, courtesy of the tradewinds, but if there has been a heavy rain, delay your hike as the stream will be dangerously swollen, and the falls will be rampaging and filled with falling rocks from above. Better wait for another day.

Walk to the end of the road -a few yards- past the 4 concrete posts and follow the clearly visible path to the right over a small footbridge. Notice the enormous leaves of the Elephant Ear plants below the bridge. A few yards past the bridge the path *veers left* into the forest and at a trail marker immediately crosses a small stream in which a rock footpath has been laid so you can keep your feet dry. Keep in mind that for the entire hike, you are following the **next stream** that you see *on your right* uphill, but you never cross it. If the trail at times seems unclear, just look down and **follow the footprints in the mud**. If you stray off the trail, which is unlikely, just stop and listen for the sound of the stream and head back toward it. The stream's source is Manoa Falls. Manoa Stream will always be close by on your *right*, and following it will lead you right to the Falls.

The Manoa Falls Trail, being only 3/4 of a mile long and taking about 2 hours for the round trip, is a favorite with *kamaainas* and their *keikis* (kids). There are a couple of places that require a scramble up over rocks or tree roots, and the muddy trail narrows at the edge of a precipice once or twice, so unruly children *could* get in trouble. But responsible kids will love it, and if its a typical weekend, you will pass numbers of supervised muddy groups along the way. Its a great opportunity for both them and the visitor to live out the classic island fantasy of swimming beneath a cool, tumbling waterfall.

Some people complain that this trail has been made to seem too easy by magazine articles and other guidebooks. This is no walk along a paved sidewalk by any means. Its muddy, slippery, and all uphill. The photographs give a good idea of what to expect. Dress appropriately. Every step should be deliberate because large boulders and remarkable networks of tangled tree roots lay across much of the trail, with mud puddles between. *This is a real rainforest,* so the hike can be hot and humid, and although there are a lot of mosquitoes, they usually aren't a major problem if you keep moving. Mosquito repellent helps, as does wearing long pants and not wearing perfume or other scented products. **Avon's Skin-So-Soft** moisturizing lotion has a strong reputation in Hawaii as a pleasant to use, non toxic, effective repellent. The best repellent of all though, is to have someone with you that the mosquitoes like better.

Normally, litter along the trail is nonexistent. This act of generosity on the part of the hikers who came before adds immeasurably to the experience. If you find litter, please pick it up if you can.

Along the path, ferns with 10 foot long fronds grow from the stream bank, and brilliant orange-cupped African Tulip Tree blossoms carpet the footfall. Nectar feeding birds can be seen clinging to clusters of these blooms high in the canopy. Mountain apples drop their bland but incredibly juicy edible fruits along the way, especially in the area right below the falls. A strong vinegar smell, as the rotting fruit ferments in the heat, sharply cuts the air. In late July the ginger begins to bloom along the section of lower trail that has been stone paved by the early Hawaiians. Incredibly enough, all the way up to the falls, pools in the stream hold live gobys and prawns which have made the astounding journey up from the sea.

If you are lucky, you may have the falls completely to yourself, even at midday. During the week there is much less activity here than on weekends. Regardless, after the sweaty hike, plunging into the pool's surprisingly chilly waters comes as a pleasant shock, and the pounding of the tumbling cascade on the back of your neck and shoulders feels better than any masseur. There is a real sense of spirituality here, where you can contemplate the fantastic setting and its lonely location in the mid Pacific, the music of the falling water, the graceful sway of the ferns that surround you and sprout from the waterfall wall, the ti leaf-wrapped stones that local people have left as offerings to the spirits and have stuck in every nook and cranny, the hot sun warming your face as the falls splash your skin...these are all things that help make Manoa Falls a place where Hawaiian dreams do come true.

5. Far Left: A Hiker takes advantage of the icy shower provided by the high mountain waters that spill over Manoa Falls.

6. Near Left: The trail to Manoa Falls is covered in some places by slippery tree roots; in others, it is bordered by blooming ginger and paved with smooth black stones, the handiwork of the early Hawaiians.

7. High in the canopy, a strangely beautiful tree blooms with vibrant color.

8. Neatly tucked into the nooks and crannies behind the Falls are stones wrapped in ti leaves which have been left by kamaainas. You will see these little packages at any spot in Hawaii that holds spiritual significance for the Islands' people.

All photos: Kodachrome 64.

TheBus
848-5555

Ask directions of the driver if in doubt.

From Waikiki:
Board bus #8 Ala Moana Center on the mauka side of Kuhio Ave. Alight at Kona St./Keeaumoku St. on the mauka side of the Ala Moana Shopping Center. Transfer to the #5 Ala Moana-Manoa bus and ride to its terminus at Paradise Park. The Manoa Falls trailhead and Lyon Arboretum are just a short walk up the road.

Return:
At Paradise Park board bus #5 Ala Moana-Manoa to the Ala Moana Shopping Center. Alight at Kona St./ Keeaumoku St. Transfer at the same bus stop to the #8 or #19 Waikiki- Beach and Hotels.

❼

❽

Tantalus and Round Top Drive

This entire area is criss-crossed with great hiking trails. Consult *Bier's Oahu map #1*, and check out the Hawaiiana Books Section at *Waldenbooks* and the *Honolulu Book Shop* for their impressive selection of local hiking books, maps and guides. Free trail maps are available from the State Division of Forestry and Wildlife.

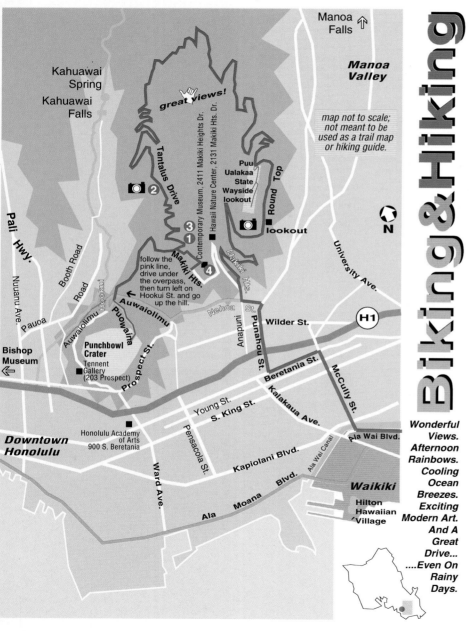

Manoa Falls ⇑

Manoa Valley

Kahuawai Spring

Kahuawai Falls

great views!

map not to scale; not meant to be used as a trail map or hiking guide.

Tantalus Drive

Contemporary Museum, 2411 Makiki Heights Dr.

Hawaii Nature Center, 2131 Makiki Hts. Dr.

Puu Ualakaa State Wayside lookout

Round Top

lookout

N

University Ave.

follow the pink line, drive under the overpass, then turn left on Hookui St. and go up the hill.

Makiki Hts.

Makiki Hts.

Pali Hwy.

Nuuanu Ave.

Booth Road

Hookui

Auwaiolimu

Pauoa

Nehoa St.

Punahou St.

Iolani St.

Wilder St.

H1

Auwaiolimu

Puowaina

Prospect St.

Bishop Museum ⇐

Punchbowl Crater

Tennent Gallery (203 Prospect)

Honolulu Academy of Arts 900 S. Beretania

Beretania St.

McCully St.

Downtown Honolulu

Young St.

S. King St.

Pensacola St.

Ward Ave.

Kalakaua Ave.

Kapiolani Blvd.

Moana Blvd.

Ala

Ala Wai Canal

Ala Wai Blvd.

Waikiki

Hilton Hawaiian Village

Wonderful Views. Afternoon Rainbows. Cooling Ocean Breezes. Exciting Modern Art. And A Great Drive... ....Even On Rainy Days.

Biking & Hiking

*R*OUND TOP ROAD is called that because it circles 'round the top of Honolulu's Mount Tantalus. Round Top/Tantalus offers the visitor many enjoyable hours of biking and jogging, hiking along trails where free snacks grow on trees and fabulous views are too numerous to count. Some of the finest art in the world is housed at the beautiful **Contemporary Museum** at the Spalding Estate, at the **Madge Tennent Gallery** on the flanks of Punchbowl Crater, and at the surprisingly impressive **Honolulu Academy of the Arts**, below Punchbowl on Beretania St.

You don't have to be in an athletic frame of mind to fully enjoy Mount Tantalus though, as the road itself is so lovely that it gets our vote for **one of Hawaii's best drives**. Even on a rainy day, when

Proceed along MC CULLY ST. for 10 blocks to BERETANIA ST. *Turn left* onto BERETANIA ST. and go a few blocks to PUNAHOU ST. *Turn right* onto PUNAHOU ST. Proceed 0.3 mile to NEHOA ST., where there is a traffic signal. *Turn left* onto NEHOA St. and go 3 short blocks to MAKIKI HTS. *Turn right*, uphill, onto MAKIKI HTS. One short block later you will see that the road forks at a little triangular park. You may go to either direction, as this is a circular route, but this guide will take you up the right fork. Five minutes into the drive a lengthy lookout shoulder appears along the right side of the road. Below to the left is Manoa Valley and out in front, all of Waikiki can be seen. The views from numerous turnouts along the road are magnificent. This is an especially wonderful place to go late in the afternoon when isolated

the enjoyment of the spectacular views are obscured somewhat, a drive on Round Top is a thoroughly enjoyable experience. The road is excellent, if at times narrow, with numerous switchbacks and hairpin turns. There are some beautiful houses scattered along the way, but due to the topographic difficulties of building here, and the lack of access to municipal water supplies, their numbers are relatively sparse. Homes of daring and utilitarian design hide in the rainforest and cling to the sides of deep gorges, or in places hang right off the edge of the precipitous road to take best advantage of the exquisite vistas.

In Waikiki, drive *north/mauka* to ALA WAI BLVD. (along the canal) and *turn left* onto it. *Turn right* onto MC CULLY ST., which is the first bridge.

rainshowers spawn ethereal transparent rainbows that bridge the mountain gulches. **It is an ideal place to come at sunset**, either alone or with a loved one, to experience nature's pyrotechnics. If you bring a camera with time exposure capabilities, you can catch the magic of a million city lights twinkling on as the horizon blazes orange and red.

About **0.5 mile** beyond this lookout, the road curves to the left through a handsome manicured park setting, and soon the tree lined entrance to the **Puu Ualakaa Park** lookout appears. **This is *the* premier Mount Tantalus view.** The park lookout provides a 230° vista from deep into Manoa Valley all the way to the Waianae Mountains at Oahu's western shore. *Be aware that car break-ins are pervasive in the parking lot at Puu*

Ualakaa, so leave nothing visible in the car interior and don't let yourself be seen placing anything in the trunk.

After leaving the park, proceed along past tantalizing peeks at homes hidden in the rain-forest as well as an impressively large number of trailheads. Many "urban wilderness" hiking trails —a contradiction in terms anywhere else but Honolulu— criss cross the area and are outlined in good detail by professionals like **Craig Chisholm** and **Robert Smith** in their respective hiking guides, available at Waldenbooks and Honolulu Book Shops. One of the best-stocked of Waldenbooks' outlets is the branch at the Ward Warehouse, Ala Moana Blvd. at Ward St. Also, **James Bier's Oahu Reference Map #1** details all hikers' routes and parking areas along Round Top Road.

Round Top Road climbs, drops and zigzags under great stands of stately, full grown trees hung with garlands of giant variegated green and yellow philodendron. It passes mature pines, ironwood, and bountiful guava. A colorful variety of large flowering trees, including the lavender blooms of jacaranda, the spectacular and showy rainbow shower tree, and the bright orange, large-cupped African Tulip tree, stand brilliant against the blue sky, while fallen blooms carpet the road with velvety hues.

The road changes names from **Round Top** to **Tantalus Drive** halfway through the journey, and near the end, two westward-facing scenic points emerge. The first offers a perfectly framed view into **Punchbowl Crater** through a clearing in a eucalyptus forest, and the second provides an expansive view of the airport area, which positively blazes at sunset. The road descends, and at the intersection of TANTALUS DR. and MAKIKI HEIGHTS you are given the choice of proceeding on either one:

A turn onto MAKIKI HTS. will take you to the **Museum of Contemporary Art**, and then back to our starting point at the little triangular park. If you continue downhill on TANTALUS DR., and make a left turn onto PUOWAINA ST., you will reach the entrance of the **National Cemetery at Punchbowl Crater.**

The Museum of Contemporary Art (tel. 526-1322) is the site of the 1920's Spalding Estate. Its mansion has been reconfigured to house the permanent collection and changing exhibits, as well as a fascinating museum shop and a pleasant but very noisy cafe. The gardens overlook the city and provide places to sit and enjoy the peace and quiet. There is a nominal admission charge, but on **Thursdays admission is free.**

Punchbowl Crater contains the National Memorial Cemetery of the Pacific **(tel. 541-1430)**, and is the #1 visitor attraction in Hawaii. The crater contains more than 30,000 graves of war dead, and the Courts Of The Missing monument names an astounding 28,000+ who are listed as missing. **Astronaut Ellison Onizuka**, killed in the 1986 explosion of the space shuttle Challenger, is buried here. The ancient Hawaiian name for this place, *Puowaina*, ironically translates to "hill of sacrifice". A sweeping view can be had from the lookout at Punchbowl's 450' summit. On an average day, 125 tour buses and 700 other vehicles pass through its gates, for a surprising total of 6 million annual visitors. Officials are working to solve the traffic problem and preserve the sanctity of Punchbowl despite its conflicting roles as both a burial place and a popular tourist attraction.

To visit Punchbowl Crater directly from Waikiki: follow the pink line on the map to the left.

TheBus
848-5555
Ask directions of the driver if in doubt.

Round Top/Tantalus from Waikiki:
Board bus #2 School-Middle St., or the #2 Liliha-Puunui Ave. to the corner of Beretania St. and Alapai St. (opposite the main police station). Walk makai on Alapai St. to the bus stop and transfer to the #15 Pacific Hts. The #2 buses run frequently, but the #15 runs only once every hour. Call for schedule. Bus #15 only travels a small section of our featured route, but passes the Contemporary Museum, and comes close to the viewpoint as seen here in the rainbow photo, located to the right of the intersection of Makiki Hts. and Tantalus Dr.

Return:
From the opposite direction, board bus #15 Pacific Hts. and transfer on King St./Ward Ave., in front of the circular Neil Blaisdell Concert Hall, to the #2 Waikiki-Kapiolani Park or #2 Waikiki-Campbell Ave.

Punchbowl Crater from Waikiki:
(Commercial tour buses visit Punchbowl directly.) Board bus #2 School-Middle St., or the #2 Liliha-Puunui Ave. to the corner of Beretania St. and Alapai St. (opposite the main police station). Walk makai on Alapai St. to the bus stop and transfer to the #15 Pacific Hts. Alight at the intersection of Puowaina St. and Hookui St. Unfortunately, its a good half mile walk uphill from here to the crater, but one with wonderful views of Honolulu and Waikiki and places to sit along the way. Bring water.

Return:
Walk back to the bus stop on Puowaina St. opposite the side of the street from where you alighted. Board the #15 Pacific Hts. and transfer to the #2 Waikiki-Kapiolani Park or #2 Waikiki-Campbell Ave. at the corner of King St. and Ward Ave. (fronting the Neil Blaisdell Concert Hall).

Photographs

1. A late afternoon rainbow appears right over Round Top Road. This view is from a hairpin turnout east of the intersection of Makiki Hts. and Tantalus Drive.

2. After sunset, a sudden shower lends an eerie moodiness to this view from the shoulder lookout on Round Top Rd. A 30 second exposure allowed the clouds to blur, and a tripod ensured the stationary objects registered clearly. The long exposure also added to the strange color due to film reciprocity failure.

3. Numerous hairpin turns, bountiful trails and memorable scenery make Mount Tantalus a favorite place with bicyclists, joggers, and hikers.

4. Punchbowl Crater is the #1 tourist attraction in Hawaii: view from Tantalus Drive.

All photos:
Kodachrome 64

25

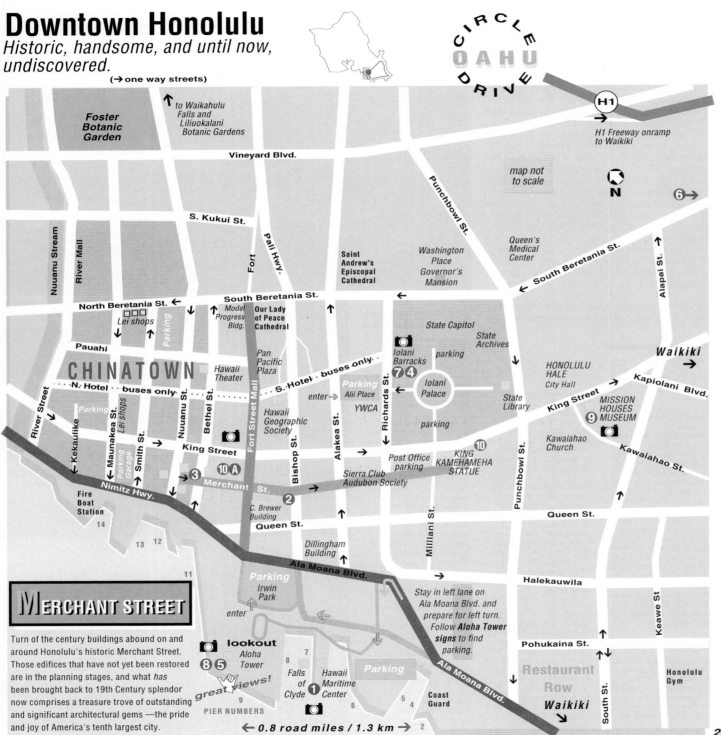

Downtown Honolulu

Historic, handsome, and until now, undiscovered.

(→ one way streets)

SOUTH SHORE

CIRCLE OAHU DRIVE

Foster Botanic Garden

to Waikahulu Falls and Liliuokalani Botanic Gardens

Vineyard Blvd.

S. Kukui St.

S. Beretania St.

Nuuanu Stream

River Mall

North Beretania St.

Lei shops

Pauahi

CHINATOWN

N. Hotel buses only

River Street

Parking

Kekaulike

Maunakea St.

Parking Garage

Smith St.

Nuuanu St.

Bethel St.

Lei shops

King Street

Fort Street Mall

Model Progress Bldg.

Our Lady of Peace Cathedral

Saint Andrew's Episcopal Cathedral

South Beretania St.

Pali Hwy.

Fort

Hawaii Theater

Pan Pacific Plaza

S. Hotel · buses only

Parking

Alii Place

YWCA

Hawaii Geographic Society

Bishop St.

Alakea St.

Richards St.

Merchant St.

C. Brewer Building

Queen St.

Sierra Club Audubon Society

Post Office parking

Dillingham Building

Nimitz Hwy.

Fire Boat Station

Ala Moana Blvd.

Irwin Park

enter

Parking

map not to scale

N

Punchbowl St.

Washington Place Governor's Mansion

State Capitol

Iolani Barracks

Iolani Palace

State Archives

State Library

Queen's Medical Center

South Beretania St.

HONOLULU HALE City Hall

King Street

MISSION HOUSES MUSEUM

Kawaiahao Church

Kawaiahao St.

KING KAMEHAMEHA STATUE

Queen St.

Millani St.

Punchbowl St.

Halekauwila

Pohukaina St.

Alapai St.

Waikiki

Kapiolani Blvd.

Waikiki

Restaurant Row

Keawe St.

South St.

Honolulu Gym

Halekauwila

H1

H1 Freeway onramp to Waikiki

Waikiki

Stay in left lane on Ala Moana Blvd. and prepare for left turn. Follow **Aloha Tower signs** to find parking.

lookout

Aloha Tower

great views!

Falls of Clyde

Hawaii Maritime Center

Parking

Coast Guard

PIER NUMBERS

Ala Moana Blvd.

← 0.8 road miles / 1.3 km →

MERCHANT STREET

Turn of the century buildings abound on and around Honolulu's historic Merchant Street. Those edifices that have not yet been restored are in the planning stages, and what *has* been brought back to 19th Century splendor now comprises a treasure trove of outstanding and significant architectural gems —the pride and joy of America's tenth largest city.

A guided morning walking tour of **Historic Downtown Honolulu** *departs from the Mission Houses Museum, 553 S. King St. The cost includes museum admission; $7 /adults, $2 /children under 17. Call for latest information and reservations* **(531-0481),** *as both the admission charge and tour days are subject to change.*

Downtown Honolulu comes as a surprise to most people. It is without a doubt one of the loveliest, most impressive and cleanest downtowns of any major US city. Downtown Honolulu exhibits a handsome mix of architecturally significant historic structures that stand tooth and jowl with ultra modern highrises and gushing waterfall-fountains. It is compact in size, human in dimension, and a delight to the eye. Downtown Honolulu is home to the **governor's mansion** ("Washington Place", on Beretania St.), the **State Capitol Building**, with its volcano-shaped roof, the nation's most vibrant and lively **Chinatown**, a lazy bougainvillea-lined river, numerous outstanding public buildings constructed in the classic red tile roof **Mediterranean Style**, and the only **Royal Palace** on United States soil.

Wandering the streets along and about and *south/makai* of the **Iolani Palace** will reveal a plethora of **superb architecture**. Drive around the area first to get an overview, then park and walk. The public parking areas on the map offer 4 hour metered parking...**bring plenty of quarters**. Parking in the **Alii Place** parking structure on ALAKEA ST. is very reasonable for **2 hours or less** only. After 2 hours, the cost skyrockets. Pay close attention to the **one way street arrows** on the map to avoid frustration.

From Waikiki:

Drive *mauka/north* in Waikiki to ALA WAI BLVD. and *turn left* onto it. *Make a right turn* at MC CULLY ST., the **first bridge**. *Go north/ mauka* on MC CULLY ST. to BERETANIA ST. *Make a left turn* onto BERETANIA. In less than five minutes, on the right, you will pass the architecturally lovely **Honolulu Academy of the Arts** at **900 S. Beretania**, which has a truly surprising and impressive collection of works, including an extensive collection of Asian and Western Art, and much by top 20th century masters. A donation is requested. The museum is famous for the beauty of its buildings and courtyards and is registered as a National Historic Place. A wonderful and inexpensive luncheon with a gourmet touch is served at the covered open air **Garden Café** in two

PIER 8

ALOHA

❶
❷ ❸ ❹

❺
❻

sittings beginning at **11:30 a. m.**, and should not be missed. For reservations call 531-8865. Thursday supper is also served. At this writing the Café is closed during summer months, but there are plans to change that. Call to check.

0.7 mile *past* the art museum on BERETANIA ST. is **Washington Place**, Hawaii's governor's mansion, on the *right/mauka* side of the street. Directly across from it is the **State Capitol Bldg.** —look for the roof peaked in the center like a volcano— after which you will make an immediate *left turn* onto RICHARDS ST. *Proceed along* RICHARDS ST. past the **Iolani Palace**, on the *left*, and the **YWCA** on the *right*. At the intersection of KING ST., notice there is short term **parking** at the Post Office Bldg. *across the street* on the *left*. A *left turn* onto KING ST. will take you past the **Iolani Palace** entrance, where on the grounds there is **more short term parking**. This area would be a good place to leave the car only for a *quick* exploration on foot. Otherwise, play it safe and choose longer term parking.

The four story **Iolani Palace**, beautifully bedecked with bunting for holidays, was constructed in 1882 by Hawaii's worldly "Merry Monarch", **King David Kalakaua,** and became the scene of lavish royal parties. Influenced by his European travels, it was the personal creation of Kalakaua, whose interest in science and technology was reflected in such modern accoutrements as indoor flush toilets, telephones, and outdoor electric lighting. After his death, his sister **Queen Liliuokalani** was imprisoned here for nine months by American businessmen who shamefully forced her abdication from the throne in 1893. During her house arrest, broken hearted, she wrote the beautiful and haunting **Aloha Oe,** still to this day the song most closely identified with Romantic Hawaii.

The handsomely restored palace is open to the public **Wednesday through Saturday** for 45 minute tours that begin every 15 minutes from **9 a.m. until 2:15 p.m.** The admission charge is $4 for adults and $1 for kids under 12. No kids under 5 years will be admitted. Call for reservations, information or price or schedule changes **(522-0832)**. Free concerts are presented at the gazebo each Friday at noon. Bring a picnic or go across the street to **JM** at the **YWCA** for take-out. **JM (533-7356)** serves great breakfasts and lunches in their courtyard eatery. The menu is on the gourmet side, but the prices aren't (JM stands for Julia Morgan, the famous architect who designed the beaux arts building).

Adjacent to the rear of the Palace on the *Diamond Head side*, is the **Archives of Hawaii**, housing

the world's largest collection of Hawaiiana and historical photographs. Copies of fascinating **photos of old Hawaii** can be ordered here by anyone, and make a great souvenir.

On the *mauka/* BERETANIA ST. side of the palace is the modern **State Capitol**, where the architecture is both impressive and symbolic of Hawaii's volcanoes and ocean environment. You can visit both the state senate and house of representatives if they are in session, and even drop in to see the office of the governor.

Across from the KING ST. Iolani Palace entrance is one of the most recognizable symbols of Hawaii, the **King Kamehameha Statue**. This replica was installed after the original, cast in **Italy**, sank to the bottom in a shipwreck while sailing around The Horn. This copy was subsequently ordered from the original artist and delivered to Hawaii safely. The lost original was recovered in a salvage operation and now stands at **Kapa'au**, Kohala, on the **Big Island**.

One block from the King's statue in the direction of Diamond Head, along KING ST. at PUNCHBOWL ST., is **Kawaiahao Church (522-1333)** circa 1841, and constructed of coral and timber. The feathered *kahilis*, signifying royalty, indicate that this church was the site of royal coronations, christenings and ceremony. On **Sunday** mornings at **10:30 a.m.**, services are conducted in the Hawaiian language and beautiful **Hawaiian hymns** are sung. The church grounds are worth a visit, especially the tiny cemetery/garden to the rear, across from the Mission Houses Museum.

The Mission House Museum (531-0481) complex is next door at 553 S. KING ST., on the *Diamond Head side* of Kawaiahao Church. Handsomely preserved, it encompasses the oldest existing buildings erected by the first missionary contingent to Honolulu. The Frame House was prefabricated and shipped around Cape Horn from New England. The detailed restoration of these houses is remarkable, and a cellar-to-bedrooms tour is offered of the Frame House. Hours are from **9 a.m. to 4 p.m., Tuesday through Saturday, Sunday, noon to 4 p.m. Closed Monday**. Admission includes a 45 minute tour and costs $3.50 /adults, $1 /children under 17. Call **(531-0481)** for possible schedule or admission charge changes.

Backtrack along S. KING ST. to RICHARDS ST., *go left* on it, and then *turn right* on MERCHANT ST. For hikers and nature lovers, both the **Sierra**

Club and **Audubon Society** have their offices at 212 MERCHANT ST. Stop by for information while you're in the neighborhood. Follow MERCHANT ST. to ALAKEA ST. *Turn left/makai* on ALAKEA ST. and go to ALA MOANA BLVD., where famous **Aloha Tower** can be seen near the harbor's edge, **2 blocks** *north/right*. (4 hour parking is available in this area —see map). *Turn left* on Bishop St. to visit the **Hawaii Maritime Center** and its crown jewel, the sailing vessel **The Falls of Clyde**.

In 1878, when **The Falls of Clyde** first set sail, it was one of the fastest vessels afloat and transported cargo to ports around the globe. In 1898 she sailed for the Matson Line fleet carrying passengers and cargo between San Francisco and Hilo, and later was refitted as a sailing oil tanker. By 1963 they were ready to deep-six her in Vancouver, when the citizens of Honolulu came to the rescue. Recently restored with authentic 19th century fittings, The Falls of Clyde is the only full-rigged, four masted ship left in the world and has been placed on the National Register of Historic Places. Your visit on board provides a wealth of **photographic opportunity**, made richer still if your camera has a macro lens, or a macro lens setting to catch all the handsome details. The ship is just one component of the *superb* **Hawaii Maritime Center**, which also includes the **Aloha Tower**, with its sweeping harbor and downtown views, the **Kalakaua Boathouse**, a museum of maritime history in the islands, and the **Hokule'a**, the double-hulled replica canoe that is believed brought the original Hawaiians to Hawaii. The Boathouse has a nice gift shop, a **great view** from its widow's walk, and is adjacent to **Coaster's**, one of Honolulu's most atmospheric and pleasant places for lunch, right at harbor's edge. The admission fee to the **Hawaii Maritime Center (536-6373** or **532-1717)** is $6 for adults and $3 for kids under 18.

After leaving the harbor, walk *back up* BISHOP ST., noticing the wealth of beautifully detailed old edifices. The first, on the *right side* of the street, is the Italian Renaissance **Dillingham Transportation Bldg.** (c.1929) with its knock-out lobby and elegant ornamentation. Next, after crossing QUEEN ST. you will *pass on the left* another superb example, the **Alexander & Baldwin Bldg**. (c.1929). Gorgeous murals face the entry way walls and depict undersea tableaux with an oriental-art deco feel. You'd think this might clash with the building's gargoyles of contented bovine faces and its Mediterranean style tiled roof —but somehow it all works. Next, turn *left* onto MERCHANT ST., and enter what is shaping up to be a location

scout's dream-come-true. From Bishop to Nuuanu St., **MERCHANT ST.** is lined with newly restored, lovingly detailed century-old commercial buildings. Its a time-warp kind of place, with a where-the-heck-are-we-anyway? feel to it, resembling streets in Old Chicago or Portland rather than Honolulu, except for the odd palm tree or two. The beautifully detailed buildings are too numerous to name, but homesick, thirsty Easterners can work their way past them for 3 blocks to **Merchant Square**, at the corner of NUUANU ST., where historic brick-faced **Murphy's Bar & Grill** awaits with its tall narrow shuttered windows, cast iron exterior decoration, and cold drinks. First opened in 1890, **Mark Twain, Robert Louis Stevenson** and **King David Kalakaua** have all tipped a glass here. Or you might want to stop in at **O'Toole's** across the street. Both look just like they did over 100 years ago when crusty sea-faring whalers frequented the area's taverns.

Backtrack along MERCHANT ST. to FORT ST. MALL, the newly refurbished pedestrian thoroughfare lined with shops, the superb old C. Brewer Bldg. (a few yards *makai* from the intersection with MERCHANT ST.), the Liberty House department store, restaurants, more historic structures, lovely Our Lady of Peace Cathedral, and beautiful new Pan Pacific Plaza. *Make a left* on HOTEL ST., and go **1/2 block** to visit the **Hawaii Geographic Society's (538-3952)** office and store at 49 S. HOTEL ST., Suite 218, to buy maps, trail guides and to get sound advice from **Willis Moore**. The store has limited hours, so call first. For great cafe au lait and croissants, stop by **Ba-Le** (the Vietnamese word for Paris, or Par-ee) at 1150 Fort St. Mall. (Phone **521-4117**).

To return to Waikiki, *drive makai* (makai means toward the ocean) on any street that allows it — **most streets are one way**. *Turn left* when you reach ALA MOANA BLVD/ NIMITZ HWY. (Confusingly, it changes names in this area). It will return you directly to the heart of Waikiki.

Photographs

5. A tugboat departs its berth in Honolulu Harbor, as seen from the Aloha Tower observation deck. The massive parking structure of the Dole Cannery looms behind, under the company's trademark pineapple-on-pylons.

6. One of the beautiful courtyards at the Honolulu Academy of the Arts.

7. Richards St. gate: the Iolani Palace.

8. A rainbow appears over the Amfac Towers in downtown Honolulu. Diamond Head and the Falls of Clyde are both partially visible in this view from the Aloha Tower.

9. The King Kamehameha statue and the State Judiciary Building.

10. The Mission Houses Museum in early morning light.

10A. In this 60 second exposure, passing car lights illuminate the Kamehameha V Post Office on Merchant Street, early evening.

All photos: Kodachrome 64.

TheBus
848-5555

From Waikiki:
On the mauka side of Kuhio Ave., board bus #2 School-Middle St. or #2 Liliha-Puunui to Hotel St. in Downtown Honolulu. Hotel St. runs parallel through the length of downtown, including Chinatown.

Return:
On the makai side of Hotel St., board TheBus #2 Waikiki-Kapiolani Park or #2 Waikiki-Campbell Ave.

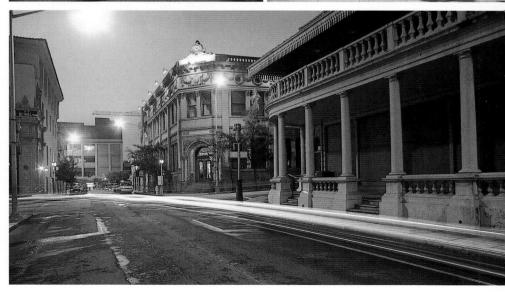

Chinatown

Great food, beautiful bargain-priced leis, and the freshest island produce and seafood.

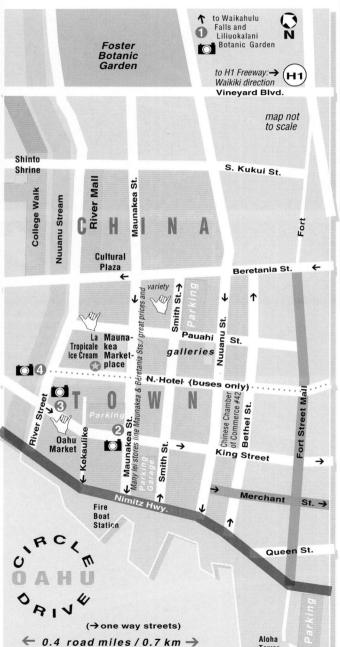

to Waikahulu Falls and Liliuokalani Botanic Garden

❶

N

Foster Botanic Garden

to H1 Freeway:→ Waikiki direction **H1**

Vineyard Blvd.

map not to scale

Shinto Shrine

S. Kukui St.

College Walk

Nuuanu Stream

River Mall

Maunakea St.

C H I N A

Fort

Cultural Plaza

Beretania St. ←

variety

Many lei stores line Maunakea & Beretania Sts./ great prices and

Smith St. →

Parking

Pauahi St.

La Tropicale Ice Cream

Mauna-kea Market-place

galleries

Nuuanu St.

◎④

N. Hotel (buses only)

T O W N

Chinese Chamber of Commerce #42

Bethel St.

River Street

Parking

◎

③

②

Oahu Market

Kekaulike

Maunakea St.

Parking Garage

Smith St.

King Street

Fort Street Mall →

Fire Boat Station

Nimitz Hwy.

Merchant St. →

C I R C L E

O A H U

D R I V E

Queen St.

(→ one way streets)

← 0.4 road miles / 0.7 km →

Aloha Tower

Parking

FOR MEN

FLOWER

IS

An amazing array of traditional and modern leis can be found in shops all along Maunakea Street, and on the makai side of Beretania St. between Maunakea and Smith Sts. Take your time browsing because making a choice isn't easy. Here you will find the official lei of Oahu, the compact ilima flower lei, with its distinctive orange color and velvet-like texture. The Ilima lei was once the lei of kings and is favored by island males. The flower was grown by the early Hawaiians especially for this one specific use.

The pua kika lei, with its unique spiral pattern, is also considered to be a male lei. It takes hundreds of blossoms to make just one garland. Another male lei is the maile vine lei. Tiny white pikake blossoms are woven around this strong, leafy vine which is worn draped over the shoulders of the groom at weddings. You will also see this "special occasion" lei worn by teen males on prom night.

❶

TheBus
848-5555

From Waikiki:
On the mauka side of Kuhio Ave., Board bus #2 School-Middle St., or #2 Liliha-Puunui to the corner of Hotel St. and Maunakea St. The #2 buses run frequently.

Return:
On the makai side of Hotel St., board #2 Waikiki-Kapiolani Park or #2 Waikiki-Campbell Ave.

Photographs

1. Just north/mauka of Chinatown, Waikahulu Falls provides peaceful respite from the noise and commotion of downtown.

2. Detail of window of a Chiatown herb shop with he window painted in English, Chinese and Korean.

3. Tattered awnings shade merchants' goods, and customers, from the hot sun.

4. Crimson Bougainvillea lines Nuuanu Stream along River Street.

All photos: Kodachrome 64

*T*he details of all tours in Hawaii are subject to change, and Chinatown's are no exception. Call first for the latest information. One of the best ways to see Chinatown is to join the **Chinese Chamber of Commerce Tour.** It leaves from the Chamber's headquarters at 42 N. KING ST. (**533-3181** or **533-6967**). The tour fills up fast and reservations are recommended. The cost is $4, with an optional lunch extra. Another tour is offered by the **Hawaii Heritage Center** (**521-2749**), at 1128 SMITH ST., 2nd floor, and also costs $4. **The Chinatown Historical Society** (**521-3045**) sponsors a 2 hour walking tour weekdays at 10:30 a.m. (donation). Please call for latest schedules and prices.

The only way you can really enjoy Chinatown is on foot. The area is compact and filled with surprises and oddities. Street parking, all short term, is limited in Chinatown, restricting you from doing much. A large long-term metered city lot (**bring lots of quarters**) is located on SMITH ST., between BERETANIA ST. and PAUAHI ST. It is close to where the Hawaii Heritage Center walking tour begins, and just a block over from the NUUANU ST. **gallery** of renowned Hawaii artist **Pegge Hopper** (at #1164). You probably noticed her giant paintings of Hawaiian women hanging at the Honolulu International Airport. **Ramsay's Galleries & Cafe** is classy and elegant, and down the street at 1128 SMITH ST., in the same building as the Hawaii Heritage center. This immediate area supports about a dozen galleries, and most are open weekdays from **10 a.m. to 4 p.m.**, and until **1 p.m. on Saturdays**.

One of planet earth's great **ice creams** is made and sold in Chinatown by two Vietnamese men who learned their skills in Paris: **La Tropicale USA (533-1393)**, located at 1120 MAUNAKEA ST., at the **Maunakea Marketplace.** There is an entrance on HOTEL ST. also. **La Tropicale** sells world class ice creams that compare quite favorably with Berthillon of Paris, which is considered the world's best by many. Its worth a special trip to Chinatown just for a taste. Also, their sandwiches —try the shredded chicken— are delicious, unique, and **very inexpensive**.

The **Maunakea Marketplace** is bordered by HOTEL, PAUAHI and MAUNAKEA ST., with the main entrance on the latter. The food court contains more than a dozen **hot food** kiosks offering mostly Asian dishes, and is a popular stop for lunch. Down the steps from the food court, the market area offers great buys in dried mushrooms, fresh watercress, bananas and papayas, live fish, and shrimp. Used styrofoam seafood containers that make great **ice chests** for your island picnics cost just $1. Extra-Jumbo size eggs, too big for the carton, cost less here than what small size eggs cost in Waikiki. Normally expensive summer harvest delicacies like local lychees, mangoes, and watermelon, are pure ambrosia and incredibly cheap here. This market also has an entrance on Hotel St., along which many other small markets are located, with wonderful and curious wares literally spilling out the doors. This plentiful concentration makes for competitive pricing where, for once, the customer wins.

Speaking of competitive pricing, shops selling good quality **T-shirts** for $5 and less are plentiful in the area adjacent to the Maunakea Marketplace, and flower shops here by the dozens display a visually stunning variety of **leis** that are priced unbelievably low. Orchid leis are priced between $3 and $5, and gorgeous floral combinations that are masterwork examples of the craft can be had for $10-$12. If you are going to pick someone up at the airport, this is the place to stop for their welcome gift. Many lei shops are concentrated along MAUNAKEA ST., like **Variety** at #1190, **Mauna Kea Leis** at #1189, **Violet** at #1165, and **Cindy's** in the pagoda-style **Wo Fat** building, but many others are sprinkled throughout Chinatown, especially along BERETANIA ST. between MAUNAKEA ST. and SMITH ST. Compare prices before buying.

The **Oahu Market**, at the corner of KING ST. and

KEKAULIKE ST., (**1 block** *down/makai*, and to the west from the Maunakea Marketplace), is a cooperatively operated, open-walled blessing to those who find Waikiki supermarket prices outrageous. The freshest of island fish, local fruits and vegetables, and exotic ethnic foods such as taro, lemon grass and fish cake can be found here. A ghastly variety of fish heads all in a row stare back from glass cases, destined for someone's gourmet soup, and crispy ducks mesmerize as they rotate slowly on spits right before your eyes. Kona crab is cheaper here than anywhere else. Fresh fruit and vegetable prices here and at the **Maunakea Marketplace** are **lower than at roadside stands** right next to the fields that grow them. Island raised chicken is more expensive than the stuff imported from California, but you can taste the difference —and its fresh, not frozen. Ready for a break? **Ba-Le (521-3973)** has a store across the street at 150 N. KING ST. for sandwiches and good French croissants and coffee. **Sea Fortune** at 111 N. KING ST. is a real popular spot for dim-sum, and believe it or not, is packed with customers as early as 7 a.m.

Other streets that invite exploring include RIVER ST., which follows the east bank of **Nuuanu Stream**, at the western border of Chinatown. A couple of very popular, tiny Vietnamese eateries are located on RIVER ST. around the corner from HOTEL ST.'s west end. The **view** up Nuuanu Stream itself is attractive, as bright crimson bougainvillea has been planted along its course. *North* of BERETANIA ST., things get seedier along RIVER WALK. RIVER ST. becomes a pedestrian mall at this point. You will pass the **Chinese Cultural Plaza**, with its interesting **Dragon Gate Bookstore**. The restaurant **Legend** (100 N. Beretania St., 532-1868) has the reputation for the best dim-sum on Oahu. Prepare to wait in line at lunchtime. If your legs are still holding out, walking another two minutes *north/mauka* delivers you to beautiful 20 acre **Foster Botanic Garden**.

Although every guidebook mentions the **Foster Botanic Garden** ($1 admission fee), none of them do justice to its beauty and location. Just minutes on foot from the craziness of central Chinatown and the stress of the downtown business district, it is a lovely and indispensable oasis of natural beauty and serenity in a surprisingly unlikely location. It must be the envy of every large city downtown in the nation. The Garden has exceptional collections of palms, orchids, heliconias and gingers, more than 20 of the city's protected "exceptional trees", a prehistoric plant collection the likes of which once fed the dino-

saurs, and a gift shop selling seeds and live plants cleared for mainland entry. Just north of the Gardens on the opposite side of the H1 FWY. is **Liliuokalani Botanical Garden**, with its two natural waterfalls and deep pool, where swimming is allowed, but not recommended due to possible contamination from runoff. Not too many city centers in the world can boast a downtown civic treasure like this. The park entrance is located on KUAKINI ST., off NUUANU ST.

Chinatown is filled with fascinating, narrow, dimly lit shops selling exotic, strange and unusual wares. Chinatown has fresh noodle factories, herbalists who dispense dried seahorse and snakeskin, Chinese delis, Vietnamese restaurants, tailors, crack seed stores, and bakeries that sell take-out dim sum. Chinatown is noisy, crazy, cool, distant and business-like, but polite, and a great deal of fun. Now, if only the same kind of civic mindedness that keeps the rest of downtown clean and tidy could be applied to Chinatown's streets and sidewalks, we'd *really* have something.

There is not enough room here to do all of Chinatown's attractions and oddities justice. The best sightseeing plan would be to freely wander at will, pacing yourself, resting when tired and eating when hungry, inspecting strange and new items with the eyes of a child, and remembering to look up and enjoy all the second story architectural details.

The easiest way to return to Waikiki from Chinatown is to drive *makai/south,* on any street that allows it, to NIMITZ HWY. /ALA MOANA BLVD. (It may be named either one —it changes names here.) Make a *left* turn onto it. The ocean will be on your right side as you drive back to Waikiki, and the mountains on your left. You will pass downtown Honolulu, (*mauka*), Ala Moana Park (*makai*), and across the boulevard from the park, the giant **Ala Moana Shopping Center**. ALA MOANA BLVD. leads directly to Waikiki's main thoroughfares, KALAKAUA AVE. and KUHIO AVE.

Pearl Harbor

Poignant Remembrances of
"The Day That Will Live In Infamy".

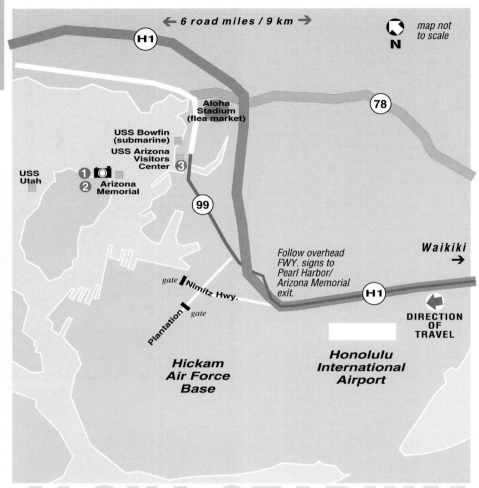

← **6 road miles / 9 km** →

map not to scale

N

H1

Aloha Stadium (flea market)

USS Bowfin (submarine)

USS Arizona Visitors Center

78

USS Utah

① 📷
② **Arizona Memorial**
③

99

Follow overhead FWY. signs to Pearl Harbor/ Arizona Memorial exit.

Waikiki →

H1

DIRECTION OF TRAVEL ←

gate **Nimitz Hwy.**

Plantation gate

Hickam Air Force Base

Honolulu International Airport

ALOHA STADIUM FLEA MARKET

The Aloha Stadium Flea Market is the largest in the islands, and attracts crowds of bargain-hungry visitors and kamaainas. Held at the Aloha Stadium (close to Pearl Harbor) every Wednesday, Saturday and Sunday, commercial tours run excursions from Waikiki. Info: 732-2437.

*F*rom **Waikiki,** take the H1 FWY. *west* to the ARIZONA MEMORIAL/STADIUM exit. Follow the signs to the **Arizona Memorial Visitor Center**. There is limited free parking, and tickets are distributed daily on a first come, first serve basis beginning at **7:30 a.m. Programs begin at 8 a.m.**, **(7:45 a.m. during the summer**), and **end at 3 p.m.** All visitors must be at least **45 inches tall**. For further information, call **422-0561**.

Although Honolulu has changed and grown dramatically since WWII, there is still enough of that time period to be found and visited today to give a veteran of the attack on Pearl Harbor a genuine sense of *deja vu*. The most obvious relic of the war era in Hawaii is, of course, **Pearl Harbor** itself, and the sunken wreckage of the **USS Arizona**. Pearl Harbor is the hub of Pacific Fleet Operations, and attracts more than **1.5 million visitors annually**.

It is not uncommon to encounter a **2 or 3 hour wait** to visit the memorial. Tickets can be picked up and questions answered in the main reception area of the **Visitor Center**, where on exhibit is an enormous 15' X 50' oil painting of the USS Arizona by artist **John Charles Roach**. There is a gift shop that does very brisk business and a museum that relates the Pearl Harbor story vividly. The visitor's first official stop is the theater, where a terrific, beautifully edited documentary film, newly produced in 1992 and movingly narrated by actress **Stockard Channing**, is viewed before boarding the Navy shuttle boat to the Memorial. National Park Rangers are stationed aboard the Memorial to provide information.

The **USS Arizona Memorial** is a simply executed, sculpted white concrete structure that ironically was designed by an Austrian P.O.W. named **Alfred Preis** who was taken prisoner by Americans in Hawaii in 1941 and interred in the P.O.W. camp close by on Sand Island.

The 184' long memorial spans the sunken battleship **USS Arizona**, and beneath the feet of the millions of visitors who have stood here, 1100 Navy men and Marines lie interred in her hull. The legacy of the attack still haunts the waters of Pearl Harbor in a very visible and tangible way, as the skeletons of aircraft, the wreck of the U.S.S. Utah, and great chunks of damaged ships litter the bottom. A toxic sediment of oil, as well as sludge containing lead, copper and zinc leaching from war debris, remain to pose an ongoing ecological threat. Stirring up this sludge by dredging would release dangerous and concentrated amounts of

pollutants into Oahu's waters.

Tied up next to the Arizona Memorial is the **USS Bowfin**, one of the last of the WWII subs. The Bowfin has been restored and the main hatch is open for public inspection. Visitors have the chance to go aboard and experience first hand the claustrophobic conditions that the crew endured for weeks at a time. Guests are invited to visit the engine room and the sleeping and eating quarters, and become involved in the hands-on fun of turning a steering wheel, pushing buttons, visiting the torpedo room... touching is not only allowed aboard the Bowfin, but encouraged. Kids love it, but must be 6 years of age or older to board. The Bowfin's illustrious history includes participation in 9 successful patrols throughout the Pacific during which she **sank 38 enemy ships**. Visitors borrow a short range radio on this self guided tour which picks up recorded tour narrative at appropriate points along the way. Admission is **$3 for adults** and **$1 for children ages 6-12**.

Next door to Pearl Harbor is **Hickam Field**, where at the **Hale Makai barracks**, rounds of enemy bullet holes have gouged the wall, remaining as a memorial of the "day that will live in infamy". Hale Makai is now a historical monument with a museum display of artifacts of the attack. **Pre-arrangements** must be made to visit Hickam, and can be by calling **449-6367 or 449-9386**.

For those wanting to further relive their memories of this era, a visit to Waikiki's **Royal Hawaiian Hotel** will reveal that although the gardens have been reduced, the architecture of the guestrooms and public spaces, where U.S. naval officers attended a dance the evening of December 6, 1941, have been preserved much the way they were. Nearby at the **Halekulani Hotel**, the 100 year old kiawe tree on the terrace stands witness to that same night, when **Admiral Kimmel**, the commander of the Pacific Fleet, ate here what would turn out to be his last peaceful dinner for quite some time. And finally, for those who have foggy memories of Saturday nights spent stumbling down Honolulu's HOTEL ST., you will find that despite recent redevelopment, a few faint shadows of war-era weekend debauchery still remain.

On your way to or from Pearl Harbor, you may want to visit the unparalleled collections of Hawaiian and Pacific artifacts at the **Bishop Museum (847-3511)**. Exit the H1 FWY. at the LIKELIKE HWY. and quickly get into the far right lane. Turn onto BERNICE ST. where the museum awaits at #1525. Weekends are best to avoid school kids.

❶

TO THE MEMORY OF THE GALLANT MEN
HERE ENTOMBED AND THEIR SHIPMATES
WHO GAVE THEIR LIVES IN ACTION
ON DECEMBER 7, 1941 ON THE U.S.S. ARIZONA

❷

❸

Photographs

1. Old Glory flies above the U.S.S. Arizona Memorial, as seen through the structure's sculptural arches.

2. Inside the Memorial the names of those killed in the attack fill an entire wall.

3. The U.S.S. Arizona Memorial as seen from the lawn of the Visitor Center.

All photos:
Kodachrome 64

TheBus
848-5555

Ask driver for directions if unsure.

From Waikiki:
On the mauka side of Kuhio Ave., heading away from Diamond Head, board the #20 Airport-Halawa Gate bus. This bus will pass along Saratoga Rd., Kalia Rd., and Ala Moana Blvd. in Waikiki on its way to Pearl Harbor. Alight on the Kamehameha HWY. at the Arizona Memorial.

Return:
Board bus #20 Waikiki-Beach and Hotels on Kamehameha HWY. at the Arizona Memorial. This bus does not run after 5 p.m. on weekdays or 4 p.m. on weekends. If you miss it, board any bus marked Honolulu-Ala Moana Center. Transfer at the Ala Moana Center to the #8 or #19 Waikiki-Beach and Hotels bus.

From Waikiki to the Bishop Museum:
Board the #2 School-Middle St. bus on the mauka side of Kuhio Ave. Ride it to Kapalama St., from which you will have to walk two blocks.

Return from Bishop Museum:
Board the #2 Waikiki-Kapiolani Park or #2 Waikiki-Campbell Ave. bus on the opposite side of the street from where you alighted.

Kapiolani Park

Right next door, but with lots more room to move on its handsome beaches.

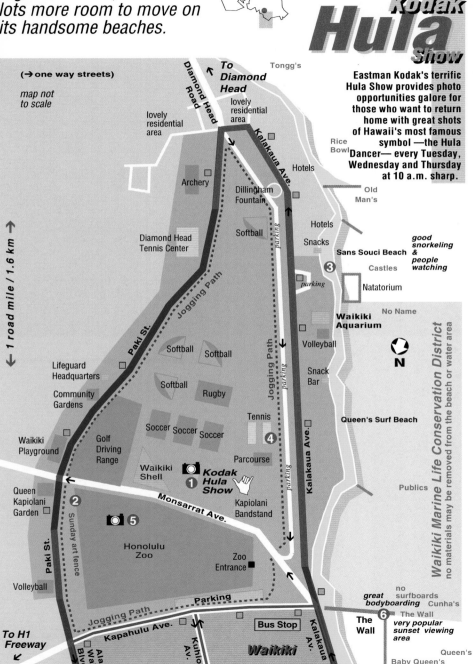

(→ one way streets)

map not to scale

← 1 road mile / 1.6 km →

To Diamond Head

Diamond Head Road

Tongg's

lovely residential area

lovely residential area

Kalakaua Ave.

Rice Bowl

Archery

Diamond Head Tennis Center

Dillingham Fountain

Hotels

Old Man's

Softball

Hotels

Snacks

Sans Souci Beach

good snorkeling & people watching

③

Castles

Natatorium

parking

Paki St.

Jogging Path

Softball Softball

Softball

Rugby

Lifeguard Headquarters

Community Gardens

Soccer Soccer Soccer

Tennis

④

Parcourse

Waikiki Playground

Golf Driving Range

Waikiki Shell

📷① **Kodak Hula Show**

Queen Kapiolani Garden ②

📷⑤

Monsarrat Ave.

Sunday art fence

Honolulu Zoo

Zoo Entrance

Kapiolani Bandstand

Volleyball

Paki St.

Parking

Jogging Path

To H1 Freeway ↙

Kapahulu Ave.

Ala Wai Blvd.

Kuhio Av.

Bus Stop

Kalakaua Av.

Waikiki

Waikiki Aquarium

No Name

Volleyball

Snack Bar

N

Queen's Surf Beach

Publics

Waikiki Marine Life Conservation District
no materials may be removed from the beach or water area

great bodyboarding

no surfboards Cunha's

⑥ The Wall

The Wall

very popular sunset viewing area

Queen's

Baby Queen's

Kodak Hula Show

Eastman Kodak's terrific Hula Show provides photo opportunities galore for those who want to return home with great shots of Hawaii's most famous symbol —the Hula Dancer— every Tuesday, Wednesday and Thursday at 10 a.m. sharp.

*A*djacent to the crowds, noise and concrete of Waikiki is a large, open sprawl of green offering welcome respite. Although Kapiolani Park is by no means deserted, there is room to move on its huge central lawn area as the familiar profile of **Diamond Head** watches over. People come here to fly kites, play ball, and pace themselves along the **2 mile long jogging path**, and to picnic, barbecue and swim at the splendid beaches with postcard Waikiki views. Weekends, as might be expected, draw the biggest crowds, and that's when most of the park's special events are scheduled. Check the daily papers to see what's happening, or pick up a free copy of the highly readable, event-savvy tabloid **Honolulu Weekly** around town. There is so much to, and happening in, Kapiolani Park that if it were set on an island all by itself, it would still be an attractive visitor destination.

Kapiolani Park is bordered on the Waikiki side by KAPAHULU AVE. and most people **enter the park** at the intersection of KALAKAUA AVE. and KAPAHULU AVE. Immediately on the *right/makai* side of this entrance is a very popular spot set aside for body surfers and belly boarders known as **"The Wall"**, because the best wave action is right alongside the wall that juts out into **Mamala Bay**. It is also a favorite place for people to come and watch the sunset and the boisterous activity in the water below. The Wall is also the NW boundary of the **Waikiki Marine Life Conservation District**, established here in 1988, and designed to conserve and replenish the area's marine resources. The MLCD extends all along the shore at Kapiolani Park from The Wall to the seawall of the Natatorium, and extends **500 yds. into the bay**. Nothing —no marine life, coral, or even sand or stones— may be taken from the water or the beach.

Across KALAKAUA AVE. from The Wall, immediately within the park, MONSARRAT AVE. branches off to the left. A short walk along MONSARRAT will bring you to the entrance of the **Honolulu Zoo**. Although small compared to some of its counterparts on the mainland, the Honolulu Zoo draws over a million visitors a year. It is open daily from **8:30 a.m. until 4:30 p.m.** The zoo is essentially a 42 acre tropical garden with over 900 kinds of mammals, amphibians, birds and reptiles, including an elephant that was a gift from India's Indira Ghandi, and which can be heard trumpeting all the way to the beach. On **Wednesdays in summer**, the zoo remains **open until 7 p.m.**, with visitors admitted **free after 4:30 p.m.** A variety of entertainment, at no charge, is scheduled beginning at 6 p.m. (tel. 971-7174)

On the *mauka* side of the zoo, outside its fence, local residents tend **community gardens**, and on the MONSARRAT ST. fence, art works are displayed on **Sundays** by **local artists** in an **outdoor exhibit and sale**. Many highly collectible Hawaii artists began their careers here, so prudent art investors might want to check it out.

Kapiolani Beach is the first beach you will pass after The Wall. With recently constructed rest rooms and new showers, it offers good swimming with a mostly sandy bottom at the Waikiki end. This is a good alternative to the jam packed Waikiki beaches close by. Along the whole length of Kapiolani Park's beaches, a paved pathway winds along the edge of the sand for joggers and strollers. A wide lawn area separates the beach from

KALAKAUA AVE. This lawn, cooled by large shade trees and dotted with picnic tables, gets quite crowded on weekends.

The next bit of strand past Kapiolani Beach is called **Queen's Surf Beach**. It has locker rooms and a snack bar. The beach is narrow, so many people sunbathe on the lawn. It is heavily frequented by local residents, and the area on the Waikiki side of the snack bar is a favorite of Honolulu's gay population. Just past Queen's Surf is the **Waikiki Aquarium**, established in 1904, and open **daily from 9 a.m. until 5 p.m.** The Waikiki Aquarium contains a very wide range of sea life, including a "flashlight fish", giant clams, the endangered Hawaiian Monk Seal, and near the ocean's edge, a hands-on tide pool exhibit with living coral and sea creatures common to Hawaii's shores. Ask about the Aquarium's field trips, tide pool walks, photography and cooking classes, and visit their unique **gift shop**. (tel. 923-9741). Next door to the Aquarium is Honolulu's disintegrating swim stadium, the **Natatorium**.

Originally dedicated as a war memorial, no final decision on its fate has been made. The waters around it are dangerous for swimming due to holes and sudden drop offs. **Beach parking** is available here but fills up early; enter from KALAKAUA AVE. On the other side of the Natatorium is **Sans Souci** (French for "without a care") **Beach**, also known locally as **"Dig Me"** beach. For people watchers, its considered to be *the* place to see and be seen, but just the same, it still plays second fiddle to the highly entertaining show-off crowd at the beach in front of the **Royal Hawaiian Hotel** in Waikiki. **Sans Souci** is a great family beach and is frequented mostly by *kamaainas* (local residents). The beach has a gradually sloping sandy shore bottom that's protected from waves by offshore reefs. **Sans Souci** (pronounced san—sue—see) also features very good snorkeling, except sometimes in summer when wave action can diminish visibility in its waters. The low wall and adjacent benches backing the beach are a favorite perch for lunch eating and people watching, with the coconut palms providing filtered shade until the early afternoon. Adding to the pleasure of this beach, the hotel building next door contains a convenience store and an ice cream parlor that face toward the park lawn. The hotel also has a renowned beachside restaurant called the **Hau Tree Lanai** that is a pleasant and popular place for breakfast and lunch. Proper casual dress is required. The grouping of hotels and apartments at this end of Waikiki is worth exploring to ascertain the wide variety of accommodations available for your next trip.

After passing Dillingham Fountain and the hotel enclave, KALAKAUA AVE. *curves to the left* at a 90° angle, and then terminates at the intersection ahead. A *right turn* here will put you on DIAMOND HEAD RD. —clearly indicated— and take you past **Diamond Head** (see next page) and onto the beginning of the fabulous, ultra-scenic **Circle Drive.**

If you'd like to return to Waikiki at this point, *turn left* onto PAKI ST., and you will pass Kapiolani Park's **tennis courts** and **archery range** as you head back to Waikiki. At the intersection of **MONSARRAT AVE.**, you will see the zoo on the left, as well as the Sunday art fence, but **do not turn** left as this is a **one way street.**

Waikiki lies straight ahead. Just stay on PAKI ST., and after it crosses KAPAHULU AVE., it becomes ALA WAI BLVD., which is the northern border of Waikiki. Any left turn from ALA WAI BLVD. —pay attention to one way streets— will take you to KUHIO AVE. and KALAKAUA AVE.

❷
❸
❹
❺

❻

Photographs

1. Dancers with the Kodak Hula Show pose for a signature portrait.

2. Sharleen Turner exhibits her work at the Sunday Art Fence in Kapiolani Park.

3. Sans Souci Beach is a favorite for families, as well as the "beautiful people" and those who like to ogle them.

4. Showertree blooms.

5. These public tennis courts in Kapiolani Park have a world famous icon as a backdrop...

6. ...and so do the monkeys in the Honolulu Zoo.

❼

7. Late day activities at The Wall include belly boarding, sunset watching, and couples making out.

All photos: Kodachrome 64

TheBus
848-5555

From Waikiki:
On the makai side of Kuhio Ave., board the #2 Waikiki-Kapiolani Park bus which circles Kapiolani Park via Kapahulu Ave., Kalakaua Ave., Poni Moi Rd. and

Paki Ave. This bus runs every 10 or 15 minutes throughout the day.

Return:
Board the same bus, the #2 Waikiki-Kapiolani Park, going in the same direction. At the corner of Poni Moi Rd. and Paki Ave., the destination sign changes to #2 School-Middle St.

Diamond Head
More than just a pretty face.

Map labels

Kahala Black Point Kaikoo St.

Hanauma Bay

Kahala Ave. Papu St. Kulamanu

3 road miles / 4.8 km

CIRCLE OAHU DRIVE

N

see next page for details about this area

triangular park

Kaalawai Beach — *a classic, palm-lined, uncrowded Hawaiian beach*

DIAMOND HEAD

tunnel

great hike!

great views!

③ lookout
② lookout
⑦ Kuilei Cliffs Beach Park
descending walkway

Diamond Head Road

① lighthouse

Beach St.

great sunset viewing on lighthouse lawn

Diamond Head Beach Park
⑤

HEAD

parking fills up quickly; come early to avoid traffic, heat, and tour buses.

DIRECTION OF TRAVEL

CRATER

TRAIL

lookout ⑥

great views!

Makalei

④

Nalaau Hawaii Arboretum (abandoned)

map not to scale; not meant to be used as a trail or hiking map

Kapahulu Ave.

Monsarrat Ave.

return to Waikiki

Paki Ave.

Paki Ave.

Kapiolani Park Dillingham Fountain

Sans Souci Beach

DIRECTION OF TRAVEL

Kapahulu Av.

Zoo

One Way

Kalakaua Ave.

Ala Wai Canal Ala Wai Blvd. Kapahulu Av. Monsarrat Ave. Kalakaua Ave. Kuhio Ave.

Waikiki

Kapahulu

A mauka turn onto Kapahulu Ave.— which acts as the eastern/ Diamond Head boundary of Waikiki— will reward with some of Honolulu's most interesting eating and shopping places. Here are just a few:

Bailey's (#758) purveys a wide selection of collectible ALOHA SHIRTS, while Snorkel Bob's (#702) rents everything you'll need for a snorkeling adventure, and also has good bargains on used equipment.

Ono Hawaiian Foods (#726) is the spot to sample traditional island favorites, and Keo's (#625) offers Thai food in an elegant, orchid-bedecked setting. To get down with the locals though, head straight for the Rainbow Drive In (#3308 Kanaina St.) for overflowing bargain plate lunches.

Main text

*D*iamond Head is more than just the distinctive natural landmark recognized around the world as a symbol of Waikiki. The area in and immediately surrounding the crater offers a good number of memorable and visually remarkable island experiences located conveniently close to Waikiki. For those who enjoy urban hiking or just a good, *long*, discovery-filled walk, you don't need any transportation other than two feet to fully enjoy Diamond Head.

From Waikiki, walk or drive along KALAKAUA AVE. parallel to the beach through **Kapiolani Park**, then continue past Dillingham Fountain on your *left/mauka* side, and Sans Souci Beach and the compact concentration of hotels on your *right/ makai* side. KALAKAUA AVE. curves to the left 90° at this point and intersects DIAMOND HEAD ROAD at the stop sign just ahead. Turn *right* onto DIAMOND HEAD ROAD. If you'd like, you can first explore this small and pretty neighborhood

with its varied cornucopia of lovely little homes, some surprisingly Midwestern looking, before continuing up along Diamond Head Road.

As you climb DIAMOND HEAD ROAD you will pass some snazzy homes on the *makai* side, and if its any typical day, a steady stream of attractive joggers as well. Keep your eye out for a steep downhill street on the *right/makai* side named BEACH ST., although usually its street sign is

missing. A low stone wall on the *makai* side begins here and a prominently placed yellow DEAD END sign otherwise marks the place. This narrow street has very limited parking along it, but offers a way to visit **Diamond Head Beach** without the long, steep walk down — and then back up— the paved pathway that most people use from the upper lighthouse area. As a bonus, the **view** from BEACH ST. is quite photogenic also.

After Diamond Head Road climbs past BEACH ST. it passes the classically handsome **Diamond Head Lighthouse**. The lawn area just to the east of the lighthouse is a favorite place for sunset viewing, and attracts a loyal and friendly little crowd each evening, some of whom bring lawn chairs and drinks. All along here the low stone wall borders the roadside and delineates the three dramatic lookout areas, from which surfers and windsurfers check out the conditions below. Carloads of tourists and kamaainas arrive to view the

brilliantly colored windsails darting across the waves, or just to sit and relax and enjoy the view, the sun or the sunset, and each other. Just east of the lighthouse lawn is the asphalt pathway trafficked by every variety of water sport enthusiast anxiously descending to enjoy the activity on **Kuilei Cliffs Beach** below. Once on the beach, be aware that sandy pockets make recreational swimming safer and more comfortable down at **Kaalawai Beach**, the beautiful strand lined with a forest of swaying coconut palms that you see toward the east end of Diamond Head Beach. Also notice the group of luxury homes at the end of the beach, including legendary **Shangri-la**, the famed estate of heiress Doris Duke.

Be cautious pulling in and out of all the lookout and parking areas due to inattentive drivers under the spell of the scenery. After the lookout areas, DIAMOND HEAD ROAD descends, and at a triangular little park it *forks off to the left.* DIAMOND HEAD ROAD now continues to circle the base of **Diamond Head** itself, heading away from the ocean and back toward Waikiki. Just ahead, on the back side of the mountain, a prominent sign directs you up a road to the *left* to the tunnel into the interior of **Diamond Head Crater**. The crater is open from **6 a.m. until 6 p.m.** but the parking lot fills up early. If you are not used to physical exertion, do not attempt this trail. The hike to the top is an increasingly popular family activity as it is fine for children under close parental supervision. Even those who are in great shape will get winded, especially near the top when you reach the **99 steps**, but the **view** is phenomenal in every direction. There are WWII bunkers to explore, and restorative breezes at the top. Don't let kids wander off the path by themselves due to drop offs. Bring a hat and water, and wear sunblock. A flashlight for the tunnel and spiral staircase is very helpful. After your hike, *return* from the parking lot through the tunnel to DIAMOND HEAD ROAD.

To continue the Circle Drive, *turn **right*** onto it. Proceed *makai* until you reach the little triangular park. *Turn left* onto KAHALA AVE. and proceed. Turn the page now to continue along the Circle Drive.

To return to Waikiki after leaving the crater through the tunnel, *turn **left*** onto DIAMOND HEAD ROAD and *proceed* along it as it descends and changes its name to MONSARRAT AVE. Stay in the right lane and prepare to *turn right* at PAKI ST. After turning right, the next main intersection is **KAPAHULU ST.**

A *left turn* onto KAPAHULU ST. will take you one block to KUHIO AVE., and then a *right turn* onto KUHIO AVE. will take you directly into the **heart of Waikiki.**

A *right turn* onto KAPAHULU AVE. takes you along an interesting thoroughfare of unusual shops, described alongside the map at left.

TheBus
848-5555

Ask driver for directions if unsure.

To Diamond Head Crater from Waikiki:
Heading in the Diamond Head (east) direction, along the makai side of Ala Moana Blvd., Kalia Rd., Saratoga Rd., or Kuhio Ave., board the #58 Hawaii Kai-Sea Life Park bus. Or, board the #22 Hawaii Kai-Sea Life Park BEACH BUS along the makai side of Kuhio Ave. Take either bus to the corner of Diamond Head Rd. and 18th Ave., and walk into the crater through the tunnel. The BEACH BUS allows surfboards and other bulky beach gear on board.

To Diamond Head Lookouts and Beaches, and Black Point, from Waikiki:
On the makai side of Kuhio Ave. board any #2, #4, #8, #19, or #20 bus heading toward Diamond Head, and alight on Kapahulu Ave. after the bus turns right from Kuhio Ave. Transfer to the #14 Maunalani Hts. bus, on the same side of the street and traveling in the same direction. The #14 only runs once an hour. The #14 bus will drive past Diamond Head's lighthouse, lookouts, and beaches, through Kahala Avenue's lush residential area, then past the Kahala Mall.

Return from Crater:
On Diamond Head Rd. heading back in the Waikiki direction, board the #58 Waikiki-Ala Moana Center or #22 Waikiki-Beach and Hotels BEACH BUS.

Return from Diamond Head Lookouts and Kahala:
In the opposite direction, board #14 St. Louis Hts. bus, and ride to the corner of Paki Ave. and Monsarrat Ave. in Kapiolani Park. Transfer to the #2, #4, #8, #19 or #20 bus back into Waikiki via Kuhio Ave.

Photographs

1. Diamond Head lighthouse is a popular place to watch the sunset.

2. Windsurfers dart among the waves as seen from a lookout along Diamond Head Road.

3. Classically beautiful palm-lined Kaalawai Beach is adjacent to Kuilei Cliffs Beach Park. This view is from a Diamond Head Road lookout.

4. This view from the Nalaau Hawaii Arboretum provides great views of Waikiki and Kapiolani Park.

5. Diamond Head Beach and offshore windsurfers are seen in this shot from Beach St.

6. The Diamond Head Crater Trail winds up the inner flanks of the famous landmark.

7. A windsurfer heads for the water at Kuilei Cliffs.

All photos: **Kodachrome 64**

Kahala to Koko Head
Hawaii's Beverly Hills

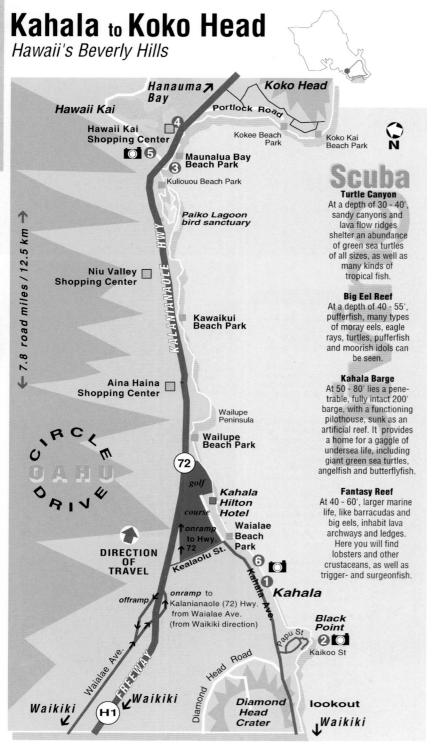

Hanauma Bay ↗

Koko Head

Hawaii Kai

Portlock Road

Hawaii Kai Shopping Center ④

Kokee Beach Park

Koko Kai Beach Park

⑤ 📷

③ Maunalua Bay Beach Park

N ↗

Kuliouou Beach Park

Paiko Lagoon bird sanctuary

Niu Valley Shopping Center

Kawaikui Beach Park

Aina Haina Shopping Center

Wailupe Peninsula

Wailupe Beach Park

72

golf

Kahala Hilton Hotel

course

Waialae Beach Park

↑ *onramp to Hwy. 72*

DIRECTION OF TRAVEL

Kealaolu St.

⑥ 📷

① **Kahala**

onramp to Kalanianaole (72) Hwy. from Waialae Ave. (from Waikiki direction)

offramp

Black Point

② 📷 Kaikoo St

Kahala Ave.

Papu St

Waialae Ave.

FREEWAY

Waikiki →

Diamond Head Road

Diamond Head Crater

lookout

Waikiki ↓

← *Waikiki*

H1

← 7.8 road miles / 12.5 km →

CIRCLE OAHU DRIVE

KALANIANAOLE HWY.

Scuba

Turtle Canyon
At a depth of 30 - 40', sandy canyons and lava flow ridges shelter an abundance of green sea turtles of all sizes, as well as many kinds of tropical fish.

Big Eel Reef
At a depth of 40 - 55', pufferfish, many types of moray eels, eagle rays, turtles, pufferfish and moorish idols can be seen.

Kahala Barge
At 50 - 80' lies a penetrable, fully intact 200' barge, with a functioning pilothouse, sunk as an artificial reef. It provides a home for a gaggle of undersea life, including giant green sea turtles, angelfish and butterflyfish.

Fantasy Reef
At 40 - 60', larger marine life, like barracudas and big eels, inhabit lava archways and ledges. Here you will find lobsters and other crustaceans, as well as trigger- and surgeonfish.

*K*ahala is Honolulu's equivalent of Beverly Hills. In recent years homes here have been bought and sold for previously unheard-of sums, only to be torn down and replaced with much grander versions. Take a look around **Kahala** to see how people with lots of money find new, and sometimes extreme, ways to spend it.

To get here, *proceed* along DIAMOND HEAD ROAD from the Waikiki direction and pass the little triangular park at the intersection of KAHALA AVE. Continue along KAHALA AVE. for just one block past the triangular park, then *turn right* onto PAPU ST., and *proceed* along it downhill to KAIKOO ST. On-street parking is not available past this point, so park uphill and take the short walk to the p.r.o.w. KAIKOO ST. is a neighborhood of exclusive homes built on a steep slope facing dreamy ocean views, and includes an interesting example constructed in the South Seas style with a steeply pitched, thatched palm frond roof. KAIKOO ST. circles around at the bottom, where there is a **public right of way (p.r.o.w.)** on the right/makai side, just past a home with a fancy verdigris metal gate and detailing.

The p.r.o.w. leads to a dramatic shore piled with huge black boulders and crashing white waves, and is a favorite water entry point for surfers. There is no beach here, but there is a wonderful and photogenic **view** back toward Diamond Head.

When finished here, *backtrack* to KAHALA AVE. and *turn right* onto it. There are **6 more p.r.o.w.s** along KAHALA AVE. in a space of less than one mile, beginning with one across from intersecting ELEPAIO ST. Further along, next door to 4477 KAHALA AVE., the p.r.o.w. leads to a favorite **eel fishing** ground. Locals set eel traps here at sunset, returning the following morning to collect their catch.

Other p.r.o.w.s provide beachside views of the homes of Honolulu's rich and famous, as does a

leisurely drive along KAHALA AVE. Despite the mansionization in recent years, many beautiful smaller homes do remain, and even a few very modest plantation style cottages can still be seen here and there. Some of the large estates leave their gates open offering a tantalizing peek at life in their privileged world for the passing tour buses and looky loos. One estate, named **Villa Kahala**, is itself hidden from street view by a beautifully designed natural-looking rock barrier with three gushing waterfalls splashing down its face. It is lushly planted with rainbows of flowers and ornamental tropicals.

❶

Located toward the end of KAHALA AVE. is **Waialae Beach Park**, perhaps not the prettiest park on the island with its murky canal, but it *is* very quiet, and the beach itself is wide and impressively well maintained. Its ace in the hole is the location in close proximity to the **Kahala Hilton** property, and all that it has to offer. The **Hilton beach** has better swimming than **Waialae** does, is open to the public, and is **lifeguard protected**. Visitors are welcome to look around the splendid Hilton property and to watch the feeding of the porpoises, and take advantage of the restaurants if properly dressed (no bathing suits).

To continue along the coast, turn *mauka* on KEALAOLU ST., which is across KAHALA AVE. from the **Waialae Beach Park**. Go straight down KEALAOLU ST. for **0.7 mile**, then turn *right* onto the **first street** past the golf course, immediately before the freeway overpass. This is the onramp to the KALANIANAOLE (72) HWY.

The KALANIANAOLE (72) HWY. skirts past the Waialae Golf Course, and **0.6 mile** later, tiny **Wailupe Beach Park** appears on the *right/makai*. The beaches all along this shore, known as **Maunalua Bay**, are mostly made up of mudflats and coral. Esthetically, you can find better recreational swimming conditions elsewhere, but the shore along the bay is attractive, wide open and uncrowded. Four parks within a 3 mile stretch of Maunalua Bay provide ample space to picnic, kite-fly, and run free. There are plenty of coconut palms, sea breezes, expansive coastal views, a bird sanctuary and lots of shopping, not to mention one of Hawaii's most internationally celebrated restaurants, **Roy's**, in Hawaii Kai.

Wailupe Beach Park is small but pretty. Its view of the bay is blocked by Wailupe Peninsula, which is a compact haven for the upscale homes whose boat piers you can see at the east end of the park. Locals crab and fish among the pilings and seem to do very well. Further along the HWY., past the Aina Haina Shopping Center, is **Kawaikui Beach Park** with similar park facilities as **Wailupe** —a restroom, some picnic tables— but with a good view of the bay and dominant **Koko Head**.

A little less than **1.0 mile** ahead, PAIKO DR. leads out to Paiko Lagoon, a good sized bird sanctuary that is, however, not especially attractive. This area silted up heavily after a disastrous 10" rainfall in Aina Haina in the late 80's. Less than half a mile past PAIKO ST. you will pass BAY ST., down which is hidden **Kuliouou Beach Park,** where you can wade in knee deep water to the end of Paiko Peninsula at low tide. Directly east is larger **Maunalua Beach Park**, with its scattered picnic tables, large lawn, and unobstructed CinemaScope bay views.

A *left/mauka turn* along here onto just about any of the streets that run up toward the mountains will give a glimpse of local homes and condo developments, small quiet neighborhood parks and commanding upland views. The affluent community of **Hawaii Kai**, located just before Koko Head, with its inland network of waterways, canals and boat slips, and homes reaching high onto the ridge flanks, is a good choice for a look-see.

Finally, just over the Hawaii Kai bridge, *turn right/ makai* onto PORTLOCK ROAD and tour **Koko Head**'s exclusive Portlock area for more examples of impressive homes and landscaping, and two miniature so called "beach parks", **Kokee** and **Kokokai** —neither of which, by the way, has any beach at all.

❷

TheBus
848-5555

Kahala From Waikiki: On the makai side of Kuhio Ave. board any #2, #4, #8, #19, or #20 bus heading toward Diamond Head, and alight on Kapahulu Ave. after the bus turns right from Kuhio Ave. Transfer to the #14 Maunalani Hts. bus, which only runs once an hour. This bus will drive past Diamond Head lighthouse and lookouts, and along Kahala Avenue's lush life, then past the Kahala Mall.

**Return:
From the opposite direction, board #14 St. Louis Hts. to the corner of Paki St. and Monsarrat Ave. in Kapiolani Park. Transfer to the #2, #4, #8, #19, or #20 bus back through Waikiki.**

Kalanianaole HWY. and Hawaii Kai from Waikiki: Board bus #58 Hawaii Kai- Sea Life Park on the makai side of Ala Moana Blvd., Kalia Rd., Saratoga Rd., or Kuhio Ave. This bus will run along Kalanianaole Hwy. and in Hawaii Kai will turn left onto Lunalilo Home Rd. and past the Hawaii Kai Shopping center. Or, board the #22 Hawaii Kai Sea Life Park BEACH BUS on Kuhio Ave.

**Return:
In the opposite direction, board the #58 Waikiki-Ala Moana Center or #22 Waikiki BEACH BUS.**

Photographs

1. Along Kahala Ave. a splendid entrance only gives a hint to passersby of what must lie behind.

2. From the p.r.o.w. at Black Point, a beautiful view of the less famous side of Diamond Head and its beaches can be seen.

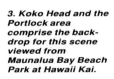

3. Koko Head and the Portlock area comprise the backdrop for this scene viewed from Maunalua Bay Beach Park at Hawaii Kai.

4. Chef Roy Yamaguchi takes a seat in front of the fabulous view in his namesake restaurant in Hawaii Kai.

5. Gracious waterside living at Hawaii Kai.

6. The beach at Kahala is quite narrow but is lined for much of the way with generous stands of coconut palm.

**All photos:
Kodachrome 64**

❸ ❹
❺ ❻

Hanauma Bay

Living rainbows swim beneath the surface.

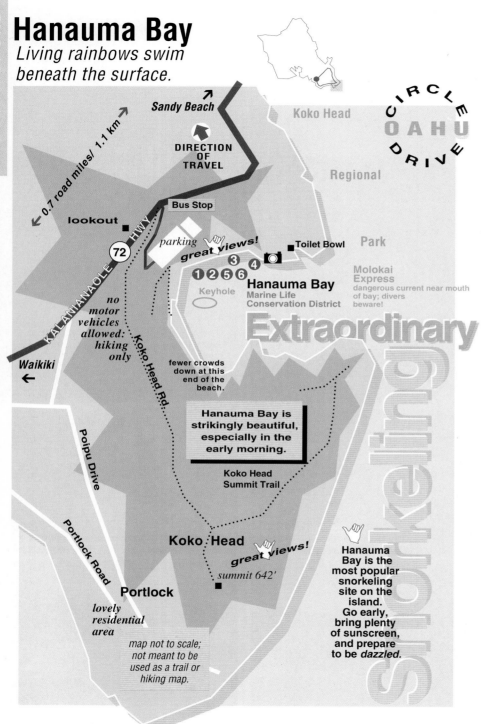

Sandy Beach

DIRECTION OF TRAVEL

Koko Head

Regional

0.7 road miles/ 1.1 km

Bus Stop

lookout

72 HWY.

parking great views!

Toilet Bowl

Park

③ ④ 📷

① ② ⑤ ⑥

Hanauma Bay
Marine Life
Conservation District

Keyhole

Molokai
Express
dangerous current near mouth
of bay; divers
beware!

KALANIANAOLE

Koko Head Rd.

*no
motor
vehicles
allowed:
hiking
only*

Waikiki

*fewer crowds
down at this
end of the
beach.*

Extraordinary

**Hanauma Bay is
strikingly beautiful,
especially in the
early morning.**

**Koko Head
Summit Trail**

Poipu Drive

Koko Head
great views!

summit 642'

Portlock Road

Portlock

*lovely
residential
area*

*map not to scale;
not meant to be
used as a trail or
hiking map.*

**Hanauma
Bay is the
most popular
snorkeling
site on the
island.
Go early,
bring plenty
of sunscreen,
and prepare
to be *dazzled*.**

Snorkeling

CIRCLE OAHU DRIVE

*H*anauma Bay is 8 miles and 20 minutes from Waikiki via the KALANIANAOLE (72) HWY.

Leaving Koko Head behind, the KALANIANAOLE (72) HWY. climbs up the grade behind the mountain, and near the crest of the hill a sign to the *right/makai* points the way to Hanauma Bay. Immediately after your right turn, notice a gated road to the extreme *right*. You can't drive on it, but an easy 15 minute walk along this road and Koko Head's summit will open up amazing views along the coast and of incomparable Hanauma Bay below. Along-highway parking is no longer allowed here. The only parking available is in the official parking lot in the park below. Plan on going to Hanauma

wet: an exquisite setting, shallow waters, calm conditions and rainbows of sea life looking for a handout all combine to create the perfect learning ground and a memorable vacation experience. At the beginning of the 1990's, tough new restrictions were placed on tour buses and the total number of visitors allowed to use Hanauma Bay. At one time, up to 10,000 people a day jammed in here. The area had become overwhelmed and the formerly crystal clear waters were clouded with bread, frozen peas, and cake that people brought to feed the fish. The health of the reef and the sealife it supports deteriorated dramatically, and it became a matter of choosing or losing. Understandably, the fish won. Daily quotas were established for visitors, automobile parking and tour

❶

Bay early, as parking is limited and fills up fast. Many people come here just for a quick look from the bluff so if the lot is full, keep your eyes open for these people returning to their cars. One of the best ways to enjoy exquisite Hanauma Bay, and avoid parking hassles, is to sign up for one of the many inexpensive snorkel excursions originating in Waikiki. See advertisements in the free streetside publications such as **This Week** and **Spotlight.**

Hanauma Bay is extraordinarily beautiful and quite deserving of its fame. It was used as a film location in **Elvis Presley's Blue Hawaii**. It is the ideal place for novice snorkelers to get their feet

groups. It is now prohibited to bring people-food to feed the sea creatures. Natural fish food is available for sale at the concession on the beach. The paved walkway down to the beach is long and steep, but there is a shuttle bus for those who wish to ride. A **schedule for TheBus** back to Waikiki is thoughtfully posted at the shuttle stop right on the beach.

The large clear sandy area beneath the azure waters as seen from the walkway is called **The Keyhole**, and is the most popular —but we're not saying the best—snorkeling area. Hanauma Bay's 2000' length of sandy beach is backed by a score of lovely palms moving in the breeze and its protective outer reef insures that the bay is always calm and safe. But as always, when bringing children, its best to check with the lifeguard about possible unseen hazards. The area at the far end of the beach is much less crowded, but the quality —if not the quantity— of vibrant sea life is just as spectacular. However, the lack of a sandy shorebottom makes entering the water here more uncomfortable than back at The Keyhole. Prepare to be startled by sea creatures both beautiful and bizarre in a variety and number existing nowhere else in Hawaii. Recovering coral is colored purple, orange and chartreuse, and between these new heads, fish of every color and shape glide by, cruising for a handout. Visibility is best away from other snorkelers whose fins stir up the sand and cloudy bits of food that have settled on the bottom. Instead of walking on the sharp, uncomfortable and fragile reef, its much easier, and much better for the reef, to glide over it. With fins and mask this is a cinch, even in water as shallow as 18 inches. Just keep your fingers out of holes as you go.

Running along the edges on both sides of the bay is a raised terrace that is popular with hikers and beachgoers. High waves have washed people off into the sea, so its best to keep alert and to read and heed the posted warning signs. This ledge makes for an interesting hike, but avoid it at high tide. The terrace to the left/east leads out to a natural phenomenon called the Toilet Bowl. It is a hole in the rocky ledge that fills and empties from the bottom in time to the wave action, like a flushing toilet. This spot accounts for the overwhelming **majority of drownings** at Hanauma Bay, so again, read and heed the posted warnings and stay out of it. Cut the week-long **tide table** from the daily **Honolulu Star Bulletin**, and carry it in your wallet so you can safely take advantage of adventures that might present themselves just about anytime and anyplace on the island.

TheBus
848-5555

From Waikiki:
On the makai side of Kuhio Ave., board the #22 Hawaii Kai-Sea Life Park BEACH BUS. The BEACH BUS allows surfboards and other bulky beach gear, so go for it. The Beach Bus also gets you to Koko Head Regional Park, Halona Blowhole, Sandy Beach, and Makapuu Beach.

Return:
In the opposite direction, board the #22 Waikiki-Beach and Hotels BEACH BUS.

❷

Photographs

1. The early morning (9 a.m.) sun delineates the shapes of the reef beneath Hanauma Bay's turquoise waters at low tide.

2. Snorkelers enjoy The Keyhole. Notice that the person whose head is visible at the center of the photo is completely surrounded by scores of fish as they gather to be fed. Walking on the reef, as some of these people are doing, kills the reef. Please don't!

3. The overwhelming number of drownings at Hanauma Bay take place because people do not heed these cautions.

4. This natural arch is located along the eastern edge of the bay.

5. People explore the eastern shelf. Note the arch at bottom of photo. Unexpected waves wash over this shelf, carrying the unwary with them.

6. To gauge for yourself the enormous rise in popularity of this beautiful place, study this shot of a typical mid-day crowd at Hanauma Bay in 1973.

Photo #6:
Kodachrome 25

All other photos:
Kodachrome 64

❸❹
❺❻

The Halona Coast

*Koko Head Regional Park:
Nature's fury unleashed*

CIRCLE
OAHU
DRIVE

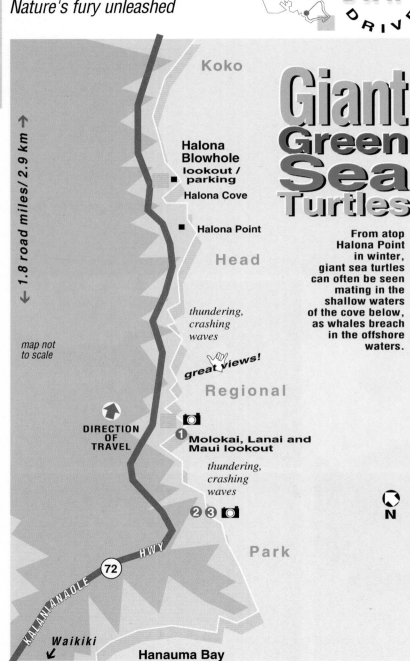

Koko

**Halona
Blowhole**
**lookout /
parking**
Halona Cove

Halona Point

Head

*thundering,
crashing
waves*

great views!

Regional

📷

❶ **Molokai, Lanai and
Maui lookout**

*thundering,
crashing
waves*

❷❸ 📷

Park

**DIRECTION
OF
TRAVEL**

↑ 1.8 road miles/2.9 km ↑

*map not
to scale*

N

72
KALANIANAOLE
HWY

Waikiki
↓
Hanauma Bay

Giant Green Sea Turtles

**From atop
Halona Point
in winter,
giant sea turtles
can often be seen
mating in the
shallow waters
of the cove below,
as whales breach
in the offshore
waters.**

*A*fter leaving Hanauma Bay Beach Park, *turn right* onto KALAIANAOLE (72) HWY. The road here is winding and very interesting as it hugs the tops of the cliffs. There are a number of places where the shoulder is wide enough to pull over and have a look. Before doing so, *be sure that the cars behind you see that you are going to stop;* people tend to get distracted from their driving by the sensational vistas.

The seashore here at **Koko Head Regional Park,** also known as the **Halona Coast,** is shamelessly magnificent. Not until you spot a fisherman standing far below on one of the bluffs, looking tiny and totally vulnerable to the elements, can you appre-

this cardinal rule prevails: **Never turn your back on the ocean**. Despite their lifelong knowledge of the area, and their vast experience with the elements, *scores of local fishermen have been swept off these rocks to their deaths* over the years, so visitors should be advised to keep well back from the edge. The rocks are covered with scree that can send the unwary flying. Don't go back home in a box.

At a small turnout at **Halona Point,** just before the turnout to the large parking area, there is a black stone monument to the Japanese god who is guardian of people who frequent dangerous coastlines and waterways. A short walk out along the

❶

ciate the sheer magnitude of this place.

Great masses of ocean water crash into the wave-carved hollows beneath the seacliffs with resounding explosions caused by rapidly displaced air. Scores of fishermen stake out their territories and rock explorers revel in the noise and the spray. Gigantic masses of elegantly layered and grooved rock, colored with minerals, sea water, and ever-changing shadows, provide a camera hungry scene just begging to be shot. A short walk in the direction of the water reveals nature's power and majesty as strong winds often carry spray as far as the roadway.

Perhaps here more than any other place on Oahu,

top of the ridge that extends from here reveals isolated little **Halona Cove**. Alas, this former hidden place and its lovely beach has been discovered by the tour buses, whose occupants walk down from the Blowhole parking area. Swimming at Halona Cove is dangerous due to the strong currents flowing out its funnel-like sea entrance.

However, from the ridge above, **giant sea turtles** can still be seen mating, literally close enough to the rocks to touch, and **whales** in the winter and early spring fly mightily out of the waters, dancing and breaching in celebration just off the Point. Next door, the **Halona Blowhole**'s performances depend on the tide and the heaviness of the seas, sending a powerful spray of salty wash some-

❸

❷

times 50' into the air. **Many** people over the years have slipped and fallen into the blowhole. Only one has ever lived. Content yourself with viewing it from the platform above. From the Blowhole viewing area, one gets a great look at **Sandy Beach**, weekend teen mecca and Wave Warrior proving ground, our next stop down the road.

TheBus
848-5555

From Waikiki:
On the makai side of Kuhio Ave., board the #22 Hawaii Kai-Sea Life Park BEACH BUS. The Beach Bus allows surfboards and other bulky beach gear, so go for it. The BEACH BUS also gets you to Hanauma Bay, Sandy Beach, and Makapuu Beach.

Return:
In the opposite direction, board the #22 Waikiki-Beach and Hotels BEACH BUS.

Photographs

1. Rock, water and sun create beautiful patterns of shadow and light along the Halona Coast.

2. Three fishermen stand perilously close to the edge as heavy seas pound the shoreline.

3. A man in shorts standing on the brink puts the magnitude of the Halona Coast into perspective.

All photos:
Kodachrome 64

Sandy Beach
Battleground for experienced wave warriors

N

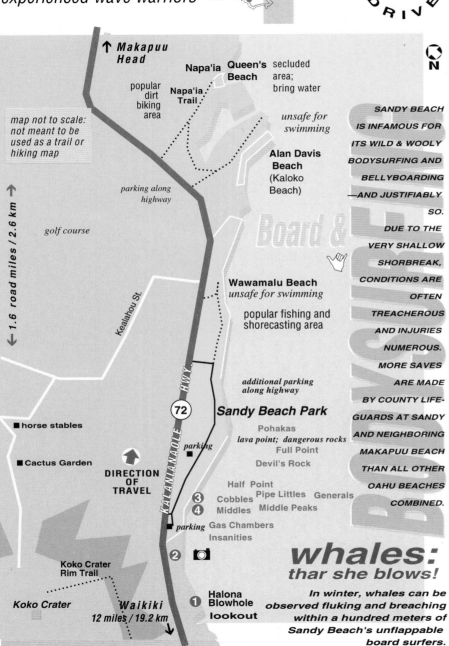

map not to scale: not meant to be used as a trail or hiking map

↑ *Makapuu Head*

Napa'ia   **Queen's Beach**   secluded area; bring water

popular dirt biking area   **Napa'ia Trail**

unsafe for swimming

Alan Davis Beach (Kaloko Beach)

parking along highway

golf course

Wawamalu Beach *unsafe for swimming*

popular fishing and shorecasting area

← 1.6 road miles / 2.6 km →

Kealahou St.

Board &

additional parking along highway

(72)

■ horse stables   *parking*

Sandy Beach Park

Pohakas *lava point; dangerous rocks*

Full Point

■ Cactus Garden   **DIRECTION OF TRAVEL**   Devil's Rock

KALANIANAOLE HWY.

Half Point

③ Cobbles   Pipe Littles   Generals

④ Middles   Middle Peaks

parking ■ Gas Chambers

Insanities

Koko Crater Rim Trail

② 📷

Koko Crater   *Waikiki* 12 miles / 19.2 km ↓

❶ **Halona Blowhole lookout**

SANDY BEACH IS INFAMOUS FOR ITS WILD & WOOLY BODYSURFING AND BELLYBOARDING —AND JUSTIFIABLY SO. DUE TO THE VERY SHALLOW SHORBREAK, CONDITIONS ARE OFTEN TREACHEROUS AND INJURIES NUMEROUS. MORE SAVES ARE MADE BY COUNTY LIFE-GUARDS AT SANDY AND NEIGHBORING MAKAPUU BEACH THAN ALL OTHER OAHU BEACHES COMBINED.

BOOGIE BOARDING BODYSURFING

whales:
thar she blows!

In winter, whales can be observed fluking and breaching within a hundred meters of Sandy Beach's unflappable board surfers.

*C*ontinue along KALANI-ANAOLE (72) HWY. from the **Halona Blowhole** and pull over on the wide shoulder just before **Sandy Beach.** *Make sure the driver behind you sees your signal.* Here you'll get a wonderful side-on vantage point from which to shoot photos of body surfers and belly boarders, especially if you have a telephoto lens. This particular view brings home the danger of the shorebreak as waves crash inexperienced –but nonetheless willing– young bodies into the sand at **Oahu's most dangerous beach.**

Sandy Beach is probably the most popular beach on Oahu with young people. The boys come to bodysurf and the girls come to watch and make fun of them when they crash. Especially on Sundays, a festive atmosphere prevails; youths gather around cars listening to music, eating, lying on the beach, and watching as the injured get hauled out of the water. Along with **Makapuu Beach**, which is located just over the next hill, Sandy is the premiere body surfing beach on the island. Sandy's wild and dangerous shorebreak, as well as the rough lava point in front of the restrooms, have made mincemeat out of many a young daredevil. But for experienced shorebreak bodysurfers, these waves are considered to be nonpareil.

Besides the danger posed by Sandy Beach's bone crushing pounders, a **powerful rip** current runs out to sea from the center of the cove to the left of the aforementioned lava point. There is much needed **daily, year 'round lifeguard** service here, and no matter what your experience level, this is one place where its wise to check with the guard for local hazards before entering the

water. More lifeguard rescues are made at Sandy and Makapuu Beaches than **all other Oahu beaches combined.**

Physically, Sandy Beach is wide and beautifully situated, with deep, comfortable sand. There is parking in designated spaces —they fill up early— as well as along the highway. The large lawn area is a favorite with kite flyers, young and old, and on weekends, lunch wagons are normally present to dispense the local favorites, saimin and plate lunches.

The annual **TDK-Gotcha Pro Surf and Bikini Contest**, held in June, is the ultimate Sandy Beach Experience, and if you are on the island then, it should not be missed. The name says it all. The people-watching at this event is Grade A, and the radical ballet out on the waves is memorable. You'll need binoculars to fully appreciate both.

Further along the HWY. adjacent to Sandy Beach is **Wawamalu Beach**, a favorite of shorecasting fishermen. Its lonely stretches attract sunbathers trying to avoid the noise and crowds at Sandy. The lack of any reef to disarm the power of the currents and incoming waves makes it unsuitable for safe swimming, but a great place for solitude and open space. At the end of Wawamalu Beach is a sizeable cove which blocks beach access to another hidden sandy gem, **Queen's Beach**. A 20-30 minute hike around the rear of the cove is required to reach it, but you still may not have it all to yourself, as this area is popular with dirt bikers and 4WD vehicles. Recreational swimming is very poor at **Queen's** due to the dangerous currents surrounding **Makapuu Point**.

Photographs

1. Sandy Beach, as seen from the Halona Blowhole Lookout.

2. On Sundays its virtual gridlock in the water as bodysurfers and bellyboarders jockey for position on the incoming breakers. The shallow shorebreak here is treacherous.

3. A bellyboarder skims past a bodysurfer who ducks under the wave to avoid getting hit...

4. ...and immediately heads right for another bodysurfer who doesn't see him coming: they missed colliding by only a hair.

All photos:
Kodachrome 64

TheBus
848-5555

From Waikiki:
On the makai side of Kuhio Ave., board the #22 Hawaii Kai-Sea Life Park BEACH BUS. The Beach Bus allows surfboards and other bulky beach gear, so go for it. The BEACH BUS also gets you to Hanauma Bay, Koko Head Regional Park, Halona Blowhole, and Makapuu Beach.

Return:
In the opposite direction, board the #22 Waikiki-Beach and Hotels BEACH BUS.

❷

❸❹

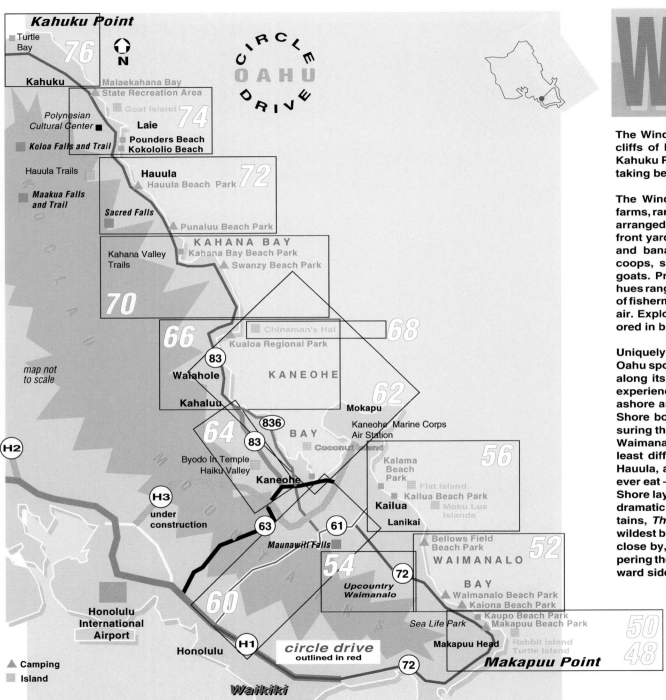

Windward *SHORE*

The Windward Shore stretches from the wild and craggy cliffs of Makapuu Head to the wild and craggy shore at Kahuku Point, with over a hundred square miles of breathtaking beach and luxuriant jungle in between.

The Windward Shore is lush and green, with countless farms, ranches and backyard agricultural enterprises neatly arranged along its marvelous roads. Moving cars flash by front yards filled with blooming red torch ginger, papayas and bananas; bronze, red and green ti plants, rooster coops, sprightly spring colts and little herds of pygmy goats. Protected bays glow beneath the sun in stunning hues ranging from cobalt to turquoise, cooling the bare legs of fishermen who throw their nets through the pure, pristine air. Explorers skim the transparent surface in kayaks colored in brilliant and primary yellows and reds.

Uniquely among the Hawaiian Isles, the Windward Shore of Oahu sports a phalanx of lovely shepherd islands that float along its coast, inviting those who've always yearned to experience true solitude on a deserted tropical isle to come ashore and claim their own private beach. The Windward Shore boasts Oahu's longest uninterrupted strand, measuring three and a half white, wide and sandy miles long at Waimanalo Bay. It shelters some of the most beautiful and least difficult hiking trails, such as those at Lanikai and Hauula, and provides the freshest jumbo shrimp you will ever eat – right out of the water– at Kahuku. The Windward Shore lays claim to some of the world's most beautiful and dramatic ramparts: the razorback cliffs of the Koolau Mountains, *The Pali.* It is pounded incessantly by some of the wildest bodysurfing waves on earth, while at the same time close by, it harbors emerald valleys, silent and still, whispering their unspeakable beauty. Welcome to Oahu's Windward side. Prepare to be amazed.

The large numbers within the rectangles on the maps indicate the page number on which the outlined area is located.

Windward Shore Beach Parks

Source: City and County of Honolulu

Windward Shore Beach Parks	Page	Lifeguard	Rest Rooms	Public Telephone	Picnic Tables	Camping	Night Security	Swimming	Snorkeling & Diving	Surfing	Bodysurfing	Windsurfing	Seasonal High Surf
Makapuu BP	48	🤙	WC	☎	XX	△	🔦	S		◣			〰
Kaupo BP	48							S	◯	◣			〰
Kaiona BP	52		WC	☎	XX			S					
Waimanalo BP	52		WC	☎	XX	△		S					〰
Waimanalo Bay SRA	52		WC	☎	XX			S	◯	◣			〰
Bellows Field BP	52	🤙	WC	☎	XX	△		S		◣			〰
Kailua BP	56	🤙	WC	☎	XX			S	◯	◣	◣		〰
Kaneohe BP	62		WC		XX								
Heeia SP	62		WC		XX								
Kualoa RP	66	🤙	WC	☎	XX	△	🔦	S					
Kalae-oio BP	70			☎	XX		🔦	S					〰
Kaaawa BP	70		WC	☎	XX			S					
Swanzy BP	70		WC	☎	XX	△		S					
Kahana Bay BP	71		WC	☎	XX	△		S	◯	◣			
Punaluu BP	72		WC	☎	XX			S					
Hauula BP	72		WC	☎	XX	△		S					〰
Laie BP (Pounders)	74							S		◣			〰
Malaekahana SRA	74		WC	☎	XX	△	🔦	S		◯			〰

Windward Shore Weather

Source: US Dept. of Commerce
National Weather Service Pacific Region
Station: Kaneohe

Oahu Weather: 836-0121
Honolulu Weather: 296-1818, X1520
Surf Report: 836-1952 or 296-1818, X1521
Marine Report: 836-3921 or 296-1818, X1522

	Daily High Temperature	Daily Low Temperature	% Of Cloud Cover	Days With 0.1" Of Rain	Days With 0.5" Of Rain	Monthly Rainfall In Inches
January	78	68	67%	16	3	6.0
February	78	68	68%	14	2	3.8
March	78	69	82%	17	2	4.3
April	79	70	80%	17	2	4.3
May	80	71	69%	16	1	2.4
June	82	73	74%	16	0	1.4
July	83	74	76%	19	1	2.0
August	84	75	69%	17	0	1.8
September	84	75	59%	14	1	1.8
October	83	74	65%	16	1	2.6
November	81	72	73%	17	2	4.3
December	79	70	70%	17	2	4.2

Because of the persistence and moderate humidity of the trade winds, August and September are usually comfortable. Unpleasant weather is more likely later in autumn or early winter when the trades may diminish or give way to a Kona condition and humidity gets opressively high.

Windward Shore weather is characterized by a persistent flow of moderate to fresh northeasterly trades, partly cloudy skies, and widely scattered light showers occurring mainly at night.

Makapuu Point

Oahu's most spectacular scenic viewpoint, and its breathtakingly beautiful beach.

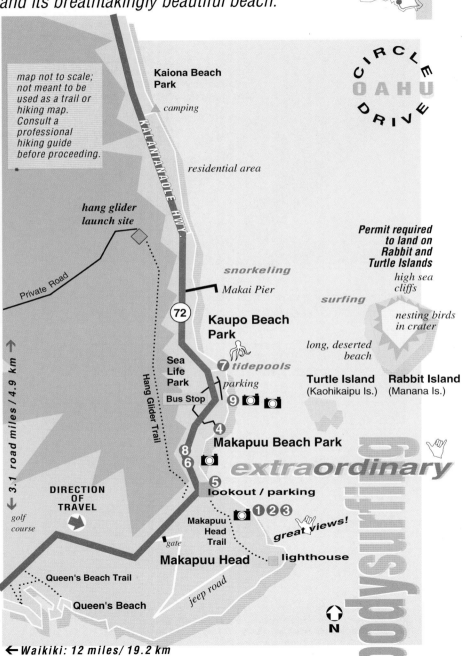

map not to scale; not meant to be used as a trail or hiking map. Consult a professional hiking guide before proceeding.

WINDWARD SHORE

Kaiona Beach Park

camping

KALANIANAOLE HWY.

residential area

hang glider launch site

Private Road

snorkeling

Makai Pier

surfing

Permit required to land on Rabbit and Turtle Islands

high sea cliffs

72

Kaupo Beach Park

nesting birds in crater

long, deserted beach

Sea Life Park

Bus Stop

Hang Glider Trail

⑦ *tidepools*

parking

⑨

Turtle Island (Kaohikaipu Is.) **Rabbit Island** (Manana Is.)

④

⑧ ⑥ **Makapuu Beach Park**

extraordinary

⑤ **lookout / parking**

DIRECTION OF TRAVEL

golf course

Makapuu Head Trail

① ② ③

great views!

gate

Makapuu Head

lighthouse

Queen's Beach Trail

jeep road

Queen's Beach

bodysurfing

N

3.1 road miles / 4.9 km

← *Waikiki: 12 miles/ 19.2 km*
← *Sandy Beach: 0.4 mile/ 0.6 km*

CIRCLE OAHU DRIVE

*M*akapuu is **12 miles and 30 minutes from Waikiki** via the KALANIANAOLE (72) HWY. No other place in the Hawaiian Islands affords such a majestic and breathtaking vista as Makapuu Head does, while at the same time being so accessible to everyone.

The approach up along the KALANIANAOLE (72) HWY. from **Sandy Beach Park** gives no inkling as to the spectacular panorama that awaits at the top of the grade. As it *passes* **Sandy** and **Wawamalu Beach Parks**, the highway climbs to the *left*, past the golf course on the *mauka* side of the road, and **Makapuu Head** on the *makai* side. The gated jeep road visible on the *makai* side is used by hikers on weekends for an easy walk up to the lighthouse at **Makapuu Point**. They park along the HWY. near the gate entrance, but off to the side and out of the way. **0.2** mile past this jeep road, prepare to *pull off to the right* at the crest of the hill when a tiny parking lot **abruptly appears** on the *makai* side.

The little parking lot can only accommodate about a dozen cars before someone gets blocked. The only alternative parking is across the highway on the wide shoulder, opposite. However, this is a very **dangerous** place to attempt to cross because just over the crest, oncoming cars are racing up the hill around a **blind curve** toward you. As you pull into the lot, there will be a low wall straight ahead, and beyond that, a truly stunning vista. You'll see fishermen hop over the wall and begin the long climb down to the rocky jetties at the base of the cliff to harvest family dinner from the sea. Far below, the ocean spreads toward the horizon in vivid shades of blue and green. Out toward the right, two uninhabited islands lie anchored side by side. The larger one, **Manana Island**, commonly known as **Rabbit Island**, is dry and barren looking. Its large crater is home to thousands of nesting seabirds. The perfect swells which break off its shore-facing beach attract **surfers**, and divers frequently ply its offshore reefs. The smaller island, **Kaohikaipu**, commonly called **Turtle Island**, is flatter, allowing rain to soak into the ground and making it a bit greener than Rabbit Island. Both islands are seabird sanctuaries and are off limits to visitors without **permits** from the Hawaii Division of Forestry

and Wildlife (call **587-0166**). Fishermen casting from boats are attracted to the protected waters off the southeast side of Turtle Island. Straight ahead from the lookout, miles and miles of some of Hawaii's most beautiful white sand beaches trail off down the coast. Directly below and to the left, photo-perfect **Makapuu Beach** lies cradled in a huge semicircle of black lava shoreline, dotted with people enjoying the sun or attempting to ride some of Oahu's best, and most hazardous, **bodysurfing** waves.

Hang around long enough, and curious things begin to happen here. A man with a small cage packed with live pigeons arrives and sets it on the wall. He removes a bird, whis-

pers something into its ear, then tosses it into the sky. It hesitates in midair for a split second while getting its bearings, then takes off at full speed, headed straight out toward Rabbit Island. Then, as it clears the sheltering bluffs of Makapuu Head, it veers sharply to the right, flying out of sight. One by one, the man repeats the ritual, with the same result, until the cage is emptied. Then he turns and leaves without looking back.

As visitors stand by the wall admiring the view, they are startled by a man dangling from a hang glider who has dropped down from out of nowhere to perform acrobatics just yards in front of them. He swoops and turns, staying aloft on the rising winds for many minutes. The group oohs and aahs in unison with each daring move, as the fly-man comes dangerously closer and closer to the jagged cliff with each turn. Then suddenly, he catches an updraft and climbs swiftly away to the applause of the growing crowd that has gathered to watch his impromptu show.

To the *right/makai* of the parking lot, a network of trails and paths lead off over the exposed rocks and climbs upward. Most of the ascent is relatively easy, with many family groups making the journey over rock which is layered like uneven steps. Loose gravel, or **scree**, as mountain climbers call it, is a possible hazard. Make sure that you avoid scraped knees by placing your foot on clean, exposed, scree-free rock with each deliberate step. No matter how far out onto Makapuu Head you choose to hike or climb, whether it be only a

❶❷❸

few paces, or all the way to the top, you will be rewarded with unforgettable views. Some of the trails follow along the lip of the cliff for a most dramatic experience. Others are placed well away from the edge, and still others cut through low brush, cactus and thorns, scratching unprotected legs. Wearing long pants here is a good idea.

The trails along the precipice pass old WWII bunkers, where sharp eyed lookouts not too long ago lay in wait, hidden from sight, watching for signs of enemy attack. At the elevation where **Balanced Rock** stands sentinel, your eyes may have difficulty gathering in the vast panorama as the view along the Windward Shore opens up considerably. The backsides of the two offshore islands, hidden from the sight of those standing at the lookout below, come into view here, and the green agricultural lands of **Upcountry Waimanalo** appear through a light atmospheric haze. Turning around 180 degrees, **Sandy Beach** and the rocky ramparts of **Koko Head Regional Park** lie far below and away. Your hike on Makapuu Head ends either when you reach the lighthouse, or when your legs give out —whichever comes first.

Another spectacular short hike with a different point of view follows the dizzying ridge on the other side of the highway opposite the parking lot. *Don't attempt to cross the road at the parking lot due to that blind curve we talked about earlier.* Instead, **backtrack** in the direction of Sandy Beach, or south, for **100'** or so until you have a full view of traffic coming from both directions. The hiking path is easy to see from the shoulder of the road as it cuts through the dry grass toward the edge of the ridge. A whole new perspective of Makapuu opens up just in the first 100' of this ascent. Above that elevation though, the trail becomes lined with lots of thorny brush and cactus, painful to unprotected legs. Also, once past the 100' level, this trail has a much steeper ascent than the Makapuu Head trails across the highway

do, and is much more difficult. It is not recommended to anyone who isn't a strong, conditioned hiker. However, **one need not climb any higher than the first 100'** to have a rewarding visual and photographic experience. As seen on James A. Bier's Oahu map #2, the trail eventually parallels the edge of the ridge all the way up to the **hang glider launch site** at the 1250' elevation. Those experienced and tireless hikers who reach the hang glider launch site with any breath left will have it taken away by the incomparable sight of daring men and women strapping themselves onto a pair of nylon wings and jumping off the cliff into thin air, almost a quarter mile above ground.

❹

TheBus
848-5555

From Waikiki:
On the makai side of Kuhio Ave., board the #22 Hawaii Kai-Sea Life Park BEACH BUS. The BEACH BUS allows surfboards and other bulky beach gear, so go for it. The BEACH BUS also gets you to Hanauma Bay, Koko Head Regional Park, Halona Blowhole, and Sandy Beach.
Or, board the #58 Hawaii Kai-Sea Life Park bus heading in the direction of Diamond Head, along the makai side of Ala Moana Blvd., Kalia Rd., Saratoga Rd., or Kuhio Ave.

Return:
In the opposite direction, board the #22 Waikiki-Beach and Hotels BEACH BUS.

Photographs

Left page: Makapuu lighthouse peeks around the Point.

1, 2, 3. A panorama taken in three parts from Makapuu Head. This view was about a 20 minute climb from the parking / lookout area. Bring water.

4. A tripod kept stationary details sharp, while the ocean water and moving clouds blurred in this sunrise view of Makapuu lighthouse. Taken from Makapuu Beach, Molokai's profile is seen on the horizon.

5. A hang glider soars above Makapuu Point. Rabbit and Turtle Islands are seen in the distance.

All photos:
Kodachrome 64

❺

6. Fishermen on the rocks below Makapuu lookout are dwarfed by the elements.

7. Exquisite Makapuu Beach attracts body-surfers and beach goers who appreciate the stunning scenery. This view is from the highway shoulder above the beach.

8. At dawn, the sun begins to light the sky behind Rabbit Island. A tripod kept stationary details sharp, while the moving ocean water blurred into a foggy mist. This is a 30 second exposure at F16 with a 14mm lens.

All photos: Kodachrome 64

*DEBORAH KERR AND BURT LANCASTER ROLLED AROUND IN THE SURF AT MAKAPUU, LOCKED TO-GETHER IN ONE OF THE SILVER SCREEN'S MOST FAMOUS EMBRACES IN **FROM HERE TO ETERNITY.***

TheBus
848-5555

Ask driver for directions if unsure.

From Waikiki:
On the makai side of Kuhio Ave., board the #22 Hawaii Kai-Sea Life Park BEACH BUS. The BEACH BUS allows surfboards and other bulky beach gear, so go for it. The BEACH BUS also gets you to Hanauma Bay, Koko Head Regional Park, Halona Blowhole, and Sandy Beach.
Or, board the #58 Hawaii Kai-Sea Life Park bus heading in the direction of Diamond Head, along the makai side of Ala Moana Blvd., Kalia Rd., Saratoga Rd., or Kuhio Ave.

Return:
In the opposite direction, board the #22 Waikiki-Beach and Hotels BEACH BUS.

*P*ulling past the little Makapuu Head parking lot, KALANIANAOLE (72) HWY. descends toward a stunning vista. Makapuu Beach is on the right, directly below the highway, and at this point on the downgrade the highway's shoulder is extra wide to allow motorists to pull over to take photographs or observe the action below.

The entrance to Makapuu Beach Park is *makai/right*, near the bottom of the grade. Sea Life Park (admission charge) is directly opposite on the *mauka/left* side of the highway. Makapuu Beach Park has two restrooms, picnic tables with superb views, showers, and one lifeguard stand that is manned 365 days a year.

Makapuu Beach Park outlaws surfboards, as well as belly boards with bottom skegs. Makapuu has for quite some time been considered the premiere bodysurfing beach in all of Hawaii. This venue boasts long, long rides and an excellent shorebreak —and there is no raised reef in its offshore waters to split young heads. The icing on the cake is its absolutely beautiful situation, where the white sandy beach slopes up toward the cliff that backs it, and numerous sand pockets between rock outcroppings provide additional privacy on an already spacious 1000' stretch of sand.

Winter surf is heavy and very hazardous at Makapuu, and seasonal wave action at this time removes sand and exposes rock along the shorebreak. The danger here to the unwary and inexperienced cannot be stressed strongly enough —especially since so many local kids play in the surf, making it look effortless and safe to the casual observer. It definitely is not. During the **summer**, the water is calmer and recreational swimming is safer, but always ask the lifeguard about hazardous conditions which may not be apparent before entering the water.

The rocky shores bordering the parking area are popular spots for beachcombing, and families bring children to play in the warm tidepools at the NW end of the park near Kaupo Cove.

Adjacent to Makapuu Beach Park, a little further along KALANIANAOLE (72) HWY, is Kaupo Beach Park (no facilities). Kaupo's calm waters attract snorkelers and escorted groups of novice scuba divers, especially in the area around the Makai Research Pier. The shore bottom here is rocky, but there are no strong currents alongshore and is safe year 'round for swimmers. Novice surfers like the gentle waves offshore.

Waimanalo Bay

Miles of exquisite, protected sandy shore.

CIRCLE OAHU DRIVE

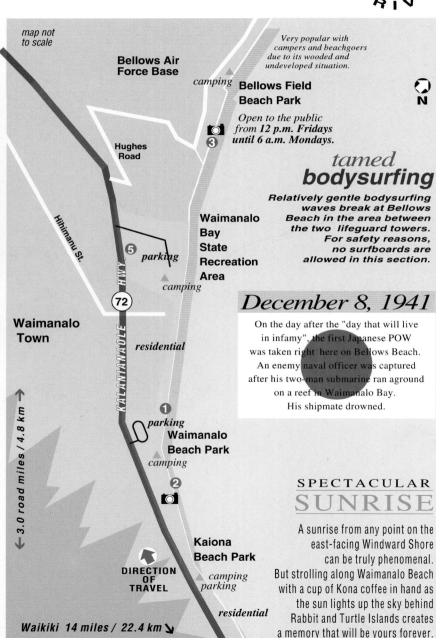

map not to scale

Bellows Air Force Base

Very popular with campers and beachgoers due to its wooded and undeveloped situation.

camping

Bellows Field Beach Park

Hughes Road

Open to the public from 12 p.m. Fridays until 6 a.m. Mondays.

③ N

Waimanalo Bay State Recreation Area

Hihimanu St.

⑤ *parking*

▲ *camping*

(72)

Waimanalo Town

residential

tamed **bodysurfing**

Relatively gentle bodysurfing waves break at Bellows Beach in the area between the two lifeguard towers. For safety reasons, no surfboards are allowed in this section.

December 8, 1941

On the day after the "day that will live in infamy", the first Japanese POW was taken right here on Bellows Beach. An enemy naval officer was captured after his two-man submarine ran aground on a reef in Waimanalo Bay. His shipmate drowned.

KALANIANAOLE HWY.

❶ *parking*

Waimanalo Beach Park

camping

❷ 📷

SPECTACULAR SUNRISE

A sunrise from any point on the east-facing Windward Shore can be truly phenomenal. But strolling along Waimanalo Beach with a cup of Kona coffee in hand as the sun lights up the sky behind Rabbit and Turtle Islands creates a memory that will be yours forever.

Kaiona Beach Park

▲ **DIRECTION OF TRAVEL**

camping parking

residential

3.0 road miles / 4.8 km

Waikiki 14 miles / 22.4 km ↘

Clean, white, sandy, sunny, wide, long, placid, protected...what more could anyone ask for in their quest for the perfect beach? **This is the real thing:** 3 1/2 miles in length, with a gradually sloping sandy bottom, an offshore reef that protects it from high surf, all kinds of facilities, acres of shade trees, and lots of picnic tables. Waimanalo Bay is the ideal family beach. Most surprising of all, it is never crowded. On holidays a few small areas will have groups of people lumped together, but with all this beach, there is plenty of space even on holidays to be off by yourself. During the week, it is virtually empty.

At Waimanalo Bay, miles of gently sloped shore allow for easy, unhampered beach walking or jogging, with plenty of time to think while traversing its length. Shade trees back the sandy beach area in many places, offering respite from the afternoon sun without having to retreat from the beach itself. The one drawback? Out of the 4 beach parks along Waimanalo Bay, *only Bellows Beach has a lifeguard on duty.*

There are four separate beach areas that share this same beautiful shoreline: Kaiona Beach Park, Waimanalo Beach Park, Waimanalo State Recreation Area, and Bellows Field Beach Park. The first, **Kaiona Beach Park**, appears just beyond the small residential enclave on the *makai* side of KALANIANAOLE (72) HWY. which you will pass after leaving Makapuu and Kaupo Beach Parks. This enclave contains the "Robin Masters" estate from the **Magnum P.I.** TV show. Kaiona Beach itself, along with the beaches fronting the residential area, was used extensively for background filming, as fans of the show will surely recognize. **Kaiona Beach Park** is the smallest of the four, and a favorite of locals. It has a restroom, picnic tables and a small parking area. Additional parking is available all along the highway, paralleling the comparatively narrow beach, so choose your

favorite patch of sand and park right close by.

The entrance to **Waimanalo Beach Park** is about **0.8** mile past Kaiona Beach Park. Waimanalo Beach Park often has a sizable population of campers on holidays and weekends, mostly families attracted by its extensive facilities: basketball courts, baseball and softball fields, a recreation building, and campside parking. *But little piles of broken glass in the main parking lot tell the tale: don't leave anything visible in your car, and don't be seen placing anything in the trunk.*

❶

Waimanalo Beach Park is an ideal place to watch the sunrise, go for a morning jog, or have a breakfast picnic. There are convenience stores just up the road that open early for your morning coffee needs. The 7-11 stocks many varieties of the addictive local favorite, **School Kine Cookies**, the new Macadamia Shortbread being, arguably, the best. The wide, safe sandy beach has a beautiful view of Rabbit and Turtle Islands as the sun rises magnificently behind them in a unique show every morning. With a cup of Kona coffee in hand, a pair of bare feet and miles of virtually deserted sand to sit on or explore, you could hardly choose a better place to start the day in Hawaii.

Further along the highway, **1.1 miles** past the entrance to Waimanalo Beach Park, is the entrance to what many think is the best beach on this part of the island, **Waimanalo State Recreation Area**. The entrance is hard to spot, so look for it just after you pass the McDonald's. The beach is backed by a grove of ironwood trees; compared to other beaches on Waimanalo Bay, the water can be rough here.

Our fourth choice, **Bellows Field Beach Park**, is attached to Bellows Air Force Station. *It is open to* the public only on weekends, from 12:00 noon on Fridays until 6:00 a.m. on Mondays, and on holidays from 6:00 a.m. until 6:00 a.m. the next day. Two lifeguards are on duty during the daylight hours on these days.

Enter Bellows Field Beach Park by making a *makai/right* turn onto HUGHES Road from the KALANIANAOLE (72) HWY, **0.2 mile** past the entrance of Waimanalo Bay State Recreation Area.

Bellows is a **great camping spot**, with its beautiful beach and neat forested interior. Camping permits are issued by the City and County of Honolulu Parks and Recreation Dept., Permit Section (**523-4525**). Bellows Beach, more than the other beaches along this shore, is physically situated to give the best effect of being enclosed in the protection of Waimanalo Bay. Wailea Point and the offshore Moku Lua Islands at the NW end seem to stand guard, while Makapuu Point and Rabbit Island to the SE echo the same effect. It is especially lovely here late in the day looking down the beach toward Makapuu as the lowering sun highlights the deep ridges in the pali, forming a stunning backdrop for the scene (see photo).

Portuguese Man o' War

Occasionally, strong offshore winds can wash the jellyfish known as the Portuguese Man o' War ashore. Although a little scary, its sting is not dangerous except perhaps for those allergic to bee stings and such. It tingles like a bad sunburn, and the sensation lasts for about twenty minutes. If you get stung, remove any visible pieces —they look like long clinging transparent threads tinged with purple— and wash the area gently with wet sand to dislodge any tiny stingers. Follow with a freshwater shower. At Oahu's beaches, showers are located in, or adjacent to, the restrooms. If medical attention is needed, continue along KALANIANAOLE (72) HWY. in the same direction we've been heading for about 2.0 miles to the main intersection, HWY. 61. Immediately ahead you will see the entrance to CASTLE MEDICAL CENTER (263-5329).

TheBus
848-5555

From Waikiki:
Board bus #58 on the side of Ala Moana Blvd., Kalia Rd., Saratoga Rd., or Kuhio Ave. heading in the Diamond Head direction. This bus will rest at Sea Life Park, so stay on board, and continue the ride to the Waimanalo Bay beaches featured in this spread. You will have a good hike into Bellows Field Beach Park from the bus stop at the Kalanianaole Hwy. entrance.

Return:
Board the #58 Waikiki-Ala Moana Center bus in the opposite direction. Wait while the bus rests at Sea Life Park, then continue on to Waikiki.

Photographs

1. A typical weekday "crowd" at beautiful Waimanalo BP.

2. The sun rises behind Rabbit Island when viewed from Waimanalo BP. Its a wonderfully peaceful time to stroll along the sand.

3. A line of bathers exits the water as the late afternoon sun dramatically shades the rifts in the distant pali: Waimanalo SRA.

4. The curve of Waimanalo Bay is backed by the beautiful pali and distinctive Olomana Peak, which said to be the oldest landform on the island of Oahu.

5. A restaurant along the coast highway has become an artist's canvas.

All photos:
Kodachrome 64

❷

❸❹
❺

Upcountry Waimanalo
Rural Hawaii at Honolulu's doorstep.

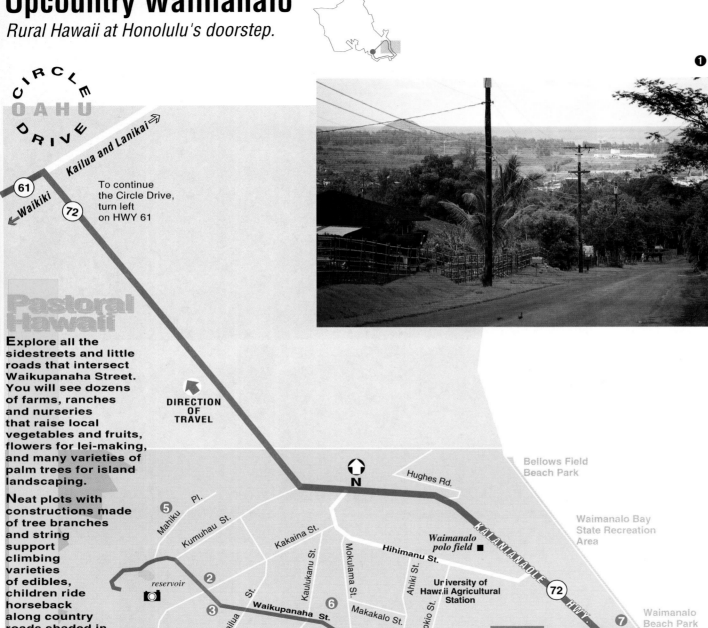

CIRCLE OAHU DRIVE

Kailua and Lanikai ➔

61

Waikiki ⬅

72

To continue
the Circle Drive,
turn left
on HWY 61

WINDWARD SHORE

Pastoral Hawaii

Explore all the
sidestreets and little
roads that intersect
Waikupanaha Street.
You will see dozens
of farms, ranches
and nurseries
that raise local
vegetables and fruits,
flowers for lei-making,
and many varieties of
palm trees for island
landscaping.

Neat plots with
constructions made
of tree branches
and string
support
climbing
varieties
of edibles,
children ride
horseback
along country
roads shaded in
the afternoon
by towering pali,
and wonderful
highland views
roll easily down to
the blue Pacific.

⬆ DIRECTION OF TRAVEL

⬆ N

Bellows Field
Beach Park

Hughes Rd.

Waimanalo Bay
State Recreation
Area

5 Mahiku Pl.

Kumuhau St.

Kakaina St.

reservoir 📷

2

Mahailua St.

3

Kaulukanu St.

6

Waikupanaha St.

Mokulama St.

Makakalo St.

Waimanalo polo field ■

Hihimanu St.

Ahiki St.

Nonokio St.

University of
Hawaii Agricultural
Station

KALANIANAOLE HWY.

72

7

Waimanalo
Beach Park

KAPU
This sign
means
keep out,
or
forbidden.

📷 1

4 📷

map not
to scale

⬅ 4.1 road miles /
6.5 km ➔

---

*T*he commercial and business district of **Waimanalo town** lies on either side of KALANIANAOLE (72) HWY., but the roads that intersect from the *left/mauka* side penetrate high into the valley. Upcountry Waimanalo is the closest rural Oahu experience to the city of Honolulu, and scores of small farming enterpri-ses grow fruits, vegetables and ornamentals, chickens, horses and dairy cows. Picture-pretty white fenced pastures sit high enough against the pali to command lovely views of the town below and the misty blue ocean in the distance. Narrow roads curve up around to the very base of the ridged pali walls, exposing bits and pieces of the lives and lifestyles of those who live and work here. The brilliant colors of red torch ginger and bronze ti leaves contrast with the lush green of the rampant foliage. Asian field workers in wide brimmed straw hats toil amidst a maze of vine-supporting string in Waimanalo's bean fields, as the towering pali rise in the background. The scene could easily be mistaken for the Far East.

On KALANIANAOLE (72) HWY, *Pass* **Kaiona Beach Park** and **Waimanalo Beach Park** on the *right/ makai*. Look for HIHIMANU ST., which crosses the HWY. **0.6** mile after passing the entrance to Waimanalo Beach Park. *Turn left/ mauka* onto HIHIMANU ST. Any of the roads that intersect Hihimanu St. will be worth a look. The **5th** road on the *left/mauka* side that you pass is named KAKAINA ST. *Turn left* onto it. Again *turn left* two streets up, onto MAHAILUA ST. Drive up MAHAILUA ST. to the end. Along the way you will pass a number of pretty little ranches. From the area of the gate at the road's end, you will see the view in photo #1.

Backtrack downhill to the first intersection: this is WAIKUPANAHA ST. which runs along the valley's width, and all roads that cross it hold surprises. Feel free to explore, respecting private property and any *no trespassing* signs. A sign with the word **KAPU** (forbidden) is a much more vehement way of saying keep out.

❷ ❸ ❹

TheBus
848-5555

From Waikiki:
TheBus does not venture into this area, so you will have a good hike uphill from the Waimanalo Town Shopping Center on the Kalanianaole Hwy.
Board bus #58 on the makai side of Ala Moana Blvd., Kalia Rd., Saratoga Rd., or Kuhio Ave., heading in the Diamond Head direction. This bus will rest at Sea Life Park, so stay on board, and continue the ride to the Waimanalo Town Shopping Center. Cross the Kalanianaole (72) HWY. and start walking up Hihimanu St. as it curves to the left. Walk uphill on Kakaina St. or any street after.

Return:
Board the #58 Waikiki-Ala Moana Center bus in the opposite direction. Wait while the bus rests at Sea Life Park, then continue on to Waikiki.

Photographs

3. Nursery grown orchid. A piece of black cardboard was placed behind the flower to isolate it from a busy background.

4. The ranches and nurseries closest to the pali enjoy both enviable views and complete privacy.

5. Looking like a scene in China, a worker pauses from chores in an upcountry bean patch.

6. All it takes is a carrot to make instant friends up here.

7. The view from the top of the ferris wheel at the annual Waimanalo Fair includes distinctive Olomana Peak.

All photos:
Kodachrome 64

❺ ❼
❻

Kailua and Lanikai

Enchanting deserted islands, a sublime beach, colorful windsurfing, and a secret little bay.

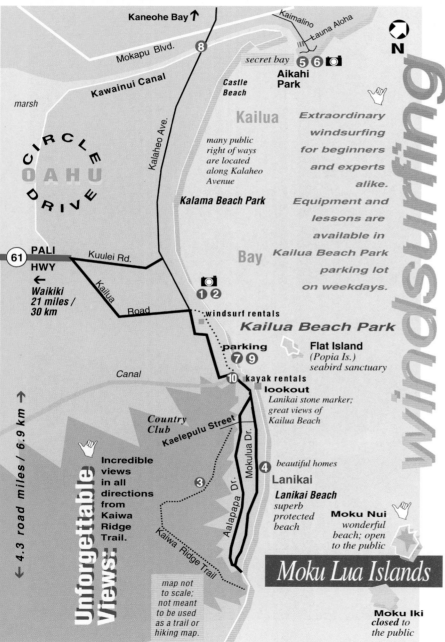

Kaneohe Bay ↑

Kaimalino
Launa Aloha

Mokapu Blvd.

8

Kawainui Canal

marsh

secret bay **5 6** 📷

Aikahi Park

Castle Beach

Kailua

many public right of ways are located along Kalaheo Avenue

Kalama Beach Park

Kalaheo Ave.

CIRCLE OAHU DRIVE

61 **PALI HWY ←**

Waikiki 21 miles / 30 km

Kuulei Rd.

Kailua Road

📷 **1 2**

Bay

windsurf rentals

Kailua Beach Park

Canal

parking **7 9**

Flat Island *(Popia Is.) seabird sanctuary*

10 kayak rentals

lookout
Lanikai stone marker; great views of Kailua Beach

Country Club
Kaelepulu Street

Mokulua Dr.

4 *beautiful homes*

Lanikai

3

Aalapapa Dr.

Lanikai Beach superb protected beach

Moku Nui *wonderful beach; open to the public*

Kaiwa Ridge Trail

← 4.3 road miles / 6.9 km ↑

Unforgettable Views: 🤙 Incredible views in all directions from Kaiwa Ridge Trail.

map not to scale; not meant to be used as a trail or hiking map.

Moku Lua Islands

Moku Iki *closed to the public*

windsurfing

WINDWARD SHORE

Extraordinary windsurfing for beginners and experts alike. Equipment and lessons are available in Kailua Beach Park parking lot on weekdays.

Kailua is **21 miles** and 50 minutes from Waikiki via the KALANIANAOLE (72) HWY., or 25 minutes via the PALI (61) HWY. **Kailua Beach Park** is a popular family favorite, with a large lawn area and welcome shade trees lining the sand, generous parking, daily lifeguard service, calm waters and perfect windsurfing conditions. The cloud-hugging pali are located farther inland here, making Kailua a sunnier beach than those of neighboring Waimanalo Bay. Offshore, little **Popoia Island**, more commonly called **Flat Island**, and the twin **Moku Lua Islands** draw local explorers on crowded weekends who paddle over on anything that floats, including surfboards, rented kayaks, and the like. Kailua is always a popular beach, but during the week the crowds are relatively sparse and you'll probably have the offshore Islands to yourself at that time.

THE EXPRESS ROUTE FROM WAIKIKI:
Follow the map on the inside back cover to get on the H1 FWY. direction: **WEST**. Take the H1 FWY to the *PALI (61) HWY. EXIT* (about 5 minutes driving time). Follow the PALI (61) HWY. uphill, over and down the other side of the pali, to the tree shaded intersection in the heart of **Kailua** town, about **1.2** miles past the intersection of the KALANIANAOLE (72) HWY. (KALANIANAOLE (72) HWY. intersects HWY 61 from the right only). See below to proceed.

FROM THE PREVIOUS PAGE:
From the intersection of HUGHES RD. (which is the entrance to **Bellows Field Beach Park**) and KALANIANAOLE (72) HWY., continue along the

HWY. in the same direction we've been heading (NW). The mountains will be on your *left,* and the ocean (not visible because of trees and brush) will be on your *right.*

About **4.0 miles** from HUGHES RD, KALANIANAOLE (72) HWY intersects HWY 61. A *left* turn onto HWY 61 will take you over the pali, back to **Honolulu**.

To reach Kailua, though, make a *right* turn onto HWY 61. In about **1.2 miles** you will approach a tree shaded intersection in the heart of Kailua town.

The road you are on now forks. One segment curves sharply to the *right*, continuing as KAILUA RD., and the other part curves slightly to the *left,* becoming KUUKEI RD. Take the *left* fork, pass through the intersection, and continue straight ahead. Almost immediately you will pass the McDonald's on the left, and then the police station and the firehouse, both on the right hand side of the street. One long block past the police station, KUULEI RD. intersects KALAHEO RD.

KALAHEO RD. parallels the beach about a block inland from it. A left turn onto KALAHEO RD. will take you through Kailua's exclusive beachside residential area. A right turn will take you to beautiful **Kailua Beach Park**, and the enclave of **Lanikai**.

First, we'll make a *left* turn onto KALAHEO ROAD. This area of beautiful homes and lush tropical landscaping will inspire you to rethink your wish list. Each of the little streets on the *right/makai* is a dead end, finishing at the backyards of those homes facing the beach. Five streets down from the intersection is tiny **Kalama Beach Park**, where you can get a look at the beach and the homes that front it.

Continue down KALAHEO ROAD, but pull over often to let through traffic pass by as you gawk at the homes. There are many **p.r.o.w.s** along here allowing access to the beach, so take your pick. About **1.1 miles** past Kalama Beach Park, the road passes over lovely wide **Kawainui Canal**, thickly lined with swaying palm trees and beautiful homes, and next, it intersects with MOKAPU BLVD. To visit the gorgeous hidden bay known as **Aikahi Park** at the NW boundary of Kailua, *turn right* onto MOKAPU BLVD. Next, *turn right* onto KAIMALINO ST., which is the first street on the right that you will see. Park four streets down on KAIMALINO, and look for the public right-of-way directly across Kaimalino St. from intersecting LAUNA ALOHA ST.

The right-of-way leads to a little beach fronted by dream homes, coconut palms, and a stunning wide angle view the likes for which *Cinerama* was created. The water in the tropical lagoon-like bay is shallow, warm and crystal clear. The gorgeous panorama of Kailua Bay, the distant pali, and all the lovely homes that share this coast are the stuff that daydreams are made of.

Now *backtrack* down KAIMALINO ST. to MOKAPU BLVD. A right turn would take you up to the gate at the Kaneohe Marine Corps Air Station, which is not open to the general public. So *turn left* onto MOKAPU BLVD. instead.

Backtrack to the main intersection. On the *right* the intersecting road is named KANEOHE BAY DRIVE, and it takes you around the westerly-facing shore of **Kaneohe Bay**. On the *left* it is named the now-familiar KALAHEO AVE., where we will backtrack the way we came in order to see Kailua Beach Park and Lanikai. *Turn left* onto KALAHEO AVE.

Backtrack along KALAHEO AVE., again past little **Kalama Beach Park** on your left and the intersection of KUULEI RD. on your right. Proceed **0.4** mile to KAILUA RD. and *turn left* onto KAILUA RD. (some maps name this little street LIHIWAI ST., but the posted street sign as of this writing says KAILUA RD.) This is a short **one way** street that will take you directly into the NW, or Kailua, end of **Kailua Beach Park**, past pedestrians (careful!) and big vans with large racks displaying a rainbow of fluorescent colored windsurfing sailboards for rent. Parking is available all along here and in the adjoining lots ahead.

Kailua Beach itself is all powdery white sand, and is steeply sloped. At the SE, or **Lanikai end**, in the vicinity of the canal, Kailua Beach is very wide, and attracts **families**. The shore bottom is sandy, but gets deep rather quickly. Especially in spring, large green sea turtles come very close to shore to revel at the submerged patches of reef rock that you see as shadows beneath the water —about 20 yards offshore— especially on the Kailua (NW) side of the canal in front of the lifeguard stand. If you have a snorkel and mask, slide in and watch them chomp on whatever seaweed the stingy reef will give up.

The picturesque **canal is deceptive** as it contains deep unseen holes, and supports dangerous bacteria growth caused by the dairy farm runoff upstream. Despite what you may see, **children should not be allowed to play in its waters**. The canal water, blocked by a barrier beach, normally does not flow into the ocean except perhaps after big storms. For some as yet unexplained reason, the city at times bulldozes the sand barrier so that the polluted stream can freely run into the clean bay waters, endangering all who swim here. If this barrier is broken when you visit, its best to swim as far away from it as possible. At this end of the beach you should be able to rent a kayak from vendors. Look for the racks of kayaks, normally yellow in color, in the tree shaded area.

Down at the opposite, NW, **Kailua end**, Kailua Beach is very narrow, steeply sloped and shaded in the afternoon by the trees that back it. At the boundary of the park, the sand is filled with windsurfers preparing to take off for a zoom around the bay. This end of the beach attracts **singles and couples**, but few families.

Kailua Beach Park has two newly refurbished comfort stations, a food concession, privately owned windsurf and kayak rental concessions, a lot of parking, and 3 lifeguard towers, which are manned 365 days of the year. It is a very popular place on weekends and holidays. Come early to get a parking space—they go fast. Across the road from the parking lot, along the bank of the canal on the Kailua side, there are often catamarans of various sizes for rent, for exploring the canal and, upstream, Enchanted Lake. On the opposite, Lanikai side of the canal, fronting the road, Buzz's Steak house is a real handy, popular place for lunch. KALAHEO AVE. changes its name when it crosses the canal, to KAWAILOA RD. Just past Buzz's Steakhouse,

❷

TheBus
848-5555
If unsure, ask the driver for directions.

From Waikiki:
On the mauka side of Kuhio Ave., heading away from Diamond Head, board bus # 8 Ala Moana Center, #19 Airport, #19 Airport-Hickam, or #20 Airport-Halawa Gate to the Ala Moana Shopping Center. Transfer to #56 Kailua-Kaneohe, #57 Kailua Sea-Life Park, or #57 Kailua-Waimanalo. Alight in Kailua Town at the corner of Kailua Rd. and Oneawa St. Transfer again to the #70 Shuttle which has a windshield sign marked "Lanikai-Maunawili". The Shuttle passes most of the places featured in this spread.

Return:
In the opposite direction, board the #70 Shuttle Bus to the corner of Kailua Rd. and Oneawa St. On Kailua Rd., transfer to #56 or #57 Honolulu-Ala Moana Ctr. Alight on Kona St. at the Ala Moana Center. Walk in the direction of Waikiki (east) to the next bus stop marked for the #8 or #19 Waikiki-Beach and Hotels.

❸

Kailua & Lanikai

it climbs past the Lanikai lookout and **stone marker** at the crest of the hill where it immediately changes its name again, to ALAPAPA DR. Don't worry about the names, though...you can't get lost here.

The view from the stone marker lookout is a winner and very camera worthy. It makes a wonderful place for a panoramic shot if you have a little **Kodak Fun Saver** Panoramic 35 single use camera. Parking is available along the road on the *mauka* side, or at the foot of the hill in the beach parking lot. Park, but don't cross the road on foot here. Oncoming cars zooming over the top of the grade make it safer for you to backtrack down KAWAILOA RD. a few yards before crossing. The view from the marker encompasses all of Kailua Beach, and you will be in luck if there is a windsurfing meet brewing, as the beach closest to your camera lens will be filled with color, and for those with **videocams**, plenty of action too. People exploring Flat Island can be clearly seen from here as can families fishing the rocks below.

Continue uphill on KAWAILOA RD. After it pulls past the stone marker that has the name **Lanikai** emblazoned on it, it changes names and then splits into a one-way-only loop. You must take the *right* fork, named ALAPAPA DR., which will loop around Lanikai and become MOKULUA DR. on its return trip to the stone marker. Explore the lovely homes along ALAPAPA ST. and the sidestreets.

One of the most superbly breathtaking views in all of Hawaii is but a brief climb up the ridge that backs this lovely community. Turn right from ALAPAPA ST. uphill onto KAELEPULU ST. and find street parking below the gated country club entrance. To the left of the gate, uphill along the chain link fence, notice a pathway bordered on the left by tall brush and on the right by the fence. This is the Kaiwa Ridge Trailhead. The further along the trail you hike, the more stunning and unforgettable the views. For those uneasy about heights, though, just a 5 minute climb will bring you to the first lookout area with amazing views of Kailua, the Windward Shore, and Lanikai and the Moku Lua Islands offshore. Its another perfect place to try out your panoramic camera, or to shoot a series of views to be assembled into a panoramic photo-mosaic later (see example in the *Magnifi-*

cent Hiking Trails article, page. 12). Its also the **ideal place for video shooters** to make great use of their camera's telephoto and wide angle capabilities, zooming in on the bountiful activity and scenic wonders below. **An impressive number and variety of gorgeous shots can be had from just this one place.** It *is* a drag to carry along a tripod usually, but bring one here. The shots you'll get from this place are too beautiful to allow them to be spoiled by camera shake —and the tradewinds funneling up the ridge can be surprisingly strong, making it difficult to hold the camera steady. Beyond this point, the trail follows the knife-edged crest of the ridge, so acrophobics may desire to go no further. Yet further along, the mind boggling views expand to include windsurfers racing around Flat Island in Kailua Bay and kayaks skimming out to the Moku Lua Islands, the wonderful properties bordering Lanikai Beach, forests of coconut palms framing aquamarine waters, and the long blowing grasses and wildflowers that edge the trail itself. Behind Kaiwa Ridge, landmark Olomana Peak oversees the region, as ant-like cars climb up the Pali Highway and over the cloud topped summit. Two WWII concrete bunkers lie sadly along the trail, remembering the day they witnessed enemy planes streaking overhead to attack Hawaii. No bullets could be fired to thwart the aircraft because their ammunition had been locked up due to a sabotage alert.

Back to the road, ALAPAPA DR. continues to circle the community and changes names to MOKULUA DR. as it loops back toward the Lanikai stone marker. Along the way there are a number of public rights-of-way on the *right/makai*, side of the street.

The beach is well worth a visit especially for the great views it frames of the **Moku Lua Islands**. The whole of Lanikai Beach, at one mile in length, is safely protected from high surf by offshore reefs, and swimming conditions here are excellent. Late in the afternoon the sun will cast palm tree shadows on the sandy shore, adding to the offshore islands' photogenic appeal. The bigger isle is named **Moku Nui**, and the smaller, **Moku Iki**. *Moku Iki is off limits to visitors*, but **Moku Nui**, with its beautiful beach backed by a pretty little double humped mountain, is open. Both islands are bird sanctuaries, and *visits to* **Moku Nui** *are*

limited to the beach area only, in order to protect the bird nests that are built right on the ground. If you intend to rent a kayak to visit Moku Nui, try to time your excursion to coincide with a **Kona condition**, that is, a day when the cooling tradewinds stop, when you will find water conditions smooth and glassy. See the *Uninhabited Hawaiian Islands* article on page 8 for a little more information on the Moku Lua Islands.

Back on MOKULUA DR., continue up past the stone marker which will now be on your right, then *backtrack* down past Buzz's Steakhouse and the canal. After crossing the canal, the road changes its name back to KALAHEO AVE. The first *left turn* after the canal, will put you on KAILUA ROAD, and into the heart of Oahu's second most populous town with its shopping center, restaurants, and busy commercial district. KAILUA ROAD intersects HWY. 61 right after passing the shopping center.

OPTION 1:
If you would like to continue the Circle Drive, and return to Honolulu over the lush and lovely NUUANU PALI (61) HWY., make a left turn onto HWY. 61, which continues with the name KAILUA

ROAD for a short distance. Turn the page to find out all you need to know about the **Nuuanu Pali Highway.**

OPTION 2:
To continue the journey around **Kaneohe Bay**, go *straight ahead* on KALAHEO AVE after crossing the canal, *backtracking* once again along KALAHEO Ave. Proceed past little Kalama Beach Park on the right, and over the Kawainui Canal. Next, proceed *straight ahead* through the intersection of MOKAPU BLVD. The road you are on is *now* called KANEOHE BAY DRIVE. Turn to page 62 to find out more about **Kaneohe Bay**.

❹

❺

❻

Photographs

1. Windsurfers flock to the near perfect conditions in Kailua Bay.

2. Part of the visual attraction for photographers to the sport, and the lifestyle it has spawned, is the brilliantly colored clothing and equipment.

3. The views from Kaiwa Ridge, also known as Lanikai Ridge, are stunning.

4. Late in the afternoon, coconut palms cast long shadows on Lanikai Beach which beautifully frame a scene of the offshore Moku Lua Islands.

5&6. From the p.r.o.w. in Aikahi Park, the expansive panorama from this little-known-to-the-public enclave proves idyllic.

7. Kailua Beach Park, the Lanikai stone marker, and offshore,

the island of Moku Nui.

8. Children rest their bikes and enjoy the beauty of Kawainui Canal, which you will cross on your way to see the above-pictured Aikahi Park.

9. To avoid the scorn and derision of other dogs, learning to handle himself on a surfboard is *de rigeur* for any island canine, as this pup demonstrates as he and his surfer girl search for the perfect wave. Or any wave, for that matter. Notice the people exploring Flat Island, just offshore of Kailua Beach Park.

10. A fisherman looks to net some dinner in the canal at the SE end of Kailua BP. This shot was taken from the bridge.

All photos:
Kodachrome 64

❼ ❽

❾ ❿

Nuuanu Pali Highway

Numerous waterfalls, a spectacular lookout, and a cool swim at Jackass Ginger Pool.

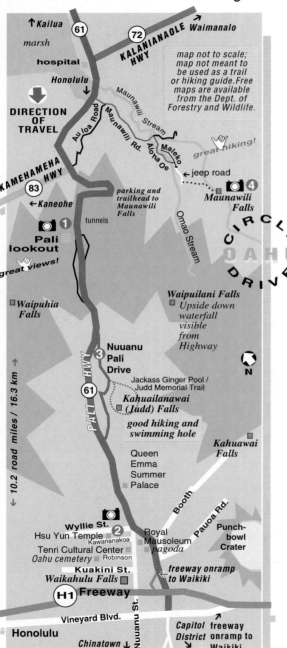

↑Kailua (61) (72) **KALANIANAOLE HWY.** Waimanalo ↗

marsh

hospital

map not to scale;
map not meant to
be used as a trail
or hiking guide. Free
maps are available
from the Dept. of
Forestry and Wildlife.

Honolulu

↓ **DIRECTION OF TRAVEL**

Maunawili Stream

great hiking!

KAMEHAMEHA HWY.

(83)

← **Kaneohe**

tunnels

Au loa Road

Maunawili Rd.

Alona Oe

Maleko

← jeep road

parking and
trailhead to
Maunawili
Falls

(4)
Maunawili Falls

Omao Stream

CIRCLE OAHU DRIVE

(1)
Pali lookout
great views!

□ *Waipuhia Falls*

PALI HWY.

Waipuilani Falls
□ *Upside down
waterfall
visible
from
Highway*

Nuuanu Pali Drive
(3)

N

*Jackass Ginger Pool /
Judd Memorial Trail*

(61)

*Kahuailanawai
(Judd) Falls*

*good hiking and
swimming hole*

Kahuawai Falls

Queen
Emma
Summer
Palace

Booth

Pauoa Rd.

Wyllie St.
(2)
Hsu Yun Temple
Kawananakoa
Tenri Cultural Center
Oahu cemetery

Royal
Mausoleum
pagoda

Robinson

Punch-
bowl
Crater

Kuakini St.
Waikahulu Falls □

(H1) **Freeway**

*freeway onramp
to Waikiki*

Honolulu

Vineyard Blvd.

Chinatown ↓

Nuuanu St.

*Capitol
District*

↗
*freeway
onramp to
Waikiki*

10.2 road miles / 16.3 km

TheBus
848-5555

TheBus does not stop anywhere near the Pali Lookout. Commercial tours will take you there, however.

From Waikiki To the Queen Emma Summer Palace: Board the #4 Nuuanu-Dowsett bus on the mauka side of Kuhio Ave. Alight at bus stop adjacent to the Palace.

Return:
Cross the Pali HWY. and take the #4 University-Waikiki bus in the downhill direction.

From Waikiki to Jackass Ginger Pool /Judd Memorial Trail: For the hike to the Jackass Ginger Pool, board the #4 Nuuanu-Dowsett bus on the mauka side of Kuhio Ave. Alight at the intersection of Nuuanu Pali Drive and Old Pali Rd. Walk up along Nuuanu Pali Dr. 0.7 mile to the trailhead.

Return:
Board Bus #4 at the same intersection you alighted. Ask the driver for instructions if unsure.

Photographs

1. The magnificent vista from the Pali lookout is at its best right after sunrise. There is often no one here at this hour.

2. Interior of the Hsu Yun Temple.

3. Nuuanu Pali Drive.

4. Maunawili: the lower falls.

*All photos:
Kodachrome 64*

---

*T*he Pali Lookout is **11 miles** and **20 minutes** from Waikiki via the PALI (61) HWY. From **Kailua**, the PALI (61) HWY. climbs quickly after passing the **Castle Medical Center** on the right.

Recently a new trailhead to Maunawili Falls was established that begins at the lookout alongside the PALI (61) HWY. which is located just below the tunnels on the Kailua side (see map). It is known as the **Maunawili Demonstration Trail**, or the **Koolaupoko Trail**. This popular trail was newly opened in 1993 and will eventually connect

(1)

to the Pali Lookout and Waimanalo when totally complete. This trailhead is reachable only when traveling *from the Honolulu side* in the *downhill direction toward Kailua*. If you are traveling in the opposite direction, *toward* Honolulu, uphill on the PALI HWY., you should exit at the **Nuuanu Pali Lookout**, and turn around. As you then leave the **Nuuanu Pali Lookout** area, follow the *direction signs toward Kailua* to return down the hill. Pull over at the hairpin curve's **scenic viewpoint/lookout** after passing through the tunnels and park there in a proper space. The trailhead begins at the uphill end of this parking area at the break in the rail. Parking is at a real premium, so have alternate plans just in case there's no parking available. This is one of the best Sierra Club hikes

to pursue. Join them for the best experience. It is recommended, if hiking without a group, that you take this hike on a weekend when other people will be on the trail to guide you to the falls, which are not visible from this trail. A free hiking map is available from the Division of Forestry and Wildlife (**587-0166**).

The Nuuanu Pali Lookout, at the head of Nuuanu Valley, is called Oahu's Scenic Masterpiece. The cliffs you see here were the site of a decisive and bloody battle between King Kamehameha the Great and the Oahuans in 1795. The Oahuans were forced by Kamehameha's army, with help from modern warfare techniques expert John Young, through the valley from the Honolulu side to the area abutting the present day lookout. Here, the embattled Oahuans were forced over these sheer cliffs to their deaths on the craggy rocks far below. Today, the lookout is one of Oahu's premiere attractions, and the parking area is often filled to overflowing with tour buses. But if you come early, **sunrise here is awe-inspiring**, and you will probably have the place **totally to yourself**. Bring a sweater –its windy, and in the morning, quite cool. Unfortunately and inexplicably, **TheBus** does not stop at the Pali Lookout.

The original **Old Pali Road**, overgrown with vegetation but quite passable on foot, begins at the downhill end of the lookout railing. The road is blocked from auto traffic by a gate. Walk around the gate and stroll down this narrow and deceptively precarious-looking roadway as it clings to the walls of the pali. This used to be the *only* way over the Pali. The views are lovely and dramatic, and since few people come here, private.

From the lookout, *return* to the PALI (61) HWY. in the direction of Honolulu (follow the direction signs posted in the parking lot) via the rainforested, mile-long transit road. Once on the HWY., a sign appears alongside announcing the turnout *to* the *left* for NUUANU PALI DR. **Get in the left lane** and make the turn when appropriate. The NUUANU PALI DRIVE is a quiet and lovely road popular with joggers and bicyclists. It first passes by lily ponds and a lovely reservoir edged by stands of tall fringe–topped papyrus. Next, massive trees with wide canopies shade the road as it passes by a number of lovely estates on the left side. Passing over a bridge by a second reservoir on the right, notice the sign for the **Judd Memorial Trail**, which leads to **Jackass Ginger Pool**.

The Judd Trail is a loop trail that takes about an hour to circle. It can be real muddy and the trail itself is at times unclear, but this a very popular place. Its best to hike this or any trail for the first time on a weekend, when there will be people around who can help you find your way. Be seen

placing nothing in the trunk and leave nothing visible in the car to tempt thieves. With-in 50' of its beginning the trail crosses **Nuuanu Stream,** continues up the other side of the gulley through a stand of bamboo, and soon reaches a great smelling little **eucalyptus** forest, then meanders into a grove of symmetrical, tiered–branch **Norfolk Pine**. Then, at the residential area the trail *loops around downhill* and returns in the direction we came. About **7 minutes** or so after leaving the residential area, *the trail forks*. The **downhill fork leads to the swimming hole and waterfall**, the other leads back up the ridge to the trail back to the trailhead. Consult a professional hiking guide for a detailed description.

After hiking the Judd Trail, Return to NUUANU PALI DRIVE, and *turn left* onto it. Continue through a lovely residential area to the PALI (61) HWY. and *turn left* onto it. A number of foreign countries have consulates along the Pali Hwy., as you will notice, and on the left side at PUIWA ROAD, historic **Queen Emma's Summer Palace (595-3167)** is located át 2913 Pali Hwy. The Palace was used by Queen Emma to escape the heat and bustle of Honolulu, and *The Daughters of Hawaii* have furnished the house with beautiful pieces belonging to the Queen and her family. Especially poignant is the cradle and bedroom of little Prince Albert, whose guilt-ridden father King Kamehameha IV had in anger drenched him with water a few days before Albert developed a fever

and died. Britain's Queen Victoria, Albert's godmother, had sent a bishop of the Church of England to Hawaii to preside over the child's christening, but Albert passed away before the bishop's arrival.

The Palace has some outstanding examples of antique **Hawaiian quilts** on display, and the gift shop has some very nice things. The museum is open daily from **9 a.m. to 4 p.m.** Call first to confirm their hours and prices. Admission $4/adult, $1/under 18.

Further along down the Pali Hwy. on the right side, past the colorful **Chinese Consulate**, exit the HWY. at WYLLIE ST. to visit the stately **Royal Mausoleum** at number 2261 Nuuanu Ave. The crypt holds the remains of the Kamehameha and Kalakaua dynasties. It is open **M-F, 8 a.m. to 4:30 p.m.** Across NUUANU ST., on KAWANAMAKOA ST., is the vibrantly colorful **Hsu Yun Temple**. Past the mausoleum is the pagoda and Japanese graveyard described below as seen from the scenic lookout. At #2236 is the **Tenri Cultural Center**, and its beautiful, impeccably landscaped teahouse. Right next door, abutting Robinson Lane, is the park-like Oahu cemetery, and in the rear, some surprising lovely old broad-lawned homes. Finally, backtracking up NUUANU ST., and entering onto the PALI HWY. again, via WYLLIE ST. in the downhill, Downtown Honolulu direction, a roadside sign will indicate a **scenic**

lookout turnoff on the *right*. From this lookout, a lovely **pagoda** and its surrounding graveyard crowded with markers presents a photogenic opportunity.

To return to Waikiki, *continue downhill* on the PALI (61) HWY., **keeping in the far right lane**. The signs indicating the H1 FWY. entrance to Waikiki aren't obvious enough, so be ready for the on ramp to appear suddenly just around the right-hand curve.

To visit historic Downtown and the Iolani Palace, continue downhill on the PALI (61) HWY., **avoiding the far right lane,** and after the FWY. overpass *turn left* onto VINEYARD BLVD., then *turn right* onto PUNCHBOWL ST. The **State Capitol** is just ahead, and next, the **Iolani Palace**. See the **Downtown Honolulu** section (page 26) for a guide to this area.

To visit **Chinatown**, continue down the PALI (61) HWY. to BERETANIA ST., and *make a right turn* onto it. **4 blocks** later, *turn left* onto MAUNAKEA ST. See the **Chinatown** section (page 30) for a guide to this area.

❷

❸

❹

Kaneohe Bay

Expansive views reminiscent of The South Seas.

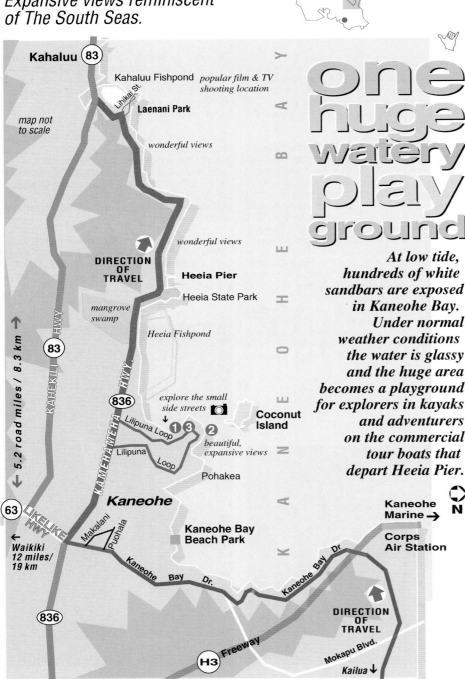

Kahaluu (83)

Kahaluu Fishpond *popular film & TV shooting location*

Lihikai St.

Laenani Park

map not to scale

B A Y

wonderful views

wonderful views

DIRECTION OF TRAVEL

Heeia Pier

Heeia State Park

mangrove swamp

Heeia Fishpond

(83)

(836)

KAHEKILI HWY

KAMEHAMEHA HWY.

explore the small side streets 📷

Lilipuna Loop

❶❸ ❷

Lilipuna

Loop

Pohakea

Coconut Island

beautiful, expansive views

Kaneohe

(63)

LIKELIKE HWY

Makalani

Puohala

← Waikiki 12 miles/ 19 km

↑ 5.2 road miles / 8.3 km ↓

Kaneohe Bay Dr.

Kaneohe Bay Beach Park

Kaneohe Bay Dr

Kaneohe Marine →

Corps Air Station

N

DIRECTION OF TRAVEL

(836)

H3 Freeway

Mokapu Blvd.

Kailua ↓

one huge watery playground

At low tide, hundreds of white sandbars are exposed in Kaneohe Bay. Under normal weather conditions the water is glassy and the huge area becomes a playground for explorers in kayaks and adventurers on the commercial tour boats that depart Heeia Pier.

❶

*E*ven on an island that's as brimming with superlatives as Oahu, its still difficult to understand why **Kaneohe Bay** receives such stingy attention. With its mind-boggling all-direction views of tranquil shoreline, sapphire waters and towering, majestic pali, its beauty is as great a surprise to visitors as is its absence from most guidebooks. Often the bay, with its transparent azure waters and pinnacled verdant Pali backdrop, recalls scenes of Tahiti and the South Seas.

In Kaneohe Bay, when the tide goes out, the fun begins. Private pleasure boats of every size, as well as small one-man kayaks and commercial craft loaded with paying customers, head out from many points along the Bay's placid shore into the bay and out toward the scores of snow white sandbars exposed by low tide waters.

The brilliant white color of the sandbars is the perfect foil for the numberless shades of emerald, cobalt and aquamarine that the water displays beneath the snorkelers who float suspended over the shallows. Boats anchor here and discharge their passengers, who promptly set up volleyball nets, umbrellas and beach blankets on the drying sandy islets.

In one designated area, jet skis zoom around with noisy abandon while overhead, jet fighters thunder in for a landing at the Kaneohe air station. Among its treasures, the bay cradles Coconut Island, the University of Hawaii's research island that you can also see in the opening credits of reruns of **Gilligan's Island**. You will also see small fishing industries here, as well as tiny jewel-like green islets that shelter seabirds, a military air base, historic fish ponds, scores of idyllic views and pockets of great beauty. Huge Kaneohe Bay accommodates all this with ease, and thanks to very vocal public outcries in recent years, it remains amazingly beautiful and serene.

KANEOHE BAY DRIVE begins at MOKAPU BLVD., the border of **Kailua** town. It quickly skirts around the base of the Oneawa Hills to the left, then under the overpass of the H3 FWY. Immediately **Kaneohe Bay** appears on the right, but along this route views are often blocked by homes and thick foliage. There are precious few public rights-of-way (**p.r.o.w.s**) along the bay, but its no real loss here as views are comparatively unre-

markable. If interested anyway, the **first street** you'll pass on the *makai/ right* side of the road is PAKU ST. **Soon after**, you'll see MALAE ST., which has a **p.r.o.w.** at its end. KANEOHE BAY DRIVE in summer is a good place to buy delicious homegrown mangoes and other fruit cheaply from people who set up stands along here to sell the bounty from their gardens. Soon KANEOHE BAY DRIVE *heads inland* to intersect with the KAMEHAMEHA (836) HWY. *Stay to the right* on KANEOHE BAY DRIVE, keeping a wary eye out for large trucks aggressively trying to make the same turn, and look for MAKALANI ST. on the *right*. The first street after MAKALANI ST. is KAMEHAMEHA (836) HWY. *Turn right* at the intersection onto KAMEHAMEHA (836) HWY. This busy commercial street will be a welcome sight if you are hungry or in need of gasoline.

In **0.9 mile**, *make a right turn* onto LILIPUNA RD. If you miss it, the next road on the right is **also** LILIPUNA. It is a **loop road** that curves around Pohakea Point through a pretty residential area, and then loops back to join the HWY. LILIPUNA RD. is elevated and provides some **really lovely** views along the way. There are just a few places to safely pull over, however. One good spot is at the entrance road that descends to the parking lot and pier that service the **University of Hawaii's Marine Laboratory** on Coconut Island, located directly offshore from the Point. Parking is available along the descending road only for short periods. The **view** from here is a winner, with its close-up look at the island, the expansive spectacle of the calm bay waters, and the fortress-like ridged pali trailing up the coast. See photo.

Back to the HWY., *turn right* from LILIPUNA ROAD onto KAMEHAMEHA (836) HWY. The commercial district is soon left behind. The HWY. crosses a bridge which passes through a swamp and an eerie mangrove forest where the trees stand above the muck on roots that look like giant spiders' legs. Right after the swamp you will encounter the entrance to **Heeia State Park**, a small peninsula jutting into the bay which provides still another round of remarkable views, including one of the adjacent and historic **Heeia Fishpond** to the south of the park.

Next door to the park as we drive along the HWY. is the **Heeia Kea Pier**, where glass bottom boats like the **Coral Queen** and **Cruiser Bob's** depart for excursions into the bay. They offer lunch, drinks, snorkeling, sandbar volleyball and other middle of the bay activities. Check out their ads in the free sidewalk magazines like **Spotlight** and **This Week**. Located at the end of the pier, **The Deli** is a convenient place for supplies for a picnic.

If you have been thinking about **kayaking**, this is *the* place on Oahu to do it. Under normal conditions, the bay waters are exceedingly calm, and at this end especially, are filled with exposed sandbars at low tide, making for great exploration opportunities and nirvana-producing perspectives. **Twogood Kayaks (262-5656)** will deliver your kayak to you if arrangements are made in advance. Bring water and something to nibble on, sunscreen and T shirt, and *especially a waterproof* **Kodak Fun Saver Weekend** camera. If you choose to bring your own camera, place it in a triple layer of gallon size Ziplock™ plastic bags for protection. Blow air into the **outermost** bag before sealing completely for buoyancy in case you drop it overboard.

After the pier entrance, the HWY. hugs the shore, and there are numerous places to view and photograph the inexhaustible beauty of Kaneohe Bay. About **2.0 winding miles** past the pier, some small commercial buildings appear on the *right/makai* side. *Turn right* on LIHIKAI DRIVE, a tiny street that descends to **Wailau Point**, passing little **Laenani Park** on the way. This community is interesting for its lilliputian size, yet it contains the park, an unobtrusive hotel complex **(Schrader's Windward Marine Resort, tel. 239-5711),** as well as a lovely gem of a little Catholic church named **St. John's By-The-Sea (239-7198)**. *The streets here are very narrow and children are usually playing, so please* **drive very slowly and attentively**.

The park is a good place for a quiet weekday picnic —there is often a lunch wagon parked up at the HWY.— and it has a number of palm shaded picnic tables, more terrific views, rest rooms, a basketball and volleyball court, and children's playground. There is no real beach to speak of.

Back up to the HWY., make a *right turn*. In **0.3 mile**, KAMEHAMEHA (836) HWY. intersects the terminus of KAHEKILI (83) HWY. We are now at the community of **Kahaluu**.

A *right turn* will put you on the continuation of KAMEHAMEHA HWY., its **number changing** from 836 to **83**. If you wish to **continue** traveling on KAMEHAMEHA (83) HWY. **along the coast**, turn to the **Kahaluu-Kualoa Park** section (page 66).

TheBus
848-5555
Ask driver for directions if unsure.

From Waikiki:
On the mauka side of Kuhio Ave., Saratoga Rd., Kalia Rd., or Ala Moana Blvd., board the #19 Airport, #19 Airport-Hickam, or #20 Airport Halwa Gate bus to the corner of Alakea St. and King St. in downtown Hon-olulu. At the same bus stop on Alakea St., board the #55 Kaneohe-Kahaluu bus, which will take you along the perimeter of the bay via the Kamehameha HWY. See map.

Return:
In the opposite direction, board the #55 Downtown-Bishop St. bus and alight at the corner of Bishop St. and King St. in downtown Honolulu. On King St., in front of the Bank of Hawaii, transfer to the #2 Waikiki-Kapiolani Park, #2 Waikiki-Campbell Ave., or the #19 or #20 Waikiki-Beach and Hotels bus.

❸

❷

A *left turn* will put you on the KAHEKILI (83) HWY., where we will now backtrack for a **4 mile** length of very interesting and lovely upcountry features, beginning on the next page.

Kahekili Highway
Haiku Valley and the serene Byodo In Temple.

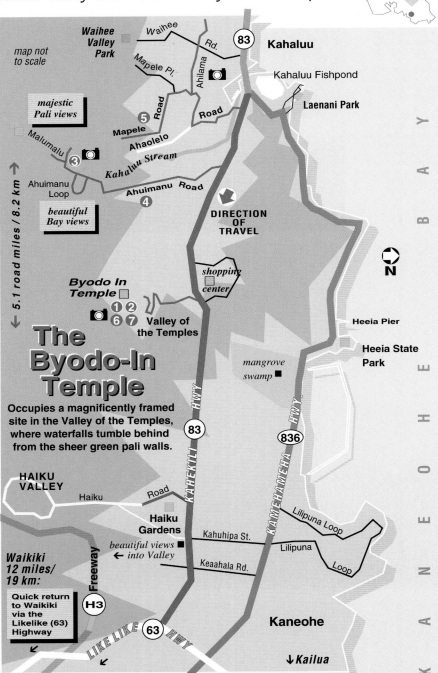

Waihee Valley Park

Waihee Rd.

83

Kahaluu

map not to scale

Kahaluu Fishpond

Mapele Pl.

Ahilama

majestic Pali views

Laenani Park

Road

Malumalu

Mapele ⑤ Road

Ahaolelo

Road

③

Kahaluu Stream

Ahuimanu Loop

Ahuimanu Road

④

DIRECTION OF TRAVEL

Byodo In Temple

① ②
⑥ ⑦

Valley of the Temples

shopping center

Heeia Pier

mangrove swamp

Heeia State Park

N

K A N E O H E   B A Y

The Byodo-In Temple

Occupies a magnificently framed site in the Valley of the Temples, where waterfalls tumble behind from the sheer green pali walls.

HAIKU VALLEY

Haiku Road

83

Haiku Gardens

beautiful views ← into Valley

Kahuhipa St.

Keaahala Rd.

KAHEKILI HWY

KAMEHAMEHA HWY

836

Lilipuna Loop

Lilipuna

Loop

Waikiki 12 miles/ 19 km:

Quick return to Waikiki via the Likelike (63) Highway

Freeway

H3

63

LIKE LIKE HWY

Kaneohe

↓*Kailua*

WINDWARD SHORE

5.1 road miles / 8.2 km

beautiful Bay views

Ahuimanu Loop

*F*rom the intersection of KAMEHAMEHA (836) HWY., which is the terminus of KAHEKILI (83) HWY. and you'll see on your left, make a *left turn* onto KAHEKILI (83) HWY. **If coming directly from Waikiki**, take the H1 FWY. *west* and exit at LIKE-LIKE (63) HWY. Drive uphill and over the pali, and make a *left turn* onto the KAHEKILI (83) HWY. You will then encounter the places described in this section in the opposite order as arranged here.

After turning left onto KAHEKILI (83) HWY., *proceed* for **0.1 mile** to AHA OLELO ROAD, and *turn right* onto it. Continue on AHA OLELO ROAD about **0.4 mile** to MAPELE ROAD. *Turn right* onto MAPELE ROAD.

This is the community of **Ahuimanu**, a place where small scale agriculture thrives, where the streams that begin life as waterfalls tumbling from the heights of the dizzying pali flood the traditional taro patches and quench the thirst of the miniature cultivated forests of brilliant red torch ginger swaying in the tradewinds. Bananas, ti plants, and all manner of edibles and ornamentals flourish here, along with horses and small livestock. Residential neighborhood homes sport a truly eclectic variety of architectural styles, ranging from traditional ranch house to... well... indescribable.

Along MAPELE RD., a number of sideroads, lined with small farming enterprises, lead *mauka / left* up into the valley. The street signs are confusing here, and so are the road maps... many of these streets are all named MAPELE, with an added RD., DR., PL., etc. MAPELE RD. **confusingly changes names** at the point *where it intersects the first road on the left*. That road to the left becomes MAPELE ROAD, and the road you are on **now** changes names from MAPELE ROAD to AHILAMA ROAD. *Make a left turn here*, heading up toward the pali.

MAPELE ROAD climbs to a surprising area of large estates and then dead ends at a circle where a number of these large homes, with beautifully landscaped grounds and blooming lily ponds, are located. As it ascends, MAPELE ROAD passes many enchanting and secluded flower farms, neat and tidy and blooming with bronze and red ti plants, anthuriums, orchid and ginger, as well as plumeria and cultivated palm trees. The little

roads branching off MAPELE are worth a looksee. Honor any **Kapu** (no trespassing) signs. When finished here, *backtrack downhill* to that confusingly named intersection, and turn *left* onto AHILAMA ROAD. Located along here are roadside taro patches where their camera-shy caretakers can be observed hard at work. Continue along, exploring this area to your curiosity's content, then *head back downhill at any street* to rejoin HWY. 83. Then, *turn right* onto HWY. 83.

Proceed along HWY. 83 (named either KAMEHAMEHA or KAHEKILI, depending where you rejoined the HWY.) after exploring uphill. *Make a right/mauka turn* at the intersection of AHUIMANU ROAD. *Continue* up AHUIMANU ROAD to the very end. The last intersecting side street is called MALUMALU ST.

Turn onto MALUMALU ST. and drive a short distance to its impressive terminus. Here, the homes are built practically touching the perpendicular face of the pali. The striking effect that these **3000'** giant, towering, sheer walls have — looming overhead and dispensing countless veils of tumbling waterfalls after a rain— is quite literally dizzying. On Oahu, you probably cannot get any closer to the pali's behemoth cliff face than this, without a difficult hike. Below MALU-MALU ST., AHUIMANU ROAD crosses a little bridge over lovely **Kahaluu Stream**, which is thickly bordered with brilliantly colored blooming impatiens. Pretty photographs can be taken right from the bridge of this picturesque stream and the valley behind it. Caring residents have hung large trash bags on the fence to encourage would-be litterers not to muck up the streambed. Further downhill, a turn onto AHUIMANU LOOP reveals the panoramic loveliness of **Kaneohe Bay** and **Mokolii Island**, popularly known as **Chinaman's Hat**.

Continue exploring at will, then *head downhill* to rejoin the KAHEKILI (83) HWY. *Turn right* onto KAHEKILI (83) HWY. and drive a little over **1.0 mile** to the entrance of the **Valley Of The Temples**, a cemetery with a large open grassy area on the *right / mauka* side of the HWY. Drive into the back of this valley to visit the beautiful **Byodo-in Temple**, an exact replica in concrete of the 900 year old Byodo-in at Uji, Japan (nominal admission charge).

Backtrack downhill from the temple parking lot again to the KAHEKILI (83) HWY., and *make a right turn* onto it, then drive **1.5 miles** to the traffic light at HAIKU ROAD. Turn *right/ mauka* onto HAIKU ROAD to visit dreamily beautiful **Haiku Gardens**, just **0.2 mile** from the intersection.

Haiku Gardens is the site of a restaurant with an incomparable view. Its lily pond, picturesque little pier, thatched roof gazebos, and gardens are strikingly framed by the often cloud-topped pali above, and it is a very popular site for **weddings**. The restaurant is one of the **Charthouse** chain, and as of this writing is open for dinner only (**247-6671**). At the rear of Haiku Valley, HAIKU ROAD dead ends at a military installation. The controversial construction of the H3 FWY. atop pilings at the back of Haiku Valley has definitely altered its beauty. But the view from the HWY. is still stunning, especially on days when the sun is in and out among the clouds, casting dramatic shadows on the pali. To see it, *return* to KAHEKILI (83) HWY., and *make a right turn* onto it. The best views can be seen right from the HWY. shoulder. Be cautious of traffic behind you if you decide to pull over.

To quickly return to Honolulu, *continue ahead* along the KAHEKILI (83) HWY. for **1 mile** to the intersection of the LIKELIKE (63) HWY., where a *right / mauka turn* will quickly take you up and over the pali and into Honolulu and the H1 FWY. To continue along the Windward Shore northward, turn around and *backtrack* the **4 miles** along KAHEKILI (83) HWY. Turn the page to proceed. ❸

TheBus
848-5555

TheBus visits lower Ahuimanu only, and the Kahekili Hwy. entrance of the Valley of the Temples.

From Waikiki:
On the mauka side of Kuhio Ave., Saratoga Rd., Kalia Rd., or Ala Moana Blvd., board the #19 Airport, #19 Airport-Hickam, or #20 Airport Halwa Gate bus to the corner of Alakea St. and King St. in Downtown Hon-olulu. At the same bus stop on Alakea St., board the #55 Kaneohe-Kahaluu bus, which will take you a short way up Ahuimanu Rd., through a

residential area not featured here, and on to the entrance of the Valley of the Temples. You will have to hike in —all uphill— to the Byodo-In Temple and the upper Ahuimanu and Mapele areas. Commercial tour buses visit Byodo In Temple.

Return:
In the opposite direction, board the #55 Downtown-Bishop St. bus and alight at the corner of Bishop & King Sts. in Downtown Honolulu. On King St., in front of the Bank of Hawaii, transfer to the #2 Waikiki-Kapiolani Park, #2 Waikiki-Campbell Ave., or the #19 or #20 Waikiki-Beach and Hotels bus.

❶ ❷

❹ ❺   ❻ ❼

Photographs

Left page: Workers tend a large taro patch along Ahilama Rd.

1. The caretaker of the Byodo-In buddha poses with his

charge: **Ektachrome 400** *film, rated at 1600 ASA. All others:* **Kodachrome 64**

2. The Temple occupies a breathtakingly beautiful site. Notice that a waterfall is

flowing in each crevasse of the pali that backs it.

3. Kahaluu Stream blooms with fluorescent-hued impatiens on its way past Ahuimanu Rd. This shot was taken below the bridge.

4. Neat little hilltop farmlets abound in Ahuimanu.

5. Plumeria.

6. Detail of the Byodo In Temple roof.

7. Peacock by the Temple's koi pond.

Kahaluu to Kualoa Park

The Hawaiian countryside is at its most beautiful here, while offshore, the kayaking is wondrous.

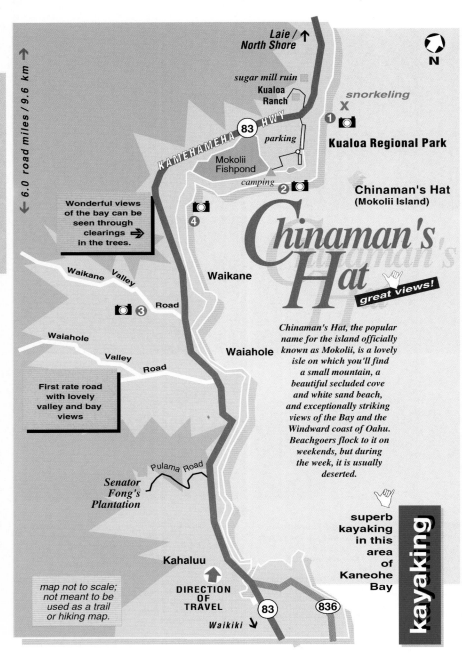

WINDWARD SHORE

← 6.0 road miles / 9.6 km →

Laie / ↑ North Shore

sugar mill ruin

Kualoa Ranch

snorkeling

X

N

KAMEHAMEHA (83) HWY

parking

Mokolii Fishpond

camping

Kualoa Regional Park

Chinaman's Hat (Mokolii Island)

Wonderful views of the bay can be seen through clearings in the trees. ➡

Waikane

Chinaman's Hat

great views!

Waikane Valley Road

Waiahole Valley Road

Waiahole

First rate road with lovely valley and bay views

Chinaman's Hat, the popular name for the island officially known as Mokolii, is a lovely isle on which you'll find a small mountain, a beautiful secluded cove and white sand beach, and exceptionally striking views of the Bay and the Windward coast of Oahu. Beachgoers flock to it on weekends, but during the week, it is usually deserted.

Pulama Road

Senator Fong's Plantation

superb kayaking in this area of Kaneohe Bay

kayaking

Kahaluu

DIRECTION OF TRAVEL

83 836

Waikiki ↓

map not to scale; not meant to be used as a trail or hiking map.

---

*I*n **Kahaluu**, at the intersection of KAHEKILI (83) HWY., and KAMEHAMEHA (836) HWY., the road continues northwest along the Windward Shore as the KAMEHAMEHA (83) HWY.

To the *right / makai* of this intersection is the palm-encircled **Kahaluu Fishpond**. This area has been the setting for numerous TV shows and films, including the village and airport scenes in **The Karate Kid.**

0.1 mile from the intersection, *on the right*, across the channel from the fishpond, is undeveloped Kahaluu Regional Park, which has a boat launching ramp, and still more impressive and photogenic **views** of the bay. Less than **2 miles** after the park, the excellent WAIAHOLE VALLEY ROAD intersects the HWY. from the *mauka / left* side, and is worthy of exploration for the look it provides into the peaceful-seeming world of those who live here. The ebony asphalt ribbon winds into verdant and beautiful Waiahole Valley, past neat papaya and banana orchards with distant views of pali waterfalls. Children set up a portable basketball hoop in the road, making the smooth surface do double duty as an impromptu court, —that's how sparse the motor traffic is here. In Waiahole Valley, the pretty views of the bay and of Chinaman's Hat never go unappreciated. Waiahole Valley's people are fiercely Hawaiian, and few islanders have fought harder, longer, or more successfully to keep their homelands from the hands of developers. Honor all **Kapu** signs.

0.2 mile beyond the KAMEHAMEHA (83) HWY. intersection, **Waiahole Beach Park** appears on the *makai* side. Frequented by fishermen and beachcombers, its mud flats make recreational swimming less than appealing. But hold on... we'll be past Kaneohe Bay soon, and there will be great beaches all over the place. **0.3 mile** past the

beach park, WAIKANE VALLEY ROAD intersects the HWY. on the *mauka/left*, and offers a similar discovery experience to Waiahole Valley Rd., above. This road, however, has not been repaved in a long, long time. Hidden just a short way up WAIKANE VALLEY RD., on the left, is a lovely and photogenic little church. See photo.

After **Waikane**, the coastline begins to hook around to the right, and on the *makai* side, through the trees, some tantalizing glimpses of houses, surrounded by their owners' agricultural specialties -bananas, papayas, torch ginger— can be seen below enjoying a phenomenal, idyllic bay view seldom seen in photographs. Offshore, **Mokolii Island**, commonly known as **Chinaman's Hat**, watches over this northwesternmost reach of Kaneohe Bay. To the *left*, **Kualoa Point** with its beautiful long shaded beach, campgrounds, and the large **Molii Fishpond** reaches out toward the little island.

❶

As we drive along, the entrance of **Kualoa Regional Park** appears *makai / right*, as does the first in a long series of gorgeous beaches that stretch all along this shore. Kualoa Regional Park enjoys one of the island's most expansive coastal views. The grounds were extensively and impressively refurbished in the late 1980's, greatly enhancing the park's beauty. The park includes an enormous lawn area dotted with still young shade trees, and a large number of picnic tables spaced well apart, as well as two comfort stations. It offers safe swimming conditions and lifeguard service daily from June to August, and on weekends the rest of the year. The beach is long and narrow, a mixture of coral and sand. The shore bottom is rocky with patches of submerged reef, interspersed with sandy areas for comfortable water entry. You may see a friendly **octopus/squid fisherman** or two employing glass-bottomed boxes for spotting their catch beneath the shallow waters, but otherwise, the park is virtually deserted during the week.

Kualoa is one of the few places on Oahu with secured nighttime camping. You can reach the **camping area** by heading *right* from the *traffic circle* located within Kualoa's huge parking area. Camping permits are necessary and are available from the **Department of Parks and Recreation (523-4525)**. They will be happy to answer any questions you have.

Offshore, **Chinaman's Hat**, with its distinctive rounded peak, a few palm trees, and lovely hidden sandy beach, beckons those who are enchanted by deserted islands. Turn the page for a full rundown on a recent visit to Chinaman's Hat.

❷

TheBus
848-5555

From Waikiki:
On the mauka side of Kuhio Ave., board the #19 Airport, #19 Airport-Hickam, or the #20 Airport-Halawa Gate bus to the Ala Moana Shopping Center. Transfer at the Ala Moana Center to the #55 Kaneohe-Circle Island bus, which will proceed along the Kamehameha (83) HWY. from Kahaluu to Kualoa Park, and then continue on to circle the island.

Return:
In the opposite direction, board the #55 Honolulu-Ala Moana Center bus and alight at Kona St. in the Ala Moana Shopping Center. Walk in the direction of Waikiki (east) to the next bus stop marked for the #8 or #19 Waikiki-Beach and Hotels bus in order to return to Waikiki.

Photographs

1. Father and son play in the shallow waters as Chinaman's Hat seems to float offshore.

2. The view from the park's campground beach area.

3. A lovely little church on Waikane Valley Road.

4. Beautiful views of the bay and the pali that ring it abound here, but there are only a few clearings in the trees that allow you to really enjoy them.

All photos:
Kodachrome 64

❸ ❹

Chinaman's HAT

by Jeanne & Harry Schwartz

*F*or many people, the idea of spending time alone —or with someone special— on a deserted island is very much a part of their vacation fantasies. But not too many people go to the trouble to seek out such an unusual destination, due to the cost, the inconvenience, and the time it takes to get there. Even though we had done quite a bit of reading about Oahu prior to our first visit to Hawaii, nowhere did we read anything about what turned out to be the most wonderful and welcome surprise of the entire trip—our discovery of Oahu's gorgeous uninhabited little Windward Isles.

Since childhood, both of us had been enchanted by the fantasy of discovering a lovely, uninhabited island to call our own, isolated from the rest of humanity by a turquoise lagoon. We recently made that dream a reality. While driving around the island on our first day in Hawaii, we kept noticing offshore islands —Rabbit Island, the Moku Lua Islands, Coconut Island. We wondered aloud if it might be possible to find a way to visit them. Our questions were soon answered when we pulled the car into Kualoa Regional Park. There, right offshore, with people exploring it, was the island called Chinaman's Hat.

As we found out, Chinaman's Hat is one of Oahu's most accessible offshore islands, and for explorers like us, one of the best for fulfilling our desire for new discoveries. This island, located about 600 yards offshore from a very popular and beautiful beach park, *does* get crowded on weekends when beachgoers paddle over on rafts or surfboards, or mostly, just wade over the connecting reef at low tide. During the week, however, it becomes a whole different place when the Park is virtually empty. Nobody can guarantee that any given location in Hawaii will be absolutely devoid of people when you visit it. But on subsequent weekday visits, we usually found Kualoa Park to be all but deserted, providing the privacy we longed for.

On that first visit, we tried to visit Chinaman's Hat, or Mokolii as it is officially known, on a crowded holiday weekend. We followed a steady stream of beachgoers as they waded over the submerged reef. The reef stretches from in front of the orange lifeguard stand and the restroom at Kualoa Point (opposite the far end of the beach parking lot) to a point near the right center of the island. Unfortunately, we didn't have any foot protection with us that day, and it was rough going. On top of that, we had forgotten to bring the tidetable from the newspaper, and no sooner did we embark on our crossing attempt when the tide began to turn against us, making it difficult to walk. We decided it would be smarter to try again on another day when we could make proper preparations. So, we returned later in the week with tidetable in hand for a much more successful experience. We were virtually alone then—only a single jogger was in Kualoa Park. We wore old sneakers to protect our feet from coral cuts. Although heavier than reef walkers, they protected better. The shadow of the reef could be plainly seen beneath the clear water to guide us across. We carried light nylon backpacks which left our hands free. Placed inside a triple layer of large Ziplock bags were wallets, keys, and dry T shirts.

We had purposely chosen a calm day for our visit, and began our wading journey two hours before lowest predicted tide. We found that the deepest that the water got —we are both 5'8" tall— was mid chest at this time and tide, which could be a little frightening for someone who's not a good swimmer. But for much of the way, it was between knee and waist deep. When we felt the water getting too deep for comfort, we saw it was because we had strayed off the reef. When this happened, we looked for the dark areas under the water and kept to them.

We headed in the direction of the tiny, shore-facing beach at the south end of the island. It took 15-20 minutes to reach it, and landing on the island via that little beach seemed to be the logical route, because a foot trail could clearly be seen climbing up from it toward the right. But this path turned out to be a false trail that soon petered out, leading nowhere. We doubled back to the tiny beach again and carefully rock-hopped along the island's park-facing shore to the north end.

Here the going got easier. A short trail appeared over the low bluff that lead to Mokolii's most magnetic feature: a lovely little cove and tiny sandy beach, very privately situated at the tip of the island, out of view of those on shore. The cove has an interesting little double-entranced sea cave that is exposed only during low tide. This seaward facing beach did not look at all safe for swimming, though. Funnel-shaped, it harbors treacherous water conditions and lots of very sharp lava rock, so we limited ourselves to beachcombing here, and were careful not to turn our backs to the sea. We sunned ourselves away from the beach due to periodic rogue waves that might have pushed us onto the jagged rocks.

Adjacent to the cove was a large flat lava shelf area with depressions that held tiny tidepool creatures. Looking up at the 206' high peak of Chinaman's Hat, we could see a large inaccessible cave almost at the very peak, mysteriously carved in its vertical face. The short trail continued around to the ocean-facing side of the island for just a few more yards. The handsome view seen from here —the islet's beach cove framed by the distant towering Koolau Mountains on Oahu's shore— looked like it was just made for photographs. A few feet ahead, the trail abruptly disappeared.

From Chinaman's Hat, the views along Oahu's Windward Shore were incomparable. We could see boats far in the distance, anchored in the translucent blue waters between Kaneohe Bay's white sandbars, which at that time of day were laid bare and gleaming by the low tide. Our eyes followed the pali as they rippled into the distance along the coast, reminding us of the many corrugated metal roofs on the simple homes we had seen in the area.

We carefully timed our stay on Chinaman's Hat to end no more than one half hour before lowest tide so that we didn't get stuck there. We returned to the park the same way we came, via the tiny, shore-facing beach at the south end of Chinaman's Hat. We headed over the dark reef straight toward the orange lifeguard stand at Kualoa Point, from where we first entered the water.

We had found our Fantasy Island pristine and spotless, except for a single chunk of styrofoam that had washed up on the rocks. We felt like we had at long last discovered our perfect little uninhabited island, just like the ones that had fascinated us since childhood, and perfect is the way we wanted to leave it. We took the styrofoam with us when we left.

For more about Chinaman's Hat, see "Uninhabited Hawaiian Islands" on page 8.

Kualoa Park to Kahana Bay

A smorgasbord of gorgeous beaches.

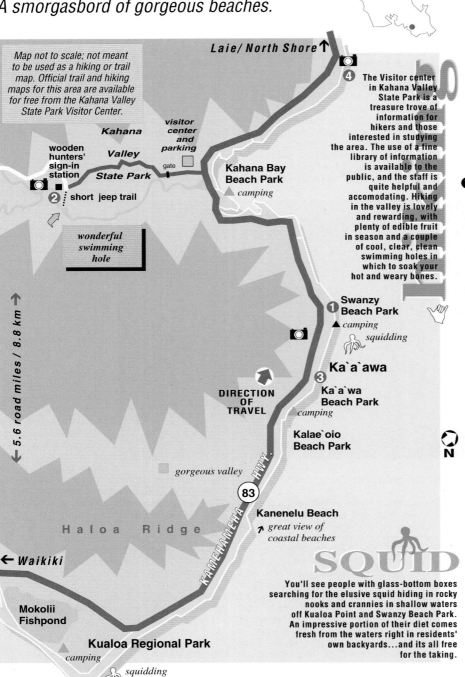

Laie / North Shore ↑

④ The Visitor center in Kahana Valley State Park is a treasure trove of information for hikers and those interested in studying the area. The use of a fine library of information is available to the public, and the staff is quite helpful and accomodating. Hiking in the valley is lovely and rewarding, with plenty of edible fruit in season and a couple of cool, clear, clean swimming holes in which to soak your hot and weary bones.

WINDWARD SHORE

Kahana

Valley

visitor center and parking

wooden hunters' sign-in station

gate

State Park

② short jeep trail

Kahana Bay Beach Park
▲ camping

wonderful swimming hole

① Swanzy Beach Park
▲ camping
🐙 *squidding*

5.6 road miles / 8.8 km

Ka`a`awa

③

Ka`a`wa Beach Park
camping

DIRECTION OF TRAVEL

Kalae`oio Beach Park

N

gorgeous valley

83

Kanenelu Beach
↗ *great view of coastal beaches*

Haloa Ridge

KAMEHAMEHA HWY.

← *Waikiki*

SQUID

You'll see people with glass-bottom boxes searching for the elusive squid hiding in rocky nooks and crannies in shallow waters off Kualoa Point and Swanzy Beach Park. An impressive portion of their diet comes fresh from the waters right in residents' own backyards...and its all free for the taking.

Mokolii Fishpond

Kualoa Regional Park
camping
🐙 *squidding*

---

*I*f you are not wearing your bathing suit, you might want to get into it; from this point on, you'll encounter a veritable smorgasbord of breathtaking beaches. For the next **10 miles** or so, the highway closely hugs the coastline, and if its sunny, you'll want to sample them all. When the urge hits, just park roadside, grab your towel, and jump in. Then quickly dry off, jump back in the car, and head for the next.

Upon leaving **Kualoa Regional Park**, make a *right turn* onto KAMEHAMEHA (83) HWY. and continue up the Windward Coast. Across the highway, attractive **Kualoa Ranch (tel. 538-7636)**

stunningly Irish green, picture-perfect, beautiful valley appears *mauka*. The combination proves irresistible to many, as you can tell by the cars almost always parked along the road here. This is **Kanenelu Beach**. It attracts surfers who like the small offshore waves, and swimmers who will find the shore bottom rocky in places, but with clear sandy areas between.

The town of **Ka'a'awa** —go ahead and try to pronounce *that*— quickly reveals itself after rounding **Makahonu Point**. Giant boulders protect the highway from storm-tossed waves, and ahead, one-acre-big **Kalae'o'io Beach Park** is a favorite,

①

at the base of the pali offers organized activities with a stunning view, including horse-back riding and helicopter rides along the coast.

The highway soon passes the disintegrating ruins of an old sugar mill on the *mauka / left* side. This was the first sugar mill to be erected on Oahu (c.1864). What *is* left of the mill is being held together by gravity and decomposing coral mortar, and is very dangerous to climb on. Notice that the neat umbrella-shaped trees here give the area a handsome *African Plains* look. Immediately ahead, the **Haloa Ridge** descends quickly to meet the road, and as you round its terminus, a sublime vision appears. Spectacular white beaches trail away endlessly up the coast, and a

judging by the mix of locals, mainlanders, and Japanese tourists, all enjoying its lovely situation. Shaded picnic tables and safe swimming conditions when calm are its main attributes. But if the stream here is running after a rain, pass by **Kalae'o'io** due to silt pollution. *Turn mauka / left*, and drive Ka'a'awa town's tiny inland streets for a few minutes. The neighborhood is green, clean and well groomed. **Ka'a'awa Beach Park** is popular with locals, with shallow, reef protected shore waters, a restroom, and a lifeguard tower that's manned daily from June through August.

0.6 mile past Ka'a'awa, **Swanzy Beach Park** makes a superb stop for some basketball or snorkeling, or to try a hand at **octopus and squid**

hunting in its shallows. There is not much of a beach beyond its handsome lava rock retaining wall. Swanzy is safe for swimming, though its toe-stubbing rocky shorebottom sends most people elsewhere. There is a sandy channel offshore that often guides dangerous **rip currents**. The park is usually empty on weekdays most of the year but attracts campers in summer. The accompanying photo was taken around New Year's Day, at the height of the tourist season when schools were closed and the kids were on the loose. Despite this, Swanzy was still completely deserted.

Beyond the Crouching Lion Inn, the HWY. rounds **Mahie Point** and a breathtaking view of expansive **Kahana Bay** materializes. Off the point, snorkelers might be seen floating suspended in the clear water, while on the *mauka* side, lei and fruit sellers often set up roadside stands. The mountains of **Kahana Valley State Park** frame the scene majestically. As beautiful as this sight is, it is even more impressive if approached from the opposite (**Punaluu**) direction. Look behind you as you go. Though very popular with locals for camping, fishing and boat launching, **Kahana Bay**'s wide sandy beach is rarely crowded, and virtually empty during the week. The beach is flat, with a gradual and gentle slope into the water, making it ideal for children and non swimmers. In addition, gentle, well formed waves provide an ideal situation for novice bodysurfers. Commercial outfits run kayak excursions in Kahana Bay and up adjacent Kahana Stream. There is a beautiful large coconut palm picnic grove across the highway from the beach.

Kahana Valley is one of the wettest Valleys on Oahu, receiving up to **300 inches of rain annually** on its peaks. **Kahana Valley State Park** is a "living park", meaning that its 100+ residents participate in a program to share with visitors their knowledge and skills pertaining to the traditional Hawaiian way of life. For specific programs, call the Honolulu Division of State Parks (**587-0300**) or Kahana Valley State Park Visitor Center (**237-8858**). Or check with the visitor Center in person upon arrival, paying special attention to the bulletin board.

Kahana Valley was once home to a very large, self-supporting community which reaped the riches of abundant schools of ahule and other fish in the bay, as well as extensive agricultural enterprises in the valley itself. Remnants of these plantings can still be seen today, and the estuary where the Kahana Stream flows into the bay is still an ideal place for fishing, squidding, crabbing, and netting opae.

Today their legacy of abundant fruit awaits hikers who walk the **Kahana Valley Trails**. Check in at the visitor center where you will find the staff very welcoming and helpful. There is an impressive library of books and publications here pertaining to this area for your reference, as well as maps and plenty of free advice. Empty the interior of your car before arriving and do not be seen placing anything in the trunk. The safest place to park is in front of the visitor center, and its free. A full valley hike lasts anywhere from **3-5 hours**, but an **easy 20-25 minute** walk up the paved park road (blocked to vehicular traffic by locked gates) leads to a wonderful, clear, deep, cool isolated swimming hole. Check in first at the Visitor Center for updated conditions and a free map, then walk uphill on the road past the first gate and continue into the valley. The road passes a few homes, **private** taro and papaya plots, then a grouping of 3 covered shelters *on the left*, and some friendly horses wandering free and hopeful of a handout. Bring apples, fallen mangoes, or—always a good idea for horses *and* barking dogs —dog biscuits.

Ignore the road that forks to the right about 10 minutes into the walk. After 20 minutes or so a second gate will appear after a dirt parking area on the *left*. Immediately to the left of the gate is a wooden hunters' **sign-in station**. To the *left* of that is a wide descending jeep road that quickly (a 3 or 4 minute shady walk) leads to the swimming hole pictured here.

Other trails deeper in the Valley also pass swimming holes, and along the way provide hungry hikers with sustaining and delicious mountain and rose apples, guava, mango and papaya.

The staff at the Visitor Center will map out a route upon request.

TheBus
848-5555

From Waikiki:
On the mauka side of Kuhio Ave., board the #19 Airport, #19 Airport-Hickam, or the #20 Airport-Halawa Gate bus to the Ala Moana Shopping Center. Transfer at the Ala Moana Center to the #55 Kaneohe-Circle Island bus, which will proceed along the Kamehameha (83) HWY. from Kualoa Park to Kahana Bay, and then continue on to circle the island.

Return:
In the opposite direction, board the #55 Honolulu-Ala Moana Center bus and alight at Kona St. in the Ala Moana Shopping Center. Walk in the direction of Waikiki (east) to the next bus stop marked for the #8 or #19 Waikiki-Beach and Hotels in order to return to Waikiki.

❷

Photographs

1. For those of us with memories of pick-up games played on gritty city lots in biting cold wind on dark gray days, this scene at Swanzy Beach Park comes pretty close to looking like heaven.

2. Local kids make a regular stop at the clear, clean, cool

swimming hole in Kahana Valley State Park.

3. Kamehameha Hwy. closely follows the shore as it passes through Ka'a'awa town.

4. Kahana Bay Beach Park.

All photos:
Kodachrome 64

❸

❹

Kahana Bay to Hauula

Stunning beaches, glorious wilderness trails, and a veritable downpour of waterfalls.

Koloa Falls

Double Waterfall

Laie / North Shore ↑

Kokololio Beach

great views!

Hauula Loop Trail ④ ⑤

③

Maakua Road

Hauula

Maakua Falls Trail (difficult)

Hauula Homestead Rd.

Hauula Beach Park

camping

Normally, there is no sign visible from the road indicating **Kokololio Beach**... just look for the low lava stone wall along the highway on the *makai* side... park roadside and walk toward the water.

Maakua Falls

Maakua Ridge Trail

parking

Sacred Falls

DIRECTION OF TRAVEL

State Park

Sacred Falls

N

whew!
The Maakua Gulch and Koloa Falls trails are both difficult full-day treks. It would be wise to join an organized guided hike led by the Sierra Club or other local hiking group.

Haleaha Rd.

②

Valley Rd.

Green Rd.

①

beautiful valley

Punaluu Valley

Punaluu Beach Park
picturesque palm-shaded beach with lovely coastal views

camping

5.6 road miles / 8.9 km

83

HWY.

KAMEHAMEHA

Waikiki ↙

map not to scale; not meant to be used as a trail map or hiking guide. Free hiking maps are available from the Dept. of Forestry & Wildlife.

WINDWARD SHORE

Kokololio Beach

As KAMEHAMEHA (83) HWY. rounds **Kahana Bay**, be sure to look behind you for the exquisite view in that direction. Looking behind as you go should become a habit on Oahu. You will surely double your pleasure, as well as your photo opportunities. Have your camera ready, as this stretch of coast continues to be some of the loveliest on an already superlative shore.

Punaluu Beach Park appears on the *makai* side. As considered from roadside, it is *deceptively* unimpressive. The park is long and narrow, and its picnic tables are alternately shaded by ironwood trees and lovely coconut groves. The beach itself is both pretty and photogenic; the trees that back it provide shade on the sand in the afternoon, and the palms cast lovely tropical shadows at water's edge. The coastal views are exceptional. It is safe for swimming, but it is best to avoid swimming at Punaluu if the streams are running, or at least swim as far away from them as possible. Punaluu has two comfort stations, and parking is available along the HWY. Across the HWY., there is an idyllic valley supporting ranch buildings, grazing horses, flocks of snow white egrets, and cultivated banana plots. About **1.0 mile** after the park, **Pat's at Punaluu** offers just about the only mainstream accommodations in this area, as well as a restaurant. Beyond Pat's, the beach is named **Kaluanui**, and is popular with fishermen and safe for swimming, with a sandy bottom. Access is alongside the stream **0.7 miles** past Pat's.

1.0 mile after **Pat's** is the entrance to **Sacred Falls State Park**, a site that gets more mixed reviews than any other on the island. Some people love it, while others are disappointed. Perhaps the problem is that it is both a very popular place and very long in getting there. Falling rocks can be a problem, especially after a rain, as is mud. Do not leave anything visible in your car, nor be seen placing anything in the trunk. The **87'** waterfall is lovely, and the pool, which can be murky after a rain, is surrounded by large flat rocks ideal for spreading a picnic on.

0.8 mile past Sacred Falls State Park is little **'Aukahi Beach Park**, where swimming is not so great due to the raised reef at the shoreline, but adjacent to the park is a tiny sand-bottomed bay with a narrow little beach.

Hauula in Hawaiian means "red hau", the name derived from the once plentiful hau trees which blossomed profusely here during the summer months. The large-cupped blossoms begin the

morning a bright yellow, transforming over the course of the day to a vivid red by evening. The numbers of these tangled trees diminished as lands were cleared for agriculture, but the name lives on.

At **Hauula Beach Park**, the striking streamline moderne-style beach pavilion remains an area landmark and an architecturally significant relic that deserves to be restored. The wide lawn between the HWY. and the beach is protected from traffic by a 3' high roadside wall which provides room for kids to run safely and to fly kites in the ocean breeze. The reef-protected beach is about 1000' in length, but the shore bottom is rocky. Lifeguard service is provided daily from June through August. The park has a restroom, a volleyball court and picnic tables.

Inland at Hauula, the lovely hills are crowned with forests of beautiful, symmetrical Norfolk pines which shelter two wonderful hiking trails. Between them, a third trail follows Maakua Stream through the gulch, ending abruptly at little Maakua Falls. Traveling *north* along KAMEHAMEHA (83) HWY., look for the 7-11 store on the *mauka* side of the road. Next door to it is a small church. The road adjacent to the church is HAUULA HOMESTEAD ROAD. The road sign is not easy to see. *Turn left/mauka* onto it. Ahead, HAUULA HOMESTEAD ROAD curves to the left 90°, but keep going *straight* along the short dirt road named MAAKUA. Park to the side being careful not to block anyone, or park along Hauula Homestead Road. At the end of MAAKUA ROAD is a distinctive **brown sign with yellow lettering** announcing the trails to the *right*. Walk to the *right* and **uphill** to the dirt road that comes in from the *left* which is bordered by a **3 1/2' yellow post** on either side. Usually a yellow cable is stretched between the posts to keep cars out. The trail is **marked** here by an **easy-to-miss brown wooden stake**, only a couple of inches wide, announcing the trail's name at the right / uphill side of the entrance. The dirt road / trail narrows and soon comes to a **streambed**, normally dry. Cross the stream bed *only* if not swollen with water. The trail *forks* about **70 yards** after the streambed crossing.

The **right fork** is the HAUULA LOOP TRAIL. A few yards along this right fork trail, it *forks once again*, but being a **loop trail**, either fork will eventually lead you right back to this spot in **2 or 3 hours**.

The **left fork** leads to the MAAKUA *GULCH* TRAIL, and a little beyond that, the PAPALI TRAIL, also called the MAAKUA *RIDGE* TRAIL, which is

2.5 **miles** in length. Continue to the PAPALI TRAIL, if taking that route. Pass on by the Papali Trailhead if heading to Maakua Falls. The MAAKUA GULCH TRAIL **follows the streambed all the way to the falls**. Much of the trail is in the streambed itself, so exercise caution to prevent slips and broken bones. The MAAKUA GULCH TRAIL should not be taken after a rain, or if it is raining in the mountains, or even if rain is predicted. *This trail is best taken the first time with a hiking organization. See the listings on page 12.*

THE HAUULA LOOP TRAIL, at 2.5 miles in length, is one of the best hiking experiences on the island of Oahu. Why? Well, its not *too* strenuous, the scenery is beautiful, the topography and flora are varied, the views breathtaking –literally– and the trail itself is very obvious, clean and well maintained. Books by professional hikers call this trail "easy", but easy *to them* means you don't have to rappel down sheer cliffs. Lets just say you're going to sweat and have to stop and catch your breath a few times. Bring water and some munchies to keep you going. The **7-11** back on Kam HWY. stocks supplies, including **School Kine cookies**.

Follow the **loop trail** via the *right fork*. It ascends through brush and trees, and is open to the sun at first, but soon leads into a heavily shaded ironwood forest which has carpeted the trail floor with a thick, comfortable, dry cushioning of long needles. The views in photos #3 & #5 were taken from here.

Abruptly, after rounding a bend, the ironwood forest changes to towering Norfolk pine, and the forest floor beneath these is populated with thousands of inches-high Norfolk pine seedlings competing with each other for the few elusive spots of dappled sunlight that manage to land on the forest floor. All along the trail, the forest's floor covering alternates –from a deep mulch of ironwood needles and natural arboral debris, to lush ferns and wild orchids on 3' spikes, to emerging tree seedlings of differing types.

Clearings through the trees which reveal the magnificent coastal views are **few and far between** as of this writing –our only complaint about the Hauula Loop Trail. But later, toward the end of the trek, back in the valley along the top of the ridge, wide open clearings provide **magical views** deep into the folds of the pali. Far into untouched valleys and well into the gorge below your eyes will wander in contemplation of the eerie stillness and distinct silence of this place, far from the ocean's roar. So protected is it from the sea

breeze that the wild orchids stand deliberate and motionless at the tops of their slender three foot tall stalks.

The **MAAKUA GULCH TRAIL** follows the streambed, normally dry, and soon traverses another small stream coming in from the right. Maakua Gulch narrows continually, and the trail crisscrosses the slippery stream bed a number of times before it just about disappears. But you can't get lost... just follow the streambed, because from here on in, the streambed *is* the trail. Watch each step you take, and avoid wet areas as much as possible. The worst thing you can do in Maakua Gulch is be in a hurry. Near the end the canyon narrows to just a few yards across, and could become a deadly place in the event of heavy rain in the mountains above. At the end of the trail, a small but lovely waterfall offers a cooling break. The pool at its deepest point is about **4'**. Watch for falling rocks from above, and bring food and water. The round trip will take about 6 hours.

Photographs

1. Punaluu Beach Park. Much of the sand is rock-free.

2. Across the Hwy. from the Beach Park, this valley of grazing horses and snow-white egrets awaits.

3. From the Hauula Loop Trail, a superb view of Hauula town and the coast looking southward appears about 15 minutes into the hike. Cutting back on branches in selected areas would boost the enjoyment of this trail, as only a few glimpses of distant beauty are now visible.

4. Pine seedlings.

5. Hauula Loop Trail. Ironwood needles carpet the way.

All photos: Kodachrome 64

TheBus
848-5555

From Waikiki:
On the mauka side of Kuhio Ave., board the #19 Airport, #19 Airport-Hickam, or the #20 Airport-Halawa Gate bus to the Ala Moana Shopping Center. Transfer at the Ala Moana Center to the #55 Kaneohe-Circle Island bus, which will proceed along the Kamehameha (83) HWY. from Kahana Bay to Hauula. Its a short walk from the HWY. up Hauula Homestead Rd. to Maakua Rd. and the trailhead for all three trails featured here.

Return:
In the opposite direction, board the #55 Honolulu-Ala Moana Center bus and alight at Kona St. in the Ala Moana Shopping Center. Walk in the direction of Waikiki (east) to the next bus stop marked for the #8 or #19 Waikiki-Beach and Hotels.

Laie and Goat Island

A lovely deserted island only a stone's throw from shore, and the area's baddest bodysurfing beach.

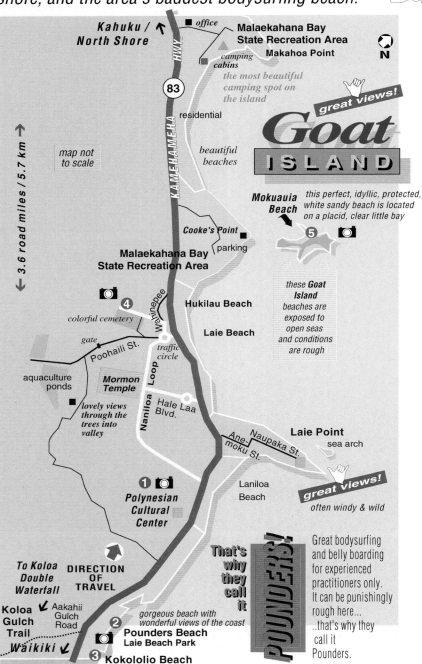

WINDWARD SHORE

As we continue along KAMEHAMEHA (83) HWY. through town, we are looking for **Kokololio Beach**, north of and adjacent to the CYO Camp Hauula. Hidden from the view of cars on the HWY., Kokololio has long kept its secret as one of the most beautiful beaches on the island of Oahu. To reach it, look for a 3' high dark stone wall along the *makai* side of the road enclosing a park-like property. Park roadside and walk to the beach. Or, you can proceed to the parking area at northerly adjacent Pounders Beach, and walk back along the shore, past the bodysurfing action and over the bluff. Kokololio boasts a gradually sloping sandy shore bottom, a lot of solitude during the week, and eye-caressing coastal views.

Next door to Kokololio Beach is the mighty and beautiful Pounders, a premier body surfing spot if there ever was one, and like its neighbor Kokololio, visually exquisite. Pounders is privately owned, but through the grand and much appreciated generosity of the land owners, its park and beach are open to the public. A dirt parking lot, its boundaries framed by large logs laid along the ground, is easy to spot on the *makai* side of the HWY. ❶

Pounders Beach is superbly framed on the south end by a distinctively-shaped low limestone bluff whose point has been undermined by the relentless sea. Powerful waves crash white against its black face, as the pine forested hills of Hauula form a hypnotic backdrop, and the majestic Koolaus in turn frame the entire scene, dreamily remindful of a Chinese landscape painting. Along this bluff, the bodysurfers, regardless of whether they ride and conquer or crash and burn, either way get soundly pounded (thus the name) by the breakers. Toward the north, the picturesque remains of a small wharf extends from the sandy beach into the ocean, and this end of the nearly quarter mile long stretch of shore that is Pounders Beach is generally safe for swimming. Use proper caution during the winter or when the water is rough. There are no lifeguards here.

After leaving Pounders Beach, the HWY. immediately rolls into Laie, the center of the Mormon community in Hawaii, home of the Polynesian Cultural Center and an interesting town in its own

right. **The Polynesian Cultural Center** (admission charge) offers an overview of customs and culture in 7 model villages, each representing a distinct Pacific area: Hawaii, Samoa, Tonga, Fiji, New Zealand, Tahiti, and the Marquesas.

Across the HWY. from the **Laie Shopping Center**, look for ANEMOKU ST. on the *makai / right* side. *Turn right* onto it, then turn *right again* on NAUPAKA ST. **Drive slowly, there are always children present**. Go the short distance to the end, and park out of the way. This is spectacular **Laie Point**.

From the end of Laie Point the **view** of the Windward Coast of Oahu is **all-encompassing**. Nowhere else on this side of the island is one so exposed to the elements. What felt only like a breeze along the HWY. feels like a gale at Laie Point. The tiny rocky islands you see are protected bird sanctuaries. The most distinctive is the sea arch **Kukuihoolua**, where during stormy seas, incoming waves entertain by crashing powerfully and noisily through the opening. Until 1946, though, there was just a cave here, visible only from the seaward side. The powerful April Fools Day tsunami (tidal wave) of that year smashed through the cave, knocking out its back wall, and forming the arch.

Back to the Kam HWY., turn *right* onto it to continue northward. The second street on the *mauka / left* side, HALE LAA BLVD., is expansively wide and continental in feel, lined with large and dignified Norfolk pines, and designed to lead impressed visitors straight up the hill to the **Mormon Temple**. From the HWY., turn *left* up HALE LAA BLVD. and explore the neat, clean streets with well-maintained homes and yards. Visitors to the Temple are welcome daily from **9 a.m. to 9 p.m.**

In front of the temple, HALE LAA BLVD. intersects NANILOA LOOP. *Make a right turn* onto it and continue until you reach the traffic circle. On the opposite side of the circle, *turn left* on POOHAILI ST. to visit the **Laie Cemetery**, with its simple graves decorated lavishly with rainbows of ribbons, natural and plastic flowers, and even balloons. Further along POOHAILI ST., pass through the gate and veer left at the intersection. The narrow road passes grazing horses, aquaculture ponds and pretty views into the valley.

②

Return to the HWY. and turn left onto it. In **about 0.4 mile**, the first of two entrances to wondrous **Malaekahana Bay State Recreation Area** appears on the *makai / right* side of the HWY. Pull into the park's enormous parking area. If its a weekday, you could very easily be the only one here. A very large, heavily shaded picnic area acts as a cool buffer between the parking lot and the superb, mile-long white sand beach. Right offshore is yet another of Oahu's uninhabited island jewels, **Mokuauia**, commonly known as **Goat Island.**

Goat Island has three beaches on its untrammeled shores. The first, to the *right* of the welcome sign as you come ashore, faces the Oahu shore toward the south. It is sandy and narrow; at its eastern end the shore bottom is sandy with rocky places. At the western end, there is submerged reef. The second beach is adjacent to it on the open ocean side of the point that divides them. It has a very rocky shore, but a nice, sandy, often windy upper beach, away from the water.

The third one is an Eden-like, first rate, sandy beach known as Mokuauia. It faces the shore to the north, and lies to the left of the welcome sign as you come ashore. Efficiently protected from ocean waves by a prominent barrier point, the shore bottom is sandy and gradually sloping. The beach itself is clean, white and free of rocks. Its an ideal and placid place for a solitary swim. Goat Island is **reachable by foot at low tide** by walking over the reef that extends from Cooke's Point to the point of Goat Island that extends **closest to shore**. You can see the welcome sign from shore: head toward it. **Check your tide table printed in the daily paper**. Wear old sneakers to protect feet from coral cuts, and please, leave nothing behind on the island. If unsure, talk about conditions with those on the beach who are about to head over to, or are returning from, Goat Island.

A second park area, also a part of Malaekahana, is located northward toward the point. Large, spacious "**cabins**", once the homes of local families, are available for rent by the state for phenomenally low prices. Their location is unparalleled for beauty, but the cabins themselves are in **extremely poor shape** and dirty, and the "bedding", consisting of piles of filthy mattresses, is a disgrace. You are supposed to bring your own linens, but take our advice: bring a tent and sleep outside instead. This place is, we think, **the most beautiful camping spot on Oahu**. Camping reservations can be made by calling **293-1736**.

Photographs

1. Polynesian Cultural Center procession.

2. Pounders, with the gorgeous Hauula loop trail pine forests covering the hills in the background.

③

3. Kokololio Beach curves toward Pounders and exquisite coastline views.

4. Laie Cemetery, alive with color, is anything but somber.

④

5. Goat Island's isolated, idyllic Mokuauia Beach is unparalelled for its beauty.

All: Kodachrome 64

⑤

Kahuku to Turtle Bay

Five long miles of unpeopled sandy shoreline.

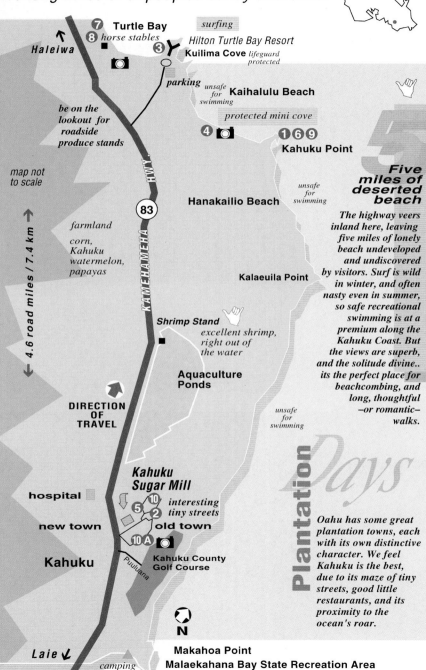

⑦ **Turtle Bay**
⑧ *horse stables*
③ *surfing*

↑ **Haleiwa**

Hilton Turtle Bay Resort
Kuilima Cove *lifeguard protected*

parking *unsafe for swimming*

Kaihalulu Beach

be on the lookout for roadside produce stands

protected mini cove

④ ①⑥⑨

Kahuku Point

map not to scale

83

KAMEHAMEHA HWY.

Hanakailio Beach *unsafe for swimming*

↑ 4.6 road miles / 7.4 km ↓

farmland
corn, Kahuku watermelon, papayas

Kalaeuila Point

Shrimp Stand *excellent shrimp, right out of the water*

Five miles of deserted beach

The highway veers inland here, leaving five miles of lonely beach undeveloped and undiscovered by visitors. Surf is wild in winter, and often nasty even in summer, so safe recreational swimming is at a premium along the Kahuku Coast. But the views are superb, and the solitude divine.. its the perfect place for beachcombing, and long, thoughtful —or romantic— walks.

Aquaculture Ponds

unsafe for swimming

▲ **DIRECTION OF TRAVEL**

Plantation Days

Kahuku Sugar Mill

⑩
⑤ ② *interesting tiny streets*

hospital

new town

⑩ Ⓐ

old town

Kahuku

Puuluana

Kahuku County Golf Course

N

Oahu has some great plantation towns, each with its own distinctive character. We feel Kahuku is the best, due to its maze of tiny streets, good little restaurants, and its proximity to the ocean's roar.

Laie ↓

camping

Makahoa Point
Malaekahana Bay State Recreation Area

Returning to the KAM HWY., *make a right turn* onto it. The town of **Kahuku** is adjacent to **Malaekahana Park**, and straddles both sides of the HWY. Usually bypassed by visitors driving the KAM HWY., except for those stopping at the sugar mill shopping complex, **Kahuku town** is an odd little treasure. With the look and somewhat unsettling feel of a *Twilight Zone* episode, the old section of town is located on the *makai / right* side of the HWY., just south of the sugar mill. Often seemingly deserted, the town is nonetheless quite inhabited and ex-

public roads leading here. The KAM (83) HWY., after Kahuku town, cuts inland more than one mile from the water, and because it bypasses the coast, that's helped keep it hidden. To take this hike, one alternative is to park your car in the Hilton's lot. Parking is inexpensive with validation from any hotel store or restaurant, and your vehicle will be more protected. Enjoy the 5 mile hike to Malaekahana State Park, then walk to the highway there to catch **TheBus**, which **runs every half hour**, back to the Hilton's front door. Or, from the Hilton, just walk part of the way along the

❶

udes a strong, albeit unusual, appeal. Explore the **tiny** streets with their movie set feel. See the town's oceanfront **public golf course**, and the enviably isolated newer homes on **Makahoa Point**, directly adjacent to the northern boundary of Malaekahana State Park.

One of Oahu's most **wild, isolated** and unvisited lengths of **shore** begins here at the golf course beach at Makahoa Point, stretching for **5 miles** up and around the coast to the North Shore and the **Turtle Bay Hilton Resort**. It is possible to walk the entire length and encounter nobody, but whether you do meet a few others or not, it is guaranteed that you will discover long, empty stretches of sand along this amazing coastline that you can call your own. What keeps these shores wild and undiscovered is the dearth of

beach until you get tired, and then simply backtrack. The other alternative is to park free at Malaekahana Park, hike to the Hilton, relax and have a bite to eat, then hop on TheBus back to Malaekahana Park.

We'll begin our hike from the north segment of Malaekahana State Park. Past the northern boundary of the park, the length of **beach along Kahuku Golf Course** is wide and sandy, with many sand dunes. Locals avoid this beach for swimming due to the **very strong offshore rip current**, but its a favorite place for beachcombers and fishermen. The rest of this shoreline for three quarters of the way to Turtle Bay consists of sandy stretches interspersed with rocky outcroppings. The shorebottom is rocky and currents can be very strong, especially in winter. Except for a few isolated places, **safe recreational swimming is poor**. However, the beaches are beautiful, sandy and isolated, with an abundance of peace and quiet. The sand is deep and your legs will get a real workout.

Hanakailio Beach, adjacent to the abandoned WWII Kahuku airfield, is the longest length of sandy beach in this area, but ahead at prominent **Kahuku Point**, bare feet are in **danger of being pierced** by the sharp appendage of a **mollusk** that is numerous and attaches itself to the rocks here. Wear foot protection, or keep off the rocks. Its a long walk to first aid.

Beyond Kahuku Point, **Kaihalulu Beach**, at one mile in length, is lovely and sandy, but its shoreline is fronted by a rocky reef, and the shore is subject to dangerous currents. Halfway down this beach is a small, lovely, protected pool for cooling off in (see photo #4).

Civilization looms as you round **Kalaeokamanu Point** to see the year-round, eminently swimmable Kuilima Cove, alive with people having a good time, a lifeguard, beach equipment rentals and the Turtle Bay Hilton Hotel. You might want to check with the hotel's front desk about the bus' schedule before you enjoy that well earned lunch.

To reach Turtle Bay from Malaekahana Park directly by car, *exit the parking lot* at Malaekahana State Park and *turn right,* onto the KAM (83) HWY. *Pass through* **Kahuku town,** noticing that the **Kahuku Mill Shopping Center** is on the *makai / right* side of the road. Outside town, in **0.2 mile** or so, you will see **Amorient Aquafarms** on the *makai / right* side, and on the *mauka / left* side, other farms growing famous Kahuku watermelon, papaya, and corn. Notice the small building on the road side of the ponds where steamed or fried shrimp are sold to passers-by right out of the water...now, *that's what we call fresh.* Continue on for about **1.0 mile** past the ponds, and the golf course of the Turtle Bay Hilton Golf & Tennis Resort will appear on the *makai / right* side, and soon, the entrance to the resort itself, lined at roadside by a low hedge of red hibiscus. *Turn right* into the hotel for a look around, or continue past it. The Turtle Bay Hilton's lifeguarded beach is only one of two on the entire North Shore that has safe, protected year-round swimming, and its open to everyone.

TheBus
848-5555

From Waikiki to Laie (previous page) and Kahuku-Turtle Bay (this page):
On the mauka side of Kuhio Ave., board the #19 Airport, #19 Airport-Hickam, or the #20 Airport-Halawa Gate bus to the Ala Moana Shopping Center. Transfer at the Ala Moana Center to the #55 Kaneohe-Circle Island bus, which will proceed along the Kamehameha (83) HWY. through Kahuku, and then continues around the island.

Return:
In the opposite direction, board the #55 Honolulu-Ala Moana Center bus and alight at Kona St. in the Ala Moana Shopping Center. Walk in the direction of Waikiki (east) to the next bus stop marked for the #8 or #19 Waikiki-Beach and Hotels in order to return to Waikiki.

Photographs

1. From Kahuku Point looking east, Hanakailio Beach, in all its isolated glory, curves to form a nameless bay.

2. An abandoned and rusting town sign.

3. Turtle Bay at dawn.

4. The lovely little protected cove at Kaihalulu Beach.

5. Kahuku Sugar Mill from the rear of the property.

6. The rocks at Kahuku Point are often covered in the ghostly remains of crabs whose flesh has long since disappeared. The slightest touch will shatter this shell.

7. Turtle Bay Beach.

8. The Hilton's riding stables become active shortly after dawn.

9. Detail of ground cover at Kahuku Pt.

10. A painted sign on an abandoned car in old Kahuku town.

10A. Old Kahuku town often looks abandoned but is quite inhabited. The old sugar mill in the background has been remodeled to include shops and a branch of Jameson's restaurant, which serves great breakfasts.

All photos:
Kodachrome 64

SHORE
North

Massive winter waves thunder ashore to the thrill of visitors and kamaainas who come to watch one of nature's great spectacles. Humans on flimsy, easily shattered fiberglass boards seek out the biggest and most powerful of these, and skim gracefully down the transparent faces of the monsters chasing them toward shore. Yet, come summer, the lion changes into a pussycat, and the same beaches that were pummeled in the wintertime are gently lapped with the arrival of mid-year.

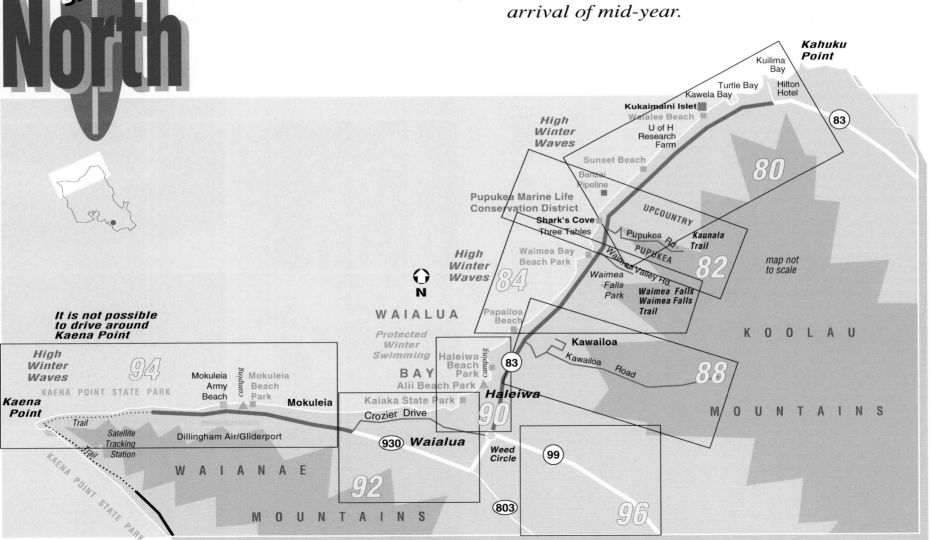

Kahuku Point

Kuilima Bay

Turtle Bay

Kawela Bay

Hilton Hotel

83

Kukaimaini Islet

Walalee Beach

U of H Research Farm

High Winter Waves

Sunset Beach

Banzai Pipeline

UPCOUNTRY

80

Pupukea Marine Life Conservation District

Shark's Cove

Three Tables

Pupukea Rd.

Kaunala Trail

map not to scale

PUPUKEA

82

Waimea Bay Beach Park

Waimea Valley Rd.

High Winter Waves

84

Waimea Falls Park

Waimea Falls

Waimea Falls Trail

N

WAIALUA

Papailoa Beach

K O O L A U

Protected Winter Swimming

Haleiwa Beach Park

camping

83

Kawailoa

Kawailoa Road

88

It is not possible to drive around Kaena Point

High Winter Waves

94

KAENA POINT STATE PARK

Mokuleia Army Beach

camping

Mokuleia Beach Park

Mokuleia

BAY

Alii Beach Park

Kaiaka State Park

Haleiwa

90

M O U N T A I N S

Kaena Point

Trail

Satellite Tracking Station

Dillingham Air/Gliderport

Crozier Drive

930 **Waialua**

99

Weed Circle

803

KAENA POINT STATE PARK

W A I A N A E

M O U N T A I N S

92

96

North Shore Beach Parks

Source: City and County of Honolulu

North Shore Beach Parks

North Shore Beach Parks	Page	Lifeguard	Rest Rooms	Public Telephone	Picnic Tables	Camping	Night Security	Swimming	Snorkeling & Diving	Surfing	Bodysurfing	Windsurfing	Seasonal High Surf
Waialee BP	80							S	◻				🌊
Sunset Beach	80	🤙		☎				S	◻			◿	🌊
Ehukai BP	80	🤙	WC	☎	XX			S		◖			🌊
Pupukea BP	82		WC	☎	XX			S	◻			◿	🌊
Waimea Bay BP	84	🤙	WC	☎	XX			S	◻	◖			🌊
Haleiwa BP	90		WC	☎	XX	△		S				◿	
Haleiwa Alii BP	90	🤙	WC	☎				S	◻				🌊
Kaiaka SRA	92		WC	☎	XX			S	◻				🌊
Mokuleia BP	94		WC	☎	XX	△		S	◻	◖		◿	🌊

North Shore Weather

Source: US Dept. of Commerce
National Weather Service Pacific Region
Station: Waialua

Oahu Weather: 836-0121
Honolulu Weather: 296-1818, X1520
Surf Report: 836-1952 or 296-1818, X1521
Marine Report: 836-3921 or 296-1818, X1522

	Daily High Temperature	Daily Low Temperature	% Of Cloud Cover	Days With 0.1" Of Rain	Days With 0.5" Of Rain	Monthly Rainfall In Inches
January	79	61	45%	7	4	5.5
February	78	60	45%	5	3	4.4
March	79	61	52%	5	3	4.4
April	80	63	59%	4	2	2.5
May	82	64	52%	2	1	1.5
June	84	66	50%	1	0	0.7
July	86	67	51%	2	0	1.0
August	86	67	47%	2	0	1.1
September	85	66	45%	2	0	0.8
October	82	65	48%	4	1	2.5
November	79	63	52%	4	2	3.5
December	79	70	48%	5	2	4.4

The sky turns black as a storm rages offshore, creating dangerous swimming conditions...but the sun still shines on Sunset Beach.

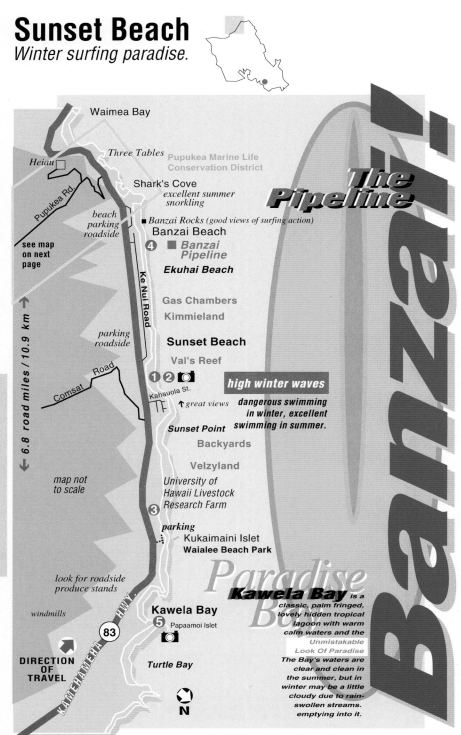

Sunset Beach
Winter surfing paradise.

Waimea Bay

Three Tables

Heiau

Pupukea Rd.

Pupukea Marine Life
Conservation District

Shark's Cove
*excellent summer
snorkling*

*beach
parking
roadside*

■ *Banzai Rocks (good views of surfing action)*

Banzai Beach

4 ■ *Banzai
Pipeline*

Ekuhai Beach

**see map
on next
page**

Ke Nui Road

Gas Chambers

Kimmieland

*parking
roadside*

Sunset Beach

Val's Reef

1 2 📷

Comsat Road

Kahauola St.

↑ *great views*

Sunset Point

Backyards

Velzyland

*University of
Hawaii Livestock
Research Farm*

3

↓ *6.8 road miles / 10.9 km* ↑

*map not
to scale*

parking

Kukaimaini Islet
Waialee Beach Park

*look for roadside
produce stands*

windmills

83

Kawela Bay

5 Papaamoi Islet
📷

Turtle Bay

**DIRECTION
OF
TRAVEL**

KAMEHAMEHA HWY.

N

high winter waves

*dangerous swimming
in winter, excellent
swimming in summer.*

Kawela Bay *is a
classic, palm fringed,
lovely hidden tropical
lagoon with warm
calm waters and the
Unmistakable
Look Of Paradise
The Bay's waters are
clear and clean in
the summer, but in
winter may be a little
cloudy due to rain-
swollen streams
emptying into it.*

*T*urtle Bay is accessible from the Hilton property. The hotel's pool is located at the extreme easterly end of the bay, and rocky little **Papaamoi Island** is at the westerly extreme. **Turtle Bay Beach** is a lovely crescent with clear aquamarine water, **treacherous conditions in the wintertime**, and a rocky shore bottom, and yes, its true...the green sea turtle still swims in Turtle Bay. The hotel's Kuilima Cove beach has safe swimming and beach gear rental year-round, and is open to the public. West of

Islet. Kukaimaini is small and rocky with no beach and only sparse vegetation. It is located offshore of **Waialee Beach Park**, which is undeveloped and unmarked at the roadside. Waialee is located right before the shockingly green pasture lands of the **University of Hawaii Livestock and Poultry Research Farm**, as seen from the KAM HWY. Just past the farm is surfing's legendary **Velzyland**, which is by no means anyplace for novices. Access is via the **public right-of-way** at the curve of KAHAUOLA ST. at **Sunset Point. Turn** *right /*

❶

Turtle Bay is idyllic **Kawela Bay**, which has a sandy, welcoming shore bottom and is ringed with swaying coconut palms. Few people will be seen on its crescent sandy beach, and the bay waters are **protected** from dangerous currents and big waves. The water tends to be **clear in summer**, but in winter can be sediment-clouded by the rain-swollen streams that flow into it. There is no access to Kawela Bay other than walking from the Hilton property.

Continuing along the KAM HWY., after passing the Hilton, produce stands selling fresh fruit and vegetables may intermittently appear, usually on the *mauka / left* side. Giant white propeller-windmills are in view along the foothills and mountain tops. Along this shore are a number of tiny islets, at least one of which can be visited at low tide, but only in the calm seas of summer: **Kukaimaini**

makai onto KAHAUOLA ST. from the KAM HWY. *Read parking restriction signs*, and then from **Sunset Point** *walk east* along the sand to reach **Velzyland. Sunset Point**, being the easternmost extreme of Sunset Beach, has a great **view** of the shore westward along the entire length of Sunset Beach.

The whole of Sunset Beach is wide, and in **winter**, deeply sloped by the **humungous waves** you see being challenged by the world's best surfers. The waves are dangerous even to beachcombers here, as they can easily knock a body down and drag him out to sea. **Children**, supervised or not, **should never be allowed to play at water's edge** during the winter here, or at any North Shore beach. The two exceptions are the Hilton's Kuilima Cove and Haleiwa Beach Park, which are **the only two winter-safe swimming beaches on**

the entire North Shore. Think twice about swimming at any other North Shore beaches except these two in the wintertime, but if you are determined, check with the lifeguard about rips and other life-and-limb threatening bugaboos. In the **summertime** however, Sunset and all other North Shore beaches are normally quite placid and offer **superlative swimming conditions**.

Parking at Sunset Beach is available roadside where the KAM HWY. skirts the sand. Oddly, there are no restrooms here, despite Sunset's popularity and worldwide fame. There is daily lifeguard service from June through August, and all year long on weekends. Sunset Beach is long and wide, with deep, comfortable sand. Its joys include strolling the strand and participating in various beach activities, such as surfing, surfer watching, jogging, sand castle building, snoozing, and daydreaming about winning the lottery and moving to Hawaii.

Where the HWY. starts to pull away from the sand at Sunset Beach, there is a very narrow road *makai / right*, named KE NUI ROAD. It runs parallel to the sand between the beach and the KAM HWY. for **1.0 mile**, to **Ekuhai Beach**. KE NUI ROAD has numerous **p.r.o.w.s** that provide access to the beach and some of Hawaii's most famous surfing spots: **Kimmieland, Gas Chambers**, and the infamous **Banzai Pipeline**. **Ekuhai Beach Park** is accessible *only* from KE NUI ROAD, and is obscured from easy view from the KAM HWY. by foliage along its flanks. Ekuhai is a developed park with restrooms and **daily lifeguard service** year 'round. Like all beaches in these parts, **swimming is very hazardous from late October through April.** Ekuhai is the best vantage point from which to watch surfers conquer the **Pipeline**.

Photographs

1. Sunset Beach.

2. At Sunset Point, surfers tackle winter waves in sunlight while an approaching storm colors the sky black.

3. U of H Research Farm, seen from the Kam Hwy.

4. The Triple Crown of Surfing attracts a large contingent of media, and a very friendly crowd.

5. Beautiful, protected palm-fringed Kawela Bay is one of Oahu's most magnetic hidden treasures.

All photos:
Kodachrome 64

TheBus
848-5555

From Waikiki:
On the mauka side of Kuhio Ave., Saratoga Rd., Kalia Rd., or Ala Moana Blvd., board the #8 Ala Moana Center, the #19 Airport, #19 Airport-Hickam, or #20 Airport-Halawa Gate bus heading away from Diamond Head, to the Ala Moana Shopping Center on Ala Moana Blvd. Transfer to the #52 Wahiawa-Circle Island bus. This bus will travel inland through the Central Plateau to the North Shore, then eastward past all of the sites included in this spread.

Return:
In the opposite direction, board the #52 Honolulu-Ala Moana Center bus and alight on Kona St. at the Ala Moana Center. To transfer, walk east toward Waikiki to the next stop marked for the #8 and #19 Waikiki-Beach and Hotels bus.

❷

❸

❹❺

Pupukea

Snorkelers explore the depths of Shark's Cove while hikers roam the cool mountain trails.

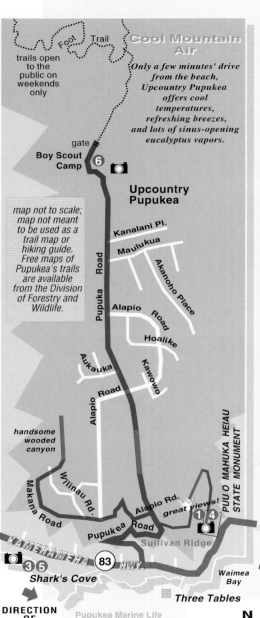

Cool Mountain Air

trails open to the public on weekends only

Only a few minutes' drive from the beach, Upcountry Pupukea offers cool temperatures, refreshing breezes, and lots of sinus-opening eucalyptus vapors.

Foot Trail

gate
Boy Scout Camp 6

Upcountry Pupukea

map not to scale; map not meant to be used as a trail map or hiking guide. Free maps of Pupukea's trails are available from the Division of Forestry and Wildlife.

Kanalani Pl.

Maulukua

Puuka Road

Akanoho Place

Alapio Road

Hoalike

Kawowo

Aukauka

Alapio Road

handsome wooded canyon

Makana Road

Wiliinau Rd.

Pupukea Road

Alapio Rd.

great views! 1 4

PUU O MAHUKA HEIAU STATE MONUMENT

Sullivan Ridge

KAMEHAMEHA 83 HWY.

3 5

Shark's Cove

Waimea Bay

Three Tables

DIRECTION OF TRAVEL

Pupukea Marine Life Conservation District 2

N

← 1.6 road miles / 2.5 km →

NORTH SHORE

You may notice in Hawaii that many people farm their yards for income. No matter how small their plot, home owners and renters alike will make clever use of every square foot of available ground to raise exotic ornamentals, herbs, and gourmet fruits and vegetables. Some people have contracts with restaurants or markets, in Hawaii and abroad, to supply them with specialty items that cannot be gotten reliably elsewhere, if at all. Many growers specialize in one or two items and build a reputation for quality and reliability. Top dollar can be earned for their efforts. Herbs from Hawaii are the latest gourmet "must-haves" for chefs from New York to Hong Kong. Herbs are fast-growing, naturally resistant to pests, don't need a lot of room and, in Hawaii, they grow year-round. They're the perfect backyard crop. Pupukea is home to many of these backyard farms.

Its always a good idea to stop at roadside produce stands —at least for a look at what's being offered— especially at those set up by non-farmers. People sell the produce from their backyard fruit trees. These are varieties that are never found in markets, varieties you have never tasted before or will again. Their seeds, cuttings and corms are only traded between friends and relatives, island-to-island.

There are dozens of varieties of bananas grown here with definite flavors of peaches, apples, oranges or nutmeg. For those who think nothing tastes better than a stringy, sour Mexican mango, you haven't lived until you have had the ultimate ambrosial taste experience —a summertime, tree-ripened, backyard Hawaiian mango. Lychees may look like dried up little chestnuts, but peel back the papery bark-like covering and feast on what looks like a grape, but tastes wonderfully like... well...like nothing you've ever tasted.

With the bright red soil in the lawn area contrasting with the green foliage and the deep blue water below, **Pupukea Beach Park** is visually striking, especially in the calm of summertime. The large protected tidepool and cove areas cradle scores of snorkelers in their shallow waters, and enthusiastic numbers of scuba divers explore the network of underwater caverns and subterranean wonders. A plethora of tidepools attracts inquisitive kids and curious beachcomb- ❶

sharp rock. For scuba divers, the area **outside** the cove is **has clearer visibility** than that within the cove, and **sea caves** are found around the cove's northeast point. Due to the danger these caves present, scuba divers should join an organized dive to familiarize themselves with the conditions here. The water at the mouth of the cove is about **20'deep**, and then slopes to about **45'** outside the cove.

ers, but be aware that as a **Marine Life Conservation District**, absolutely nothing may be taken from the water or the shore, not even a pebble. Pupukea was designated a Marine Life Conservation District in 1983, meaning that its waters have been set aside as a protected area to encourage a healthy and abundant population of sea creatures.

A convenient parking area is located roadside, adjacent to the lawn. Stand facing the sea, and you'll see **Shark's Cove** to the *right,* at the eastern, Turtle Bay end. **Shark's Cove is a mecca for scuba divers**. Its sandy beach provides a comfortable water entry in an otherwise very rocky area. During the calm of summer, the cove provides excellent **snorkeling** and **swimming** in its placid, clear waters. During the **winter** however, the entire area is **extremely hazardous** due to the deadly combination of high, rough seas and

At the park's southern end, toward the *left* as you face the sea, the area of Pupukea Beach known as **Three Tables** also has a somewhat protected beach. Three Tables is named for the 3 or 4 flat sections of reef visible at low tide. **Snorkeling** is good around and just outside the tables area, and diving conditions improve farther out. Near the Tables, water averages **15' deep**. Many **lava tubes, ledges and arches** are found nearby and outside the tables. The park's elevated lawn area is a popular place for beach goers to set up shop for the vantage point it provides of the action in the water below. Pupukea is a large park —over 80 acres total– and has two comfort stations and a basketball and volleyball court. It is **not** lifeguard protected, but a **firehouse** is located directly across the KAM HWY. from the park.

PUPUKEA ROAD is located across the KAM HWY. from the park, near the **fire station**. *Make* a mauka / left turn onto it. As Pupukea Road climbs from sea level, it zigs, then zags quickly (watch that hairpin turn!) up the Ridge. The road, narrow and winding, demands caution, which is made all the more difficult by the beautiful, sweeping **panoramic view** of the North Shore below. It is especially lovely on a sunny morning. It is said that the brush along the roadside is left to grow so that it obscures this view, helping drivers keep their eyes on the road.

As PUPUKEA RD. straightens out near the top, a road appears on the *right* side, with a sign indicating the **Puu O Mahuka Heiau State Monument**. This ancient Hawaiian sacred place of ceremony was constructed high above **Waimea Bay** and boasts a **magnificent view** all along the North Shore from Waimea to **Kaena Point**. The side road leading to the heiau winds through heavy brush. Its surface is colored red from the soil washed over it by the rains, and numerous speed bumps jolt cars along the way. The heiau parking lot is small but ample. **This is a favorite place for car break-ins**, so be sure not to leave anything visible in the car, nor be seen placing anything in the trunk. Stay on the pathways, as the rocks that make up the construction of the low walls are held together only by gravity and are **unstable**. Notice the ti-leaf wrapped stones that have been left everywhere around here by the faithful, as well as offerings of flower leis and fruit. Walk to the Kaena Point side of the property along the pathway and marvel at the **vista** of **Waimea Bay, Waimea Valley**, the upcountry pineapple fields on the opposite bluff, and the seemingly endless view of sea and pali trailing away down the coast.

Backtrack to PUPUKEA RD. and *make a right turn* onto it, **continuing uphill**. You will pass many very well kept, handsome homes with lushly maintained landscaping. Visible from the side roads, many people have turned their large yards over to agricultural enterprise, growing vegetables or ornamentals. Near the top of PUPUKEA RD. a few larger properties support livestock, and the *left* side of the road becomes heavily forested with trees supporting great garlands of giant climbing philodendron. The paved road ends at the entrance to the **Boy Scout Camp**, but a pretty tree-lined dirt road continues ahead for a few hundred yards to a gate that is locked to keep vehicles out. Hiking the **2.5 mile Kaunala Trail** is allowed on **weekends and holidays only**, as it crosses military property. Park next door at the Boy Scout camp parking lot. Past the gate, the dirt road continues as a trail for **1/2 mile** to a grove of paperbark trees. At the grove, the trail takes off to the *left*, and runs over the valleys and ridges of the

Pupukea Forest Reserve. It joins a jeep road which leads *makai / seaward* to the **Girl Scout Camp Paumalu**. Check with the **Sierra Club (538-6616)** or the **Hawaii Geographic Society (538-3952)** for more information on this and other island trails before hiking. A free **Island Of Oahu Recreation Map** of this trail and others is available from the Division of Forestry, 1151 Punchbowl St., Room 325, Honolulu HI 96813 **(587-0166)**.

Return partway down PUPUKEA RD., and *make a right turn* onto ALAPIO ROAD. This is the exclusive **Sunset Hills** area. You will pass a large home surrounded by a tall boxwood hedge known locally as The Mansion, which was Elvis Presley's Hawaiian retreat. ALAPIO RD. continues at a 90 degree right turn, but proceed ahead along MAKENA RD. to see some great houses with pretty canyon and sea views.

Return to the KAM HWY. by *backtracking down the ridge* the same way you came up. *Make a left turn* onto the KAM HWY. to continue toward **Waimea Bay**.

TheBus
848-5555

Ask the driver for directions if unsure.

From Waikiki:
On the mauka side of Kuhio Ave., Saratoga Rd., Kalia Rd., or Ala Moana Blvd., board the #8 Ala Moana Center, the #19 Airport, #19 Airport-Hickam, or #20 Airport-Halawa Gate heading away from Diamond Head, to the Ala Moana Shopping Center on Ala Moana Blvd. Transfer to the #52 Wahiawa-Circle Island bus. This bus will travel inland through the Central Plateau to the North Shore, then eastward along the Kamehameha (83) HWY. to Pupukea, and then continue circling the

island. This bus does not turn inland to visit Pupukea's upcountry. After you are finished here, to continue circling the island, reboard the next #52 bus that comes along on the same side of the HWY. from which you alighted.

Return:
In the opposite direction, board the #52 Honolulu-Ala Moana Center bus and alight on Kona St. at the Ala Moana Center. To transfer, walk east toward Waikiki to the next stop marked for the #8 and #19 Waikiki-Beach and Hotels bus.

❷

Photographs

1. This exposure was taken in late afternoon from the Puu O Mahuka State Monument. The view is from the hill on the west side of the heiau, and includes Waimea Bay and the shoreline all the way to Kaena Point.

2. Pupukea Road climbs from the Kam Hwy. toward the upcountry in this aerial shot. Shark's Cove can be seen at left, and Three Tables Beach on the right.

3. Snorkelers check out the shallow waters in front of Shark's Cove beach.

4. A rainbow appears in late afternoon over the Puu O Mahuka Heiau.

5. Shark's Cove.

6. High in the cool Ucountry, Pupukea Road ends at this lovely tree-lined dirt road. A gate prevents cars from entering; park at the Boy Scout Camp and walk uphill on this road to reach the Kaunala Trailhead.

All photos:
Kodachrome 64 except #2:
Ektachrome 400 rated at 800 ASA/ISO

❸

❹

❻

❺

Waimea Bay
Ride, ride, ride the wild surf.

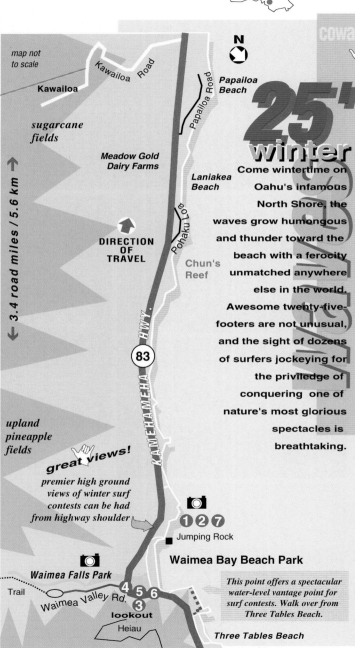

SURF'S UP!

25'
winter

Come wintertime on Oahu's infamous North Shore, the waves grow humongous and thunder toward the beach with a ferocity unmatched anywhere else in the world. Awesome twenty-five-footers are not unusual, and the sight of dozens of surfers jockeying for the priviledge of conquering one of nature's most glorious spectacles is breathtaking.

Surf contests are a great island activity for visitors to partake in... they have a carnival-like atmosphere, you get to see a lot of interesting people you otherwise might not encounter, and its truly exciting to witness spectacular board maneuvers by master surfers riding those mammoth breakers. Here's a partial list of contests:

March.
Buffalo's Annual Big Board Surfing Classic is a 2 day event with food and Hawaiian entertainment at the Leeward Shore's Makaha Beach.

June.
The Gotcha Pro Surfing Championship takes place at Sandy Beach on the South Shore. A bikini contest helps draw major crowds.

July.
The Beachtown Hawaiian Pro Am Contest is held on the South Shore. The Blue Hawaii State Amateur Surfing Championships are held at Kuhio Beach in Waikiki, Diamond Head, and Sandy Beach.

November & December.
The Triple Crown of Surfing on Oahu's North Shore adds to the area's already heady party atmosphere with a 1-2-3 punch that includes the Billabong Hawaiian Pro Contest at Sunset Beach, and the Marui Masters at Pipeline.

great views!
premier high ground views of winter surf contests can be had from highway shoulder

Jumping Rock

Waimea Bay Beach Park

This point offers a spectacular water-level vantage point for surf contests. Walk over from Three Tables Beach.

Waimea Falls Park
Trail
Waimea Valley Rd.
lookout
Heiau

Three Tables Beach
Pupukea

---

*T*he **KAM (83) HWY.** leaves Pupukea Beach Park behind at the **Three Tables** area across from little KAPUHI ST. If you would like a unique profile perspective for photographing the sizzling **winter** surf action in Waimea Bay, walk to the **Waimea / west end** of Three Tables Beach, hop on the rocks, well away from crashing waves, and walk around in front of the private residences on *your left* out to the **point** and join other observers perched there, watching in awe.

After Three Tables, the KAM HWY. passes the tower of **Sts. Peter and Paul Catholic Mission**, looking like a bit of Tuscany transplanted to the middle of the Pacific. It is a photogenic center-piece and symbol for the town of Waimea, and few would guess that it is a former rock-crushing plant. The HWY. quickly de-scends and curves to the left, following the contour of Waimea Bay. On the *makai* side, the impressive profile of Waimea Beach provokes love at first sight, and then the bright green **marsh** at the delta of the **Waimea River** appears. The HWY. then curves sharply toward the right, but at this point on the *mauka / left* side, WAIMEA VALLEY RD. inter-sects and leads to **Waimea Falls Park** (admission charge).

After WAIMEA VALLEY RD., the KAM HWY. crosses the bridge, and for those on foot, the **view** from the bridge toward the beach is lush and pretty. Directly after crossing the bridge, look *makai / right* for the entrance to **Waimea Bay Beach Park**. There is a good amount of parking here, but on weekends or during surfing season, when the lot fills up early, you will find **roadside parking** along the KAM HWY. After *passing* the beach park entrance, *continue uphill*. The road-side as it reaches the top of the bluff is a **great place** from which **to watch surfers** and the winter contests at Waimea. The area becomes quite busy then and a party atmosphere prevails. Bring food and cold drinks, or buy from one of the lunch wagons who come to supply the crowd, make friends and have fun...this kind of event is what the North Shore is all about. Waimea Bay Beach Park provides daily lifeguard service throughout the year. It has a restroom, outdoor shower, and a large lawn with trees and picnic tables. Waves

and backwash are **treacherous** in the winter, but in summer Waimea Bay is a favorite place for families. Then, the water is calm and swimming conditions excellent.

The **Waimea River** flows toward the sea but a barrier beach keeps it from reaching the ocean. Only after a strong rain does it break through. When the water is flowing, a condition develops as the water flows over a depression in the river bottom that is like a stationary wave going no place. Local children on boogie boards catch this "wave" and ride it endlessly, or until bored. At the opposite, or Kaena Point end of the beach, **Jumping Rock** at times accommodates scores of people who cling to it and watch as others catapult themselves off the top into a carefully timed incoming wave. This can be observed well from along the KAM HWY. roadside above it.

The rest of this shore, from the Kaena Point end of Waimea Beach, to Haleiwa Beach Park (a distance of about **3.5 miles**) is known as **Kawailoa Beach**. Not visible from the HWY. and without easy public access for much of its length, the area with its rocky shorebottom is unwelcoming to swimmers...which makes Kawailoa Beach an *attractive* place to those who wish to avoid crowds. **4 p.r.o.w.s** extend from PAPAILOA ROAD to the beach. Look for PAPAILOA ROAD on the *makai / right* side, about **2.4 miles** past Waimea Bay's beach parking lot. PAPAILOA ROAD intersects the Kam Hwy. across the road from the **Meadow Gold Dairy Farm**. **Papailoa Beach** has several good sand pockets between its reefs where swimming is safe, except during high surf.

Photographs

1. Jumping Rock swarms with kids watching dare-devils catapult themselves off it.

2. In a direct challenge to nature, four surfers compete to conquer one of Waimea's mammoth

winter waves: 300mm lens w/1.4 extender.

3. Moving traffic creates light trails along the Kam Hwy. in this 60 second time exposure: 24mm lens. Taken from Pupukea's Puu O Mahukka heiau lookout.

Waimea Bay

4. Waimea River delta view from the bridge.

5. Waimea Beach's beauty holds a crowd captive until well after sunset.

6. Late afternoon's golden light illuminates the delta grasses.

7. As seen from the Kam Hwy. lookout, the entire expanse of Waimea Bay is captured in this shot: 24mm lens.

All photos:
Kodachrome 64
except #2:
Kodachrome 200

TheBus
848-5555
Ask the driver for directions if unsure.

From Waikiki:
On the mauka side of Kuhio Ave., Saratoga Rd., Kalia Rd., or Ala Moana Blvd., board the #8 Ala Moana Center, the #19 Airport, #19 Airport-Hickam, or #20 Airport-Halawa Gate bus heading away from Diamond Head, to the Ala Moana Shopping Center on Ala Moana Blvd. Transfer to the #52 Wahiawa-Circle Island bus. This bus will travel inland through the Central Plateau to the North Shore, then eastward along the Kamehameha (83) HWY. to Waimea Bay, and then continues circling the island. After you are finished here, to continue circling the island, reboard the next #52 bus that comes along on the same side of the HWY. from which you alighted.

Return:
In the opposite direction, board the #52 Honolulu-Ala Moana Center bus and alight on Kona St. at the Ala Moana Moana Center. To transfer, walk east toward Waikiki to the next stop marked for the #8 and #19 Waikiki-Beach and Hotels bus.

❻
❼

❹

❺

Kawailoa

Oceans of waving sugar cane surround a tiny plantation town frozen in time.

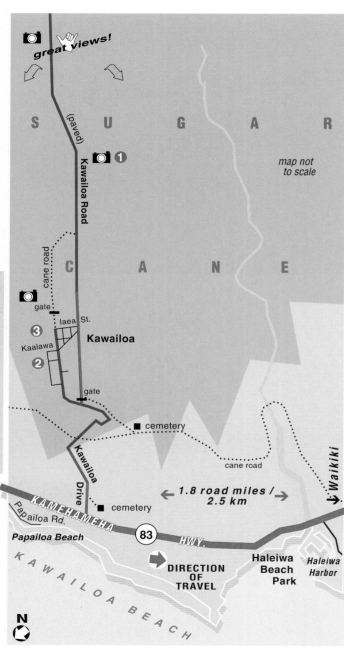

great views!

S U G A R

(paved)

Kawailoa Road

map not to scale

cane road

C A N E

gate

Iaea St.

Kawailoa

Kaalawa

cemetery

cane road

gate

Kawailoa Drive

← **1.8 road miles / 2.5 km** →

cemetery

Papailoa Rd.

KAMEHAMEHA

Papailoa Beach

83 HWY.

DIRECTION OF TRAVEL

Haleiwa Beach Park

Haleiwa Harbor

→ Waikiki

K A W A I L O A   B E A C H

N

To reach **Kawailoa**, make a *mauka/left turn* from the KAM HWY. onto KAWAILOA DRIVE, after passing the **Meadow Gold Dairy Farms**. Drive *past* the dump on your *left*, and up the ridge. You will *pass* paved KAWAILOA ROAD, which intersects from the right. You need permission —easy to receive— from the **Waialua Sugar Company (637-3521)** to enter the vast property and its deep green sea of sugarcane. They want to know you are up there so they don't lock the gates on you. If you **do** get locked in, they charge you a **small fortune** to come and get you out. Park your car just past this intersection to visit the town. Its tiny streets can't accommodate outside traffic.

Truly one of the last real plantation towns, Kawailoa deserves protection and inclusion by the National Register of Historic Places before it completely burns down in *yet another* in a long series of sugar cane field fires gone wrong. Kawailoa perches on the edge of a waving sugar cane world of long flowing green fronds and sapphire sky. At one time this was the biggest town on the North Shore, physically much larger than it is today. There were many more homes, stores, a church, a Buddhist temple, theater, recreation center and public swimming pool. But today, the theater stands in ruins at the back of town, overgrown and unrecognizable. The pool is in there too, someplace, filled with years of debris. The temple and church were destroyed in the most recent fire calamity, in the early 1980's. An abandoned plantation store still stands, but the town is now too small to support a business there.

But what *is* left has enough downtrodden charm to still interest the visitor, and the little plantation homes are of attractive architectural design. Almost all have little gardens alive with brilliant color amidst their accumulations of rusting artifacts. Little verandas allow the occupants to catch the cooling afternoon trades blowing up from the sea. Children peer from behind window screens or ride fat-tire bikes through the compact maze of town streets. The residents are friendly, and some of the older ones are alive with stories and town history, and are happy to share. All of Kawailoa's townsfolk are active or retired employees of the Waialua Sugar Company. An employee becomes eligible to rent a home here after ten years' employment with the company, for a token rent of about $100 a month, including utilities. Kawailoa has played an important part in the making of Hawaii, and still hangs on despite hard times in the sugar industry. It should not be allowed to slip away . It is a living, breathing piece of island history, and deserves care and restoration.

If you have received permission to visit the cane fields, backtrack to the gate at Kawailoa Road, and use your key to enter. The Kawailoa sugar cane road is one of the few such roads on any Hawaiian island that is paved and in good repair. It climbs quite high toward the **Koolau Mountains**, and the views you experience will depend on whether a particular field was harvested recently or if it is at full height. As you climb, remember to look behind you for spectacular views and great photo opportunities. Notice the air is cooler here, and that the clouds fly swiftly overhead almost close enough to touch. The all-encompassing vistas of the North Shore, and of the distant **Waianae Mountains** beyond the sea of undulating sugar cane, are breathtaking. The colors are primary and brilliant: cobalt blue sky, pure white clouds, shimmering green cane, and red sienna earth. No photograph can truly capture the feeling and scope of wide open spaces, and this is especially true here in the cane fields of Kawailoa. Save for the rustle of fully grown sugarcane grass in the trades, the silence, the brilliance and clarity of the sky, and the astringent cleanliness of the breeze are things that can only be experienced and appreciated first hand. When finished here, return to the KAM HWY. by just driving downhill. You can't get lost.

Photographs

1. Kawailoa backstreet.
All: **Kodachrome 64**

2. Mailbox amid bougainvillea.

3. Kawailoa's endless cane fields.

Haleiwa
Oahu's quintessential beach town.

NORTH SHORE

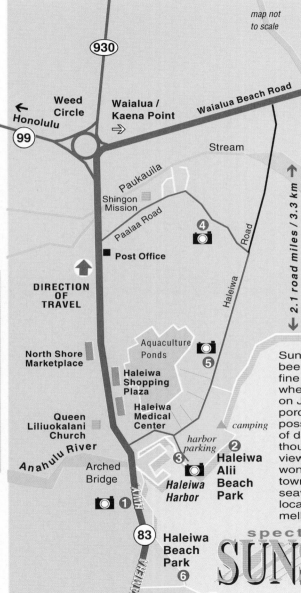

Map labels

930

← Honolulu
99

Weed Circle

Waialua / Kaena Point ⇒

Waialua Beach Road

Stream

Paukauila

Shingon Mission

Paalaa Road

Haleiwa Road

2.1 road miles / 3.3 km

4 📷

■ Post Office

⬆ DIRECTION OF TRAVEL

North Shore Marketplace

Aquaculture Ponds

📷 **5**

Haleiwa Shopping Plaza

Haleiwa Medical Center

Queen Liliuokalani Church

▲ camping

harbor parking

Anahulu River

Arched Bridge

📷 **3** **2** 📷

Haleiwa Alii Beach Park

Haleiwa Harbor

📷 **1** HWY

83 **Haleiwa Beach Park** **6**

KAMEHAMEHA

Kawailoa ⇓⇓

N

map not to scale

Photographs

1. The last hint of sunset colors blaze at the horizon as a lone figure sits on the beach contemplating its beauty. This was taken right across the Hwy. from Jameson's.

2. Surfbords stacked at Haleiwa All'i Beach Park.

3. Late day midweek traffic ambles over the double arched bridge along the Kam Hwy., past surfshops and shave ice emporiums.

4. Smoke rises from a sugar cane field fire behind town in this view from Haleiwa harbor.

5. Stately old trees line the road and frame pretty upland views along Paalaa Rd.

6. Crystal clear morning view of Haleiwa Beach Park.

All: **Kodachrome 64**

Sunset watching has been honed into a fine art in Haleiwa, where getting a seat on Jameson's front porch is nearly impossible at this time of day. Don't despair though, because the view is even more wonderful from the town's 800' rock seawall. Join the locals as they fish, mellow out, or neck.

spectacular
SUNSETS

---

*I*f coming from visiting Kawailoa, make a left turn from KAWAILOA DRIVE onto the Kam Hwy. In **0.6 mile**, you will reach Haleiwa Beach Park and its host of recreational facilities, not the least of which is a safe and sandy year-round swimming beach. There are basketball and volleyball courts, baseball and softball fields, daily lifeguard service from June through August, a food concession, and usually a few roadside jet ski and kayak rental concessions. **Jameson's** restaurant is across the HWY., where the determined somehow manage the strength to come in and mellow out on the front porch after a

number of surfwear shops, quality and quantity of people-watching, and just plain goodtime fun.

The prevailing architectural style in Haleiwa is Early Paniolo, or Hawaiian cowboy, with ubiquitous western town false-front wooden buildings and an absence of sidewalks. New construction has been faithful to this style, giving this crazy quilt town's look a semblance of visual harmony. You will notice the long lines outside shop doors attesting to the addictive powers of Hawaiian shave-ice, not to be confused with the laughingly inadequate mainland snow cone. Traffic on any day along the

❶

hard day of suntanning. Just past **Jameson's** are other points of interest, like great surf shops, eating places, and, after crossing the arched bridge, downtown Haleiwa itself to the *left*, and the entrance to the harbor area on the *right*.

Haleiwa (pronounced Holly-Eve-Uh) is at its best —or worst— on any Sunday or major holiday. Traffic can be a major problem unless you arrive early and leave late. Honolulu residents flock to the North Shore on weekends, and Haleiwa is the center of all the action. Virtual gridlock can extend from beyond the traffic circle at HWY. 99, through town, and all the way to Shark's Cove, in a worst case scenario. The positive side, though, is that nothing says fun in the sun like Haleiwa does. On weekends, it outdoes all other beach towns for brilliant color, great tans, variety of food, the

KAM HWY. has to slow to a crawl to negotiate the narrow, double-arched bridge that crosses the Anahulu River. After crossing the bridge, a *right turn* will bring you past the steak house to the harbor, where the enormous seawall provides a perch for the daily numbers of people who come to fish and watch the sunset. Fishing boats and pleasure craft fill Haleiwa's harbor, which has for a long time been a favorite layover for modern explorers piloting their sailing craft across the Pacific. The flags of various nations flutter from masts in the breeze, proudly proclaiming the origins of their romantic adventures. Under appreciated elsewhere, sunsets are revered and celebrated daily from the seawall in Haleiwa.

Double back from the harbor, and follow the KAM HWY. through town, past beautiful Liliuokalani

Church, and a wide choice of places to eat and shop. At the end of town, across the HWY. from the post office is the venerable **Haleiwa Cafe**, where every surf star of note on this planet has eaten breakfast. Haleiwa should really be sampled twice: once during the week when its quiet, and again on a crazed Sunday afternoon when the place is jammin'. You will then discover two completely different towns, each with its own charm.

Continuing along the KAM HWY., across the road from the Haleiwa Cafe look for PAALAA ROAD, and *turn right* onto it for a short jaunt through a quiet residential part of town. You'll first pass the Shingon Mission with its beautiful architectural detailing, then the tiny side streets leading past little houses to Paukauila Stream, and finally you'll pass through a tunnel of venerable old trees bordering a sugar cane field with a pretty mountain backdrop. Make a right turn onto HALEIWA ROAD and you will end up back at the double arched bridge and the KAM HWY. A *right turn* onto the KAM HWY. will take you through Haleiwa again, past the post office and over the bridge to the traffic circle (WEED CIRCLE).

To return to Honolulu, follow the sign at WEED CIRCLE that directs you to Honolulu, via the KAMEHAMEHA (99) HWY., and up through the Central Plateau's rainbow festooned pineapple fields.

To continue along the North Shore, follow the sign at WEED CIRCLE *to the immediate right* directing you to **Waialua**.

TheBus
848-5555

Ask the driver for directions if unsure.

From Waikiki:
On the mauka side of Kuhio Ave., Saratoga Rd., Kalia Rd., or Ala Moana Blvd., board the #8 Ala Moana Center, the #19 Airport, #19 Airport-Hickam, or #20 Airport-Halawa Gate bus heading away from Diamond Head, to the Ala Moana Shopping Center on Ala Moana Blvd. Transfer to the #52 Wahiawa-Circle Island bus. This bus travels inland through the Central Plateau to Haleiwa, and then turns eastward along the North Shore and the Kamehameha (83) HWY. to continue circling the island. After you are finished here, to continue circling the island, reboard the next #52 bus that comes along on the same side of the HWY. from which you alighted.

Return:
In the opposite direction, board the #52 Honolulu-Ala Moana Center bus and alight on Kona St. at the Ala Moana Center. To transfer, walk east toward Waikiki to the next stop marked for the #8 and #19 Waikiki-Beach and Hotels bus.

❷❸
❹❻
❺

Waialua Town and Crozier Drive

An old sugarmill town and its lovely beach colony neighbor.

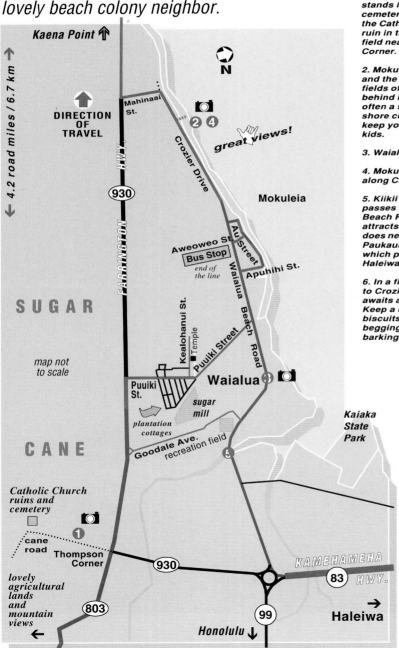

Kaena Point ⇧

4.2 road miles / 6.7 km

↑ **DIRECTION OF TRAVEL**

930 FARRINGTON HWY.

Mahinaai St.

Crozier Drive

🎥 ②④ ⤳ **great views!**

Mokuleia

Aweoweo St.

Au Street

Bus Stop

end of the line

Apuhihi St.

Kealohanui St. ■ Temple

Puuiki Street

Waialua Beach Road

Waialua 🎥

map not to scale

S U G A R

Puuiki St.

sugar mill

plantation cottages

C A N E

Goodale Ave. *recreation field* ⑤

Kaiaka State Park

Catholic Church ruins and cemetery 🎥

cane road ① **Thompson Corner**

930

lovely agricultural lands and mountain views ←

803

99

Honolulu ↓

KAMEHAMEHA HWY.

83

→ **Haleiwa**

NORTH SHORE

N

Photographs

1. An iron cross stands in the cemetery adjacent to the Catholic church ruin in the sugar cane field near Thompson Corner.

2. Mokuleia Beach and the upland sugar fields of Haleiwa behind it. There is often a strong along-shore current here, so keep your eye on the kids.

3. Waialua Sugar Mill.

4. Mokuleia Beach along Crozier Drive.

5. Kiikii Stream passes under Waialua Beach Rd. and attracts kayakers, as does neighboring Paukauila Stream, which passes under Haleiwa Rd.

6. In a field adjacent to Crozier Dr., a horse awaits a handout. Keep a box of dog biscuits in the car for begging horses and barking dogs.

*F*rom **WEED CIRCLE** and the Waialua direction sign there, drive along WAIALUA BEACH ROAD, which crosses the bridge over **Kiikii Stream** in **0.8 mile**, then passes **Waialua Elementary School** on the *left*. Just past the school's adjacent playing field, GOODALE AVE. intersects from the left. *Turn left* onto GOODALE AVE., which runs straight through **Waialua** to the sleepy tree-lined town center, passing the huge rusting **sugar mill** on the way. At the town's center, the columned, stately former Bank of Hawaii building is now the locally famous **Sugar Bar**, still *the* place to be on Sunday afternoons on the North Shore. *Continue* along GOODALE AVE. through town to the FARRINGTON (930) HWY. You now have two options:

Option #1:

Make a *left turn* onto FARRINGTON (930) HWY. In a little over **0.6 mile** you will reach an intersection named THOMPSON CORNER. HWY. 930 **intersects** it from the *left*. *Continue ahead* on what was FARRINGTON (930) HWY., but has now **changed names and number**, to KAUKONAHUA (803) ROAD. In about **1.5 miles** on this pretty road you will pass through a stand of **ironwood trees** lining the way. Drive a little further to the **University of Hawaii Experimental Farm**, or thereabouts, then *turn around* when you feel like it. *Heading back downhill*, you will see that the area to the *left/mauka* of the road is beautiful farmland which backs up to the foot of the **Waianae Mountains**. The sun and clouds cast lovely light effects on the foothills, and the higher mountainsides behind. When you reach THOMPSON CORNER again, notice that there is a dirt **sugarcane road** to the *left/mauka*. Down this road lies the **ruins** of a stone **Catholic Church**, and next to it is a cemetery with a number of well kept graves and two large palm trees. You may be able to visit this ruin by asking permission from the **Waialua Sugar Company (637-3521)**. If you do, take heed of this first-hand experience: The ruin is crumbling, and large boulders may easily crash down on you, smashing your camera and gashing your leg, so be content to just look. *Continue back* along the highway, past GOODALE AVE., then past **Waialua High School** on your *left/mauka*, to PUUIKI ST. on your *right*. Continue below*.

Option #2:

Turn right from GOODALE AVE. onto FARRINGTON (930) HWY.; drive about **0.4 mile**, *passing* **Waialua High School**, to PUUIKI ST.

* *Turn right* onto PUUIKI ST. You will *pass* a pretty, but very weathered, **wooden church** on the *left*. The small streets on the right are lined with **tiny plantation homes** with even tinier gardens. *Continue* up PUUIKI ST. and *turn left* on KEALOHANUI ST. to the equally weathered and forlorn **Hongwanji Buddhist temple**. Across the street from the temple is an oddly interesting old **general store** from days gone by, where the neighbors still sit out front, trading stories and sipping **Diamond Head Cola**.

Return to PUUIKI ST., *turn left* and *continue* to WAIALUA BEACH ROAD/CROZIER DR. (**it changes names here**), and *turn left* onto it. In **0.1 mile**, privately owned **Puuiki Park** appears on the *makai* side. No one will fault you if you want to pull in and have a look. *Continue* past the park a few yards to APUHIHI ST. Turn *right* onto it and *continue* **3 short blocks** to AU ST. *Straight ahead* is a **p.r.o.w.**, if you'd like to walk to the beach and have a look. There are **2** other **p.r.o.w.s** in quick secession, then AU ST. *turns left* to intersect CROZIER DR.

Turn right from AU ST. onto CROZIER DR. and *continue* through a delightful **beach colony** of homes, weekend cottages, lovely beaches, a children's camp, and rewarding **views** from the beach along the curve of the North Shore, especially back toward the direction of Haleiwa.

The only **p.r.o.w.** in this area is about **0.2 mile** past OLOHIO ST., which intersects Crozier Dr. from the *left/mauka*. Walk along it *makai* to see the **view** and the strand, and to see how the residents have set up outdoor seating and entertaining areas on their lawns at the edge of the sand for celebrating the sunsets.

CROZIER DR. ends at a gated compound, and a left turn onto MAHINAAI ST. brings you back to join FARRINGTON HWY. A *right turn* onto FARRINGTON (930) HWY. begins your journey along this uncluttered, sparsely traveled coast.

TheBus
848-5555

Ask the driver for
directions if unsure.

From Waikiki:
On the mauka side of
Kuhio Ave., Saratoga Rd.,
Kalia Rd., or Ala Moana
Blvd., board the #8 Ala
Moana Center, the #19
Airport, #19 Airport-
Hickam, or #20 Airport-
Halawa Gate bus heading
away from Diamond Head,
to the Ala Moana
Shopping Center on Ala
Moana Blvd. Transfer to
the #52 Wahiawa-Circle
Island bus. This bus
travels inland through the
Central Plateau to
Haleiwa, where right after
Weed Circle, you will
alight opposite the
Haleiwa Town post office.
Cross the HWY. and wait
at the side of the HWY. in
front of the post office for
the #76 Shuttle, with a
windshield sign marked
"WAIALUA". This Shuttle
route will pass by many of

the sites featured in this
spread (you can obtain a
map of this and all island
bus routes by calling the
above telephone
number).You will have to
walk along Crozier Drive
from the intersection of
little Aweoweo St. (see
map), but its quite a
pleasant jaunt. After you
are finished here, to
continue circling the
island, reboard the next
#52 bus back in Haleiwa
that comes along on the
same side of the HWY.
from which you alighted.

Return:
In the opposite direction,
board the #76 Shuttle with
a windshield sign marked
"HALEIWA" to the
Kamehameha (83) HWY. in
the heart of Haleiwa town.
Transfer to the #52
Honolulu-Ala Moana
Center bus and alight on
Kona St. at the Ala Moana
Center. To transfer, walk
east toward Waikiki to the
next stop marked for the
#8 and #19 Waikiki-Beach
and Hotels bus.

93

Mokuleia and The Kaena Point North Shore Trail

Oahu's wildest spot.

HAWAII
MALAMA KA AINA

Kaena Point
white coral beaches

great views!

The entire vicinity of Kaena Point is unsafe for swimming

satellite tracking station

gate

During winter, when big north swells run, Kaena Point has the largest, most consistent, most perfectly shaped, but unrideable, waves to be found anywhere in the world. These monsters *average* **30' - 40'**! Beautiful, terrifying mountains of water that reach 50' — and more— are not unheard of. Listen for reports of big surf. Bring a light picnic, *sit well back from the shore,* and be amazed.

KAENA POINT STATE PARK

N

roadside parking

930

YMCA Camp Erdman

Mokuleia

Army

Beach

Mokuleia Beach Park
picnic tables crystal clear water

SHORECASTING

The entire Mokuleia Shore west of the YMCA camp is a very popular fishing area on weekends.

WINDSURFING

Consistently favorable winds, uncrowded conditions, transparent waters and beautiful coastline views draw avid windsurfers to the Mokuleia Shore.

GLIDER RIDES

Incomparable and breathtaking vistas of the North Shore can be seen from the silence of a soaring, unfettered manmade bird. Unforgettable.

6.8 road miles / 10.9 km

Dillingham Airfield and Gliderport

map not to scale

DIRECTION OF TRAVEL

FARRINGTON HWY.

Mokuleia Beach Colony

polo fields

---

*F*ARRINGTON (930) HWY. edges toward the shore, bypassing handsome Crowbar Ranch on the *left/mauka* side, and the Mokuleia Polo field on the *right/makai*. A 12-16 goal polo match is held here each Sunday from March through August.

1.1 miles past the polo field is **Mokuleia Beach Park**, with a large lawn area and unshaded picnic tables, a restroom, and generally during the week, plenty of privacy. A sand dune held in place by naupaka shields the narrow, sloping beach from view of the picnic tables, so **children should be closely watched**. Summer is the only safe swim-

①

ming time, and although much of the park shore waters have a rocky reef bottom, there are a few sand pockets for comfortable entry. Steady breezes attract **windsurfers** who ready their craft on the park lawn, and then follow each other into the ocean zooming quickly out into open water. Summer's calming influence on the North Shore's waves and currents attract **snorkelers** to the clear aquamarine shallows and purplish reefs. Next door along the HWY., abutting the beach park, is wide and beautiful **Mokuleia Army Beach**, which is open to the public, and during the week, generally deserted. Unprotected by any offshore reef, the waters can be dangerous for swimmers during winter or stormy conditions. Just across the highway is the entrance to the **Dillingham**

Airfield and Gliderport, where one of Hawaii's most majestic experiences awaits as your glider is towed to an altitude of 5,000', and then released. You and your pilot glide silently through the air along the North Shore as the breathtaking island topography unfolds beneath. No reservations are taken over the phone for glider rides, but you might want to call to check on the weather conditions before driving out. See their ads in the free giveaways. Before continuing, If you plan to make the Kaena Point Hike, here might be a good place to make all your preparations. Take whatever you'll need for the hike from the trunk and place items left behind out of view.

The whole Mokuleia area is a haven of quiet during the week, but once the paved road ends, isolation is almost assured. Beyond, Kaena Point State Park awaits with secluded sandy coves and enormous wide open spaces. The trail follows a deeply rutted jeep road with dozens of small seaward trails branching off to the ocean's edge. See page 110 for more about the Kaena Point Trail.

Photographs

1. The Brilliant Colors of Nature soothe the soul and senses at deserted Mokuleia Army Beach.

2. The trail to Kaena Pt. is a jeep road that traverses exceptionally lovely terrain.

Both photos: Kodachrome 64

TheBus

TheBus does not come any closer to Mokuleia than the Crozier Dr. area. See bus directions on previous page.

②

Central Plateau
Oahu's Rainbow Alley.

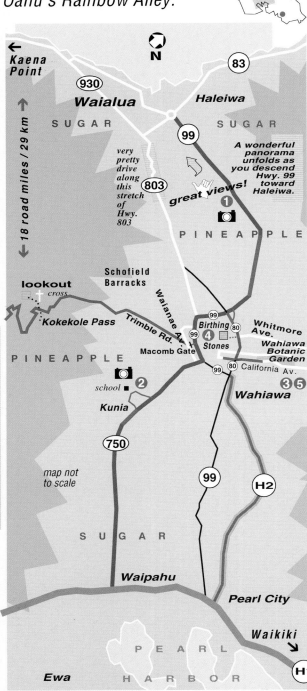

18 road miles / 29 km

← **Kaena Point**

N

930

83

Waialua   **Haleiwa**

S U G A R   S U G A R

99

very pretty drive along this stretch of Hwy. 803

A wonderful panorama unfolds as you descend Hwy. 99 toward Haleiwa.

803

great views!   **❶** 📷

P I N E A P P L E

Schofield Barracks

lookout   ✝ *cross*

Kokekole Pass

Waianae Av.   *Trimble Rd.*

99

Birthing **99** **❹** 🔲 **80** ... **Whitmore Ave.**

Macomb Gate   **Stones**   **Wahiawa Botanic Garden**

P I N E A P P L E

📷   **99** **80** California Av.   **❸❺**

school ■ **❷**

Wahiawa

Kunia

750

map not to scale

99   **H2**

S U G A R

Waipahu

Pearl City

Waikiki ↘

Ewa   P E A R L   H A R B O R

H1

❶

TheBus
848-5555
Ask the driver for directions if unsure.
TheBus does not go to Kunia.

From Waikiki :
On the mauka side of Kuhio Ave., Saratoga Rd., Kalia Rd., or Ala Moana Blvd., board the #8 Ala Moana Center, the #19 Airport, #19 Airport-Hickam, or #20 Airport-Halawa Gate bus heading away from Diamond Head, to the Ala Moana Shopping Center on Ala Moana Blvd. Transfer to the #52 Wahiawa Hts. to visit the Botanical Gardens directly. This bus stops across the street from the Gardens' entrance.
To visit Schofield Barracks or the Birthing Stones: board the #52 Wahiawa-Circle Island or #52 Wahiawa Hts. Ride to the corner of Kamehameha HWY. and Avocado St. in Wahiawa, after the Wilson Bridge. To visit Schofield: Cross Kamehameha HWY. to the opposite side and transfer to the #72 Shuttle bus with the windshield sign marked "SCHO-FIELD", which will take you into Schofield Barracks via Macomb Gate. The Shuttle runs once an hour with no service after 7 p.m. To visit the Birthing Stones: Change at the same bus stop you alighted from to the #72 Shuttle with the windshield sign marked "WAIALUA" to the intersection of Whitmore and Kamehameha Hwy. Walk from there down the dirt cane road to the grove of palm trees that you will see ahead on the right.

Return:
From the Botanical Gardens: in the opposite direction board the #52 Honolulu-Ala Moana Center bus and alight on Kona St. at the Ala Moana Center. To transfer, walk east toward Waikiki to the next stop marked for the #8 and #19 Waikiki-Beach and Hotels bus.

From Schofield Barracks and the Birthing Stones: In the opposite direction, board the #72 Shuttle and ride to the corner of Kameha-meha (83) HWY. and Avocado St. in Wahiawa Town after the Wilson Bridge. Transfer to the #52 Hono-lulu-Ala Moana Center bus and alight on Kona St. at the Ala Moana Center. Transfer again, walking east toward Waikiki to the next stop marked for the #8 and #19 Waikiki-Beach and Hotels bus.

*A*fter rounding WEED CIRCLE, KAMEHAMEHA (99) HWY. climbs steadily up through Oahu's Central Plateau past neatly rowed pineapple fields. Legend says this is the birthplace of Oahu's rainbows. With the Koolau Mountains on the east, and the Waianae Mountains on the west—both often topped by cloud cover— rainbows materialize continually, especially in the afternoon. The combination of elements creates a rich and impressive scene, and even without a rainbow or two in the picture, it is quite photogenic. As you drive along don't forget to look behind you. If driving from Honolulu *north* to Haleiwa, the scene is even more wondrous, especially as the HWY. descends toward the

North Shore. Endless expanses of sugar cane and the lovely geometry of pineapple fields reach from roadside to infinity, climbing from the blue Pacific to the emerald green flanks of the Koolau and Waianae Mountains.

After the long climb up from WEED CIRCLE you will eventually see a small grove of trees on the *left* marking the **Dole Pineapple Pavilion**, and then **0.8 mile** after, the turnoff for the city of **Wahiawa** toward the *left*. Because few tourists stop here, you will find prices in the supermarkets and other stores very reasonable by island standards, and certainly a bargain compared to those in Waikiki. Wahiawa is a town that caters to the military, so

charm and beauty are hard to come by in this homely little place. But like a hidden family jewel, the 27 acre **Wahiawa Botanical Gardens** await at **#1396 California Ave.** *Turn left* onto California Ave. when you reach the center of town. Over 40 years old now, with most species well established, the Garden shelters exotic and beautiful trees from Africa, Asia, New Guinea, and Australia. Wahiawa Botanical Gardens, just like other botanical gardens on Oahu, offers a multitude of photo opportunities concentrated in one compact space. Get in close for details of leaves, bark, and blooms. Keep a piece of matte black mount board in your trunk (pick one up at a five and dime or art supply store) to use as a backdrop to isolate

blooms or foliage from background distractions. Tilt the board slightly toward the camera to avoid reflecting the light so it will read pitch black on film, being careful not to break or damage any plants in the process.

Just *north* of town, the **Kukaniloko Birthing Stones** —not to be confused with Wahiawa town's Healing Stone– are arranged in a very pretty location among a grove of palm trees in the middle of a pineapple field with a distant mountain backdrop. Hawaiian ali'i (royalty) gave birth here, and you can see sculpted indentations in the rocks just the right size and shape to cradle the form of a female in labor. To reach the Birthing Stones after leaving the botanical gardens, *backtrack* along the KAM (80) HWY *north* out of town and *turn left* onto the cane road at the Whitmore Ave. traffic signal. The petroglyph-adorned stones lie directly ahead, down the dirt cane road, just 0.2 mile from the intersection. Often you will see a fascinating variety of offerings that the faithful have left behind, including intricate woven grass skirts, leis, fresh fruit, and even children's toys. You may see beautiful packages made from the leaves of ti or banana and tied artfully with raffia. Called **puolo** they contain gifts for the spirits. Please leave them in place.

To visit **Schofield Barracks**, considered to be the

There are two short trails at Kolekole Pass, indicated by large signs roadside. One trail leads to the base of a large white steel cross, and the other leads to Kolekole Rock. Each has a grand view of Oahu's Central Plain. First though, visit the sentry gate a short distance ahead and ask specifically if any machine gun or artillery practice exercises are planned. We were caught totally off guard by these while on a precarious part of the slippery trail behind the cross. Suddenly, very frightening and seriously deafening explosions commenced with no warning whatsoever. Rocks rained down on the cars parked at the trails' parking lot, and it was easy to see how unsuspecting visitors could have been seriously injured. (Special permission

edifice from vandalism. An equally lovely but smaller back building appears to be used merely for storage. Both buildings share an idyllic setting. The verdant Waianae Mountains loom in the near distance beyond the neat patterns formed by purposely arranged pineapple rows. The main building is U-shaped and has a large wrap-around porch enclosing a small coconut grove and fronted by a large lawn area used as a playing field. These handsome buildings have played an important role in Hawaii's vanishing plantation history, and need —and deserve— respectful preservation and restoration. In the vicinity of the school, little bougainvillea-lined roads beckon the visitor to explore the village. The sounds of a Saturday

FWY., or west to continue on up to Makakilo's cool forests and amazing upland views, and the Leeward Shore's unbroken string of infamous surfing beaches.

Photographs

1. View from Hwy. 99.

2. Kunia's photogenic recreation center.

3. Detail of eucalyptus bark at the Wahiawa Botanic Garden.

4. At Wahiawa's Birthing Stones, packages called puolo are left as gifts to the spirits.

5. Berries and leaves from the Australian Blue Marble tree: Wahiawa Botanic Garden.

All: **Kodachrome 64**

most beautiful military base in the world, *backtrack* from the stones to the intersection of WHITMORE AVE. and KAMEHAMEHA (80) HWY. again, then *turn left* onto the KAM HWY., and *make another left turn at the next intersection,* which is KAMANANUI (99) RD. Then follow the signs to close-by Schofield Barracks. Enter the base at **Macomb Gate**, and go *straight ahead* to visit the **Tropic Lightning Museum**. To visit **Kolekole Pass**, *turn right* at the museum onto WAIANAE AVE., then make an immediate *left* onto HEARD AVE. One block ahead there is a V-shaped intersection. *Take the right fork,* called TRIMBLE ROAD, all the way up to Kolekole Pass high in the Waianaes for a **sweeping view.**

from the military is needed to pass through the sentry gate and over the top of the pass, and if you receive it, you'll emerge at the Leeward Shore's Nanakuli Beach).

Backtrack down TRIMBLE ROAD and exit Macomb Gate the same way you entered. *Turn right* onto HWY 99, and in **0.6 mile**, *turn right* onto KUNIA (750) ROAD. Proceed along through the sugarcane fields that border its flanks for **2.0 miles**. *Turn right* onto little KUNIA DRIVE, which is a loop road that encircles the town. Drive directly toward the back of town to the **school**. Unfortunately, a homely chain link fence is needed to protect this beautiful classic plantation-style

morning basketball game echo from inside the photogenic tin-roofed recreation center. Along improbably tiny MOA ST., roosters run and squawk as the Filipino residents look on in suspicion at the intrusion on their quiet lives. Everywhere, flowering plants pour forth blossoms from any available vessel, blooming in incessant and unbridled volumes from the deep red earth.

The town store faces the highway and is a fascinating hodgepodge of merchandise and local people trading gossip, so stop in for something to eat or drink. Afterward, *turn right* onto the highway and head downhill for about **5.0 miles** to the H1 FWY. **To return to Waikiki**, head *east* on the H1

❷❸❹
❺

The Ewa District

Where did all the tourists go?

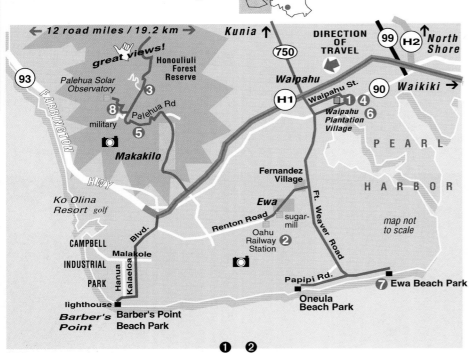

← 12 road miles / 19.2 km →

Kunia ↑

DIRECTION OF TRAVEL

99 H2 ↑North Shore

750

great views!

Honouliuli Forest Reserve

93

Palehua Solar Observatory

3

Waipahu

H1

Waipahu St.

90 Waikiki →

8

Palehua Rd

military

5

Makakilo

Waipahu Plantation Village

PEARL

Fernandez Village

HARBOR

Ewa

Renton Road

sugar-mill

Ko Olina Resort golf

Ft. Weaver Road

map not to scale

Blvd.

CAMPBELL

Malakole

Oahu Railway Station

2

INDUSTRIAL

Hanua Kalaeloa

PARK

Papipi Rd.

7 Ewa Beach Park

lighthouse

Oneula Beach Park

Barber's Point

Barber's Point Beach Park

❶ ❷
❸ ❹

*W*aipahu town sure doesn't look like the idyllic place identified as such in those beautiful **C&H Sugar** commercials we see on the mainland, but is interesting just the same. If approached from Waikiki via the Farrington (90) HWY., a *right turn* onto WAIPAHU DEPOT RD. will take you uphill through the movie set-like downtown area of Waipahu, with its giant sugar mill looming above. A left turn onto WAIPAHU ST. at the mill intersection will take you past the lovingly maintained and fascinating **Waipahu Cultural Garden Park and Plantation Village**, one of Oahu's best kept secrets.

The Village consists of a museum dedicated to plantation life, as well as a beautiful collection of restored plantation houses, places of religious worship, plantation offices, and businesses representing all of the ethnic groups who have worked Hawaii's sugar plantations. Well informed, enthusiastic volunteers guide visitors through the complex. Its a great place for photographs, and the possiblities for pretty detail shots are endless, as there is so much memorabilia, –including furnishings, tools and artifacts– used throughout. A tremendous amount of love, creativity, good taste, and dedication has obviously been poured into this place, so if Hawaii's plantation history interests you even remotely, **don't miss it**. Call **677-0110** for information (donation requested).

Continue along Waipahu St. to KUNIA RD., and *turn left*. Quickly, it changes names to FT. WEAVER RD. and continues *south*. After passing MANGO TREE ROAD on the *right*, then a high school, and then a forlorn little dirt cemetery, look for KARAYAN ST. right after the cemetery. *Turn right* onto KARAYAN ST.

You've now arrived at the oddly endearing little hamlet of **Fernandez Village**, a neighborhood of small, tightly packed homes built on tiny lots, where every square inch of extra ground is given over to a riot of colorful flowers, shrubs, and blossoming trees. Minuscule homes have been embellished with gates and fences of wrought iron grill work and filigree, their decorous balconies and balustrades more befitting of epic structures on sprawling country estates than these modest structures.

If, after touring Fernandez Village you emerge at FT. WEAVER ROAD, *turn right* onto it, then make another *right turn* onto RENTON ROAD.
If you emerge from Fernandez Village at RENTON ROAD, *make a right turn* onto it.
Either way, you'll enter the shaded, quiet world of giant banyan trees, pretty homes and handsome

company buildings known as **Ewa** town. On the right, across the street from the Baptist School, **PEPPER ROW**'s large common lawn is almost hidden from street view by an enormous banyan near its center. The lovely little plantation homes that ring the perimeter all face in toward the green. Each has a ruler-straight royal palm standing guard out front. After passing the rusting sugar mill, RENTON RD. leads into an area of tiny streets lined with simple plantation cottages, crowing roosters and dogs that bark at strangers.

Beyond, you will come upon the **Hawaiian Railway Society**'s working train yard. The yard has about 40 pieces of rolling stock in its collection and includes Waialua #6, a plantation engine put together from spare parts sometime around 1918. The Oahu Railway's volunteers are currently restoring additional miles of track as well as railroad cars, preserving island history while at the same time giving residents and visitors the opportunity to ride the train on weekends. The train travels west to the Ko Olina Resort, then returns. The money earned through these rides and the sale of **souvenirs** in the rail yard **gift shop** support the ongoing effort of an extremely loyal and dedicated group of historical preservationists. For reservations and information, call **681-5461** or **833-5878**. It would be gratifying to see greater appreciation and interest shown by local businesses, like those located in nearby Campbell industrial Park, as well as the visitor industry, in the group's unwavering efforts. Closer policing of the property along the railroad's right-of-way should be a priority, as in a number of places people have used it to dump their unwanted rubbish, at times spoiling the enjoyment of the ride.

After visiting the railyard, *backtrack* along RENTON ROAD through town again to FT. WEAVER ROAD, then *turn right* onto it. The road will curve to the *left* in about **2.5 miles**, and **1 mile** after that, near its terminus, will pull past **Ewa Beach Park**. Ewa Beach is a favorite of locals and off duty military. Small but pretty, the large lawn accommodates weekend volleyball games and the ubiquitous blue tarps used to shelter picnickers from brief and sudden showers. The beach is lovely; trees provide shade for many of the picnic tables and the shoreline draws people from all over the island who come to harvest the locally famous edible seaweed. You will see few tourists here.

Backtrack about **1 mile** along FT. WEAVER ROAD to where it curves to the *right*. At this point you can go straight ahead on POHAKUPUNA RD. to visit **Oneula Beach Park**, but we suggest you pass this one up. *The area is a disgrace of rubbish and* *household discards.* Instead continue *north* on FT. WEAVER ROAD past the town of **Ewa**, to the H1 FWY. Head *west* on the H1 FWY. to the Makakilo offramp. Exit here, and drive uphill on MAKAKILO DR. After the road curves to the *right*, look for KIKIAHA ST., and *turn left* onto it. At its end, *turn left* onto UMENA ST.

The gate across UMENA ST. is normally open and a sign pleads with people not to abandon their pets here. After the gate, the road name changes to PALEHUA RD. and climbs through lovely rural hilly pasture land very reminiscent of California, first dry and golden, then becoming greener as it reaches the **Honouliuli Forest Reserve**. At different points along PALEHUA RD., three distinct views can be seen: a sweeping vista of distant Honolulu and Waikiki, the entire Ewa Plain including the island's industrial area, and the adjacent canyons descending toward the Leeward Shore.

About **1 mile** beyond the gate, a picturesque road comes in from the *right* and climbs steeply for another mile to the Forest reserve entrance. Normally the gate is kept locked, but hiking organizations schedule treks here at regular intervals. At this altitude temperatures are cool and the views memorable, but in places sheltered from the tradewinds, mosquitoes can be a problem. Don't forget your **Avon Skin So Soft**, or other repellent.

Backtrack downhill and turn right at the intersection that you will see —it has stone walls built roadside. Continue uphill to the entrance of the camp, remembering to look behind you, when safe, for great views. If the camp's road gate is open, drive up the road a short way to the curve and a lookout with dizzying views into deep gullies and of the Pacific far below. Then, backtracking to the camp road entrance, continue a short distance to road's end and the **Palehua Solar Observatory**, which offers yet another commanding view of the Pacific. The mission of this U.S. Air Force facility is to monitor all solar activity from sunrise to sunset, 365 days a year. The unit has several sophisticated telescope and computer systems to accomplish its task. Tours of the facility are available by calling the public affairs office of Hickam AFB in advance.

Return downhill to the H1 FWY., and turn onto it heading *west*. Get off at the Campbell Industrial Park/KALAEIOA BLVD. exit. **Campbell Industrial Park** is notable chiefly for being what is probably the most attractive industrial area in the country. You may want to avoid unattractive **Barber's Point Beach Park** due to the double whammy of stench resulting from both industrial

air pollution, and the offshore sewage outfall.

Backtrack along KALAEIOA BLVD. to the H1 FWY, enter the freeway and head *west*. The freeway soon ends and seamlessly joins FARRINGTON (93) HWY., as it skirts around the Waianae Mountain foothills to the sunny, dry and beautiful Leeward Shore.

TheBus
848-5555
Ask the driver for directions if unsure.

From Waikiki :
On the mauka side of Kuhio Ave., Saratoga Rd., Kalia Rd., or Ala Moana Blvd., board the #8 Ala Moana Center, the #19 Airport, #19 Airport-Hickam, or #20 Airport-Halawa Gate bus heading away from Diamond Head, to the Ala Moana Shopping Center on Ala Moana Blvd. To go to:
Waipahu/Plantation Village: transfer to the #50 Waipahu-Ewa Mill bus and alight on Waipahu Rd. near the Village entrance.
Ewa: transfer to the #50 Waipahu-Ewa Mill bus. Ride along Renton Rd. through old Ewa Town to the Oahu Railway yard.
Ewa Beach: transfer to the #50 Ewa Beach bus.
Makakilo: transfer to the #50 Waipahu-Makakilo bus.TheBus will take you all the way up to the corner of Kikaha and Hunekai Streeets. From there, its a 5 minute uphill hike to the gate at Palehua Rd.

Return:
In the opposite direction, board the #50 Honolulu-Ala Moana Center bus and ride it to Kona St. in the Ala Moana Shopping Center. Walk toward Waikiki (east) to the next bus stop marked for the #8 and #19 Waikiki-Beach and Hotels bus.

Photographs

1. Detail of Chinese cookhouse at Waipahu Plantation Village.

2. Engine #12, Oahu Railway Yard in Ewa.

3. Palehua Rd. climbs toward the Honouliuli Forest Reserve.

4. Interior of sugar plantation office at the Waipahu Plantation Village.

5. In the far distance, Waikiki and Diamond Head can be seen from Palehua Rd. No wider than a driveway all along its route, use caution here. Notice the differnece in the micro-climate between this photo and photo # 3. Both shots were taken on the same day. These two areas are only one road mile apart, yet this one is very dry and reminiscent of East Africa, while the other is green and lush.

6. Waipahu Plantation Village is tidy, handsome and rich in culture and history.

7. Ewa Beach.

8. Camp Lookout off Palehua Rd. provides sweeping views of adjacent gullies and the Pacific far below.

All photos:
Kodachrome 64

❼❽

Leeward SHORE

Clear and dry, the Leeward Shore attracts sun worshippers who know that when the sun is playing hide and seek with the clouds on the Windward Shore, it is usually sunny and bright on the Leeward Side. This also means that with far less rain, the Leeward Shore can't boast the lushness and green found elsewhere on Oahu. However, the beaches are unparalleled for their beauty and solitude, and, unprotected by offshore reefs, nature buffets the Leeward Coast with perfect surfing swells. When a storm is brewing, the foaming jet black lava shoreline north of Makaha becomes reminiscent of California's wild and isolated Big Sur.

Sunsets from this west-facing shore are always reliably magnificent, and the sight at Makaha and elsewhere of a solitary surfer silhouetted against the sunset is the perfect icon for the Leeward Coast experience. The Leeward Side is almost tourist-free, and the residents have earned a reputation for being tough and unfriendly –a tag which they thoroughly and unabashedly enjoy. But don't believe it. Just keep an eye on families having a picnic at the numberless places set aside for this purpose along the shore, or watch island fathers fishing and playing with their kids, and the true character of the Leeward Local shines through. If you encounter someone with a less than welcoming attitude, give him a big smile and a couple of friendly words, and just watch him melt.

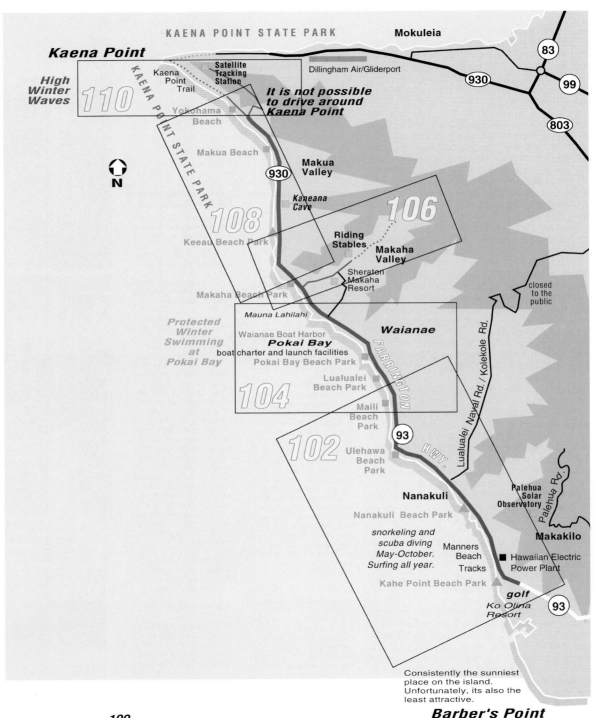

Leeward Shore Beach Parks

Source: City and County of Honolulu

Leeward Shore Beach Parks	Page	Lifeguard	Rest Rooms	Public Telephone	Picnic Tables	Camping	Night Security	Swimming	Snorkeling & Diving	Surfing	Bodysurfing	Windsurfing	Seasonal High Surf
Barber's Point BP	99		WC		XX				╲				∿
Kahe Point BP	102		WC	☎	XX	△			╲	◯			∿
Haw'n Electric/ Tracks	102				XX			S	╲	◯	◣		∿
Nanakuli BP	102	🤙	WC	☎	XX	△		S	╲	◯	◣		∿
Ulehawa BP	102		WC	☎	XX			S	╲	◯	◣		
Maili BP	102	🤙	WC	☎	XX			S	╲	◯	◣		∿
Lualualei BP	104		WC	☎	XX	△							∿
Pokai Bay BP	104	🤙	WC	☎	XX			S					
Waianae Park	104		WC	☎					╲				
Maunalahilahi BP	104		WC	☎	XX			S		◯			∿
Makaha BP	106	🤙	WC	☎	XX			S			◣		∿
Keaau BP	108		WC	☎	XX	△		S	╲				∿
Kaena Point SP	109		WC	☎				S	╲		◣		∿

Balmy trade wind weather with infrequent light showers is the rule at Barber's Point. The north trades are moist when they reach the islands, but through orographic lifting, the air is relieved of most of its moisture as it passes over eastern Oahu's Koolau Mountains. As a result, the Leeward Shore has sunny skies and few showers during a trade regime. The humidity is rarely uncomfortably high at Barber's Point, and the higher humidities are recorded during the cooler months of the year. From May through September there is practically no rain at Barber's Point.

Leeward Shore Weather

Source: US Dept. of Commerce
National Weather Service Pacific Region
Station: Barber's Point

Oahu Weather: 836-0121
Honolulu Weather: 296-1818, X1520
Surf Report: 836-1952 or 296-1818, X1521
Marine Report: 836-3921 or 296-1818, X1522

	Daily High Temperature	Daily Low Temperature	% Of Cloud Cover	Days With 0.1" Of Rain	Days With 0.5" Of Rain	Monthly Rainfall In Inches
January	79	66	35%	10	2	4.3
February	79	65	29%	7	1	2.4
March	80	66	28%	7	1	2.3
April	81	68	25%	7	1	1.4
May	82	69	25%	4	0	1.0
June	84	71	28%	3	0	0.3
July	85	72	27%	4	0	0.3
August	86	73	21%	4	0	0.4
September	86	72	16%	4	0	0.4
October	85	71	21%	5	1	1.8
November	82	70	26%	7	1	2.4
December	80	67	29%	8	2	2.8

Kahe Point to Maili
Uncrowded beaches lie end to end along Oahu's sunniest shore.

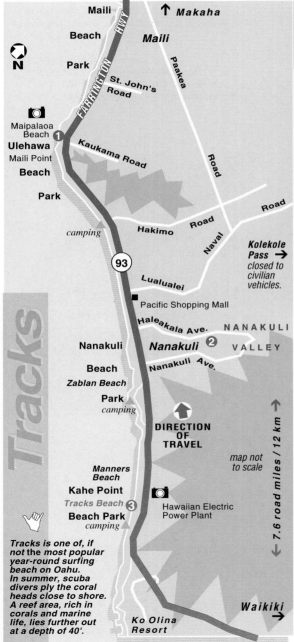

Maili
Makaha
Maili Beach Park
St. John's Road
FARRINGTON HWY
Paakea
Maipalaoa Beach
Ulehawa
Maili Point
Beach
Park
Kaukama Road
Road
camping
Hakimo Road
Naval Road
93
Road
Kolekole Pass → closed to civilian vehicles.
Lualualei
Pacific Shopping Mall
Haleakala Ave.
NANAKULI VALLEY
Nanakuli
Nanakuli Ave.
Nanakuli
Beach
Zablan Beach
Park
camping
DIRECTION OF TRAVEL
map not to scale
Manners Beach
Kahe Point
Tracks Beach
Beach Park
camping
Hawaiian Electric Power Plant
7.6 road miles / 12 km
Ko Olina Resort
Waikiki →
N

Tracks is one of, if not the most popular year-round surfing beach on Oahu. In summer, scuba divers ply the coral heads close to shore. A reef area, rich in corals and marine life, lies further out at a depth of 40'.

Tracks

LEEWARD SHORE

Dive The
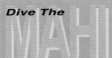
MAHI

The M/V Mahi was sunk one mile off Maili Point as the first planned artficial reef in Hawaii. At a depth of 90', the ship is intact and penetrable, and has attracted a wide variety of marine life, including sponges, corals, goatfish, tame lemon butterfly fish, blue-stripe snapper, sea turtles, rays, and a six foot moray eel that likes being hand fed. For the best and safest experience, join one of many daily dive tours that visit this spot.

*T*raveling west from **Makakilo,** the H1 FWY. ends and seamlessly joins FARRINGTON (93) HWY. As it approaches the sea, FARRINGTON (93) HWY. curves northwest toward **Kahe Point Beach Park,** which despite its name does not have much of a beach. It does offer good fishing, though, and 14 campsites with parking, A lawn area with picnic tables is located on a low bluff above the rocky shoreline. Because of the rocks, recreational swimming opportunities are poor.

Adjacent to Kahe Point Beach Park is the **Hawaiian Electric Beach Park**, also known as "**Tracks**", directly across the highway from the looming Hawaiian Electric Co. **Power Plant**. Tracks' beach is wide and sandy with a gentle slope and sandy bottom. As with all leeward beaches —the only exception being **Pokai Bay Beach Park**— the same high winter waves that bring potentially dangerous conditions and strong currents also attract plenty of surfers. **Summer** often brings beautiful little swells, making Tracks and the adjacent Manners Beach more or less reliable year-round surfing spots. At the southernmost end of Tracks, groups of scuba divers arrive in summer to make shore dives and explore the subsurface wonders. From late spring to early autumn, conditions on the Leeward Shore are reliably placid, making it very popular with families.

Next along FARRINGTON (93) HWY., **Nanakuli Beach Park** lies **1.3 miles** past the Hawaiian Electric Plant. It has a wide sandy beach, and a complete and impressive array of facilities, including a softball field, children's playground, combination volleyball/basketball courts and three restrooms. Because of its location in a residential area, it is heavily used by local families. Swimming, snorkeling and scuba diving during the non-winter months are excellent at Nanakuli, which has two lifeguard towers.

Ulehawa Beach Park is just *northwest* of Nanakuli and is the next beach park that we encounter along the shore. The lifeguard stand is manned here on all weekends, and daily during the summer. The best swimming area is located in front of the lifeguard tower. The safest area is around

②

①

Maili Point at **Maipalaoa Beach** which has a protective offshore reef.

Next along FARRINGTON (93) HWY. we encounter well maintained **Maili Beach Park**. Maili has a large parking lot and a great expanse of lawn dotted with picnic tables which overlooks the beach. More shade trees would be helpful here at midday as there are only a few, but its a great spot for a pre-sunset picnic and swim. Whatever the time of day, the beach is beautiful, with deep, clean sand. After a storm, there are often lots of tiny *puka* ("hole") shells to be found for those interested in collecting them for stringing their own necklaces.

The hill known as **Puu Mailiili** creates a distinctive rounded backdrop toward the beach's northerly end, where the most popular swimming area is located near the mouth of **Mailiili Stream**. But remember, **strong backwashes** and **forceful rip currents** are the rule in **winter** for this entire length of beach.

TheBus
848-5555
Ask the driver for directions if unsure.

From Waikiki :
On the mauka side of Kuhio Ave., Saratoga Rd., Kalia Rd., or Ala Moana Blvd., board the #8 Ala Moana Center, the #19 Airport, #19 Airport-Hickam, or #20 Airport-Halawa Gate bus heading away from Diamond Head, to the Ala Moana Shopping Center on Ala Moana Blvd. Transfer there to the #51 Makaha bus. This bus will pass every Leeward Shore beach all the way to Makaha.

Return:
In the opposite direction, board bus #51 Honolulu-Ala Moana Center and ride to Kona St. in the Ala Moana Shopping Center. Walk toward Waikiki (east) to the next bus stop marked for the #8 and #19 Waikiki-Beach and Hotels bus.

Photographs

1. At Maipalaoa Beach, local kids hunt for sea delicacies in the exposed reef at low tide.

2 . Plumeria

3. A group of scuba divers emerges from the clear turquoise summer waters at beautiful Tracks, the popular name for Hawaiian Electric Beach.

All photos: Kodachrome 64

③

Waianae

*Lualualei and Pokai Bay Beach Parks,
and the beautifully situated
Ku'ilioloa Heiau.*

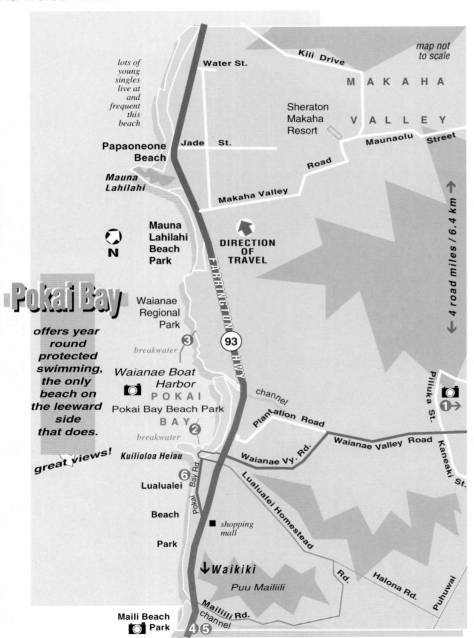

MAKAHA VALLEY

map not
to scale

*lots of
young
singles
live at
and
frequent
this
beach*

Water St.

Kili Drive

Jade St.

**Papaoneone
Beach**

*Mauna
Lahilahi*

Sheraton
Makaha
Resort

Maunaolu Street

Road

**Mauna
Lahilahi
Beach
Park**

Makaha Valley

N

**DIRECTION
OF
TRAVEL**

FARRINGTON HWY

4 road miles / 6.4 km

Pokai Bay

Waianae
Regional
Park

*offers year
round
protected
swimming,
the only
beach on
the leeward
side
that does.*

93

breakwater
③

*Waianae Boat
Harbor*

POKAI

Pokai Bay Beach Park

BAY

breakwater
②

Kuilioloa Heiau

great views!

channel

Plantation Road

Waianae Vy. Rd.

Waianae Valley Road

Piliuka St.

①➡

Lualualei

Beach

Park

⑥

Pokai Bay Rd.

*shopping
mall*

Lualualei Homestead

Kaneaki St.

↓*Waikiki*

Puu Mailiili

Rd.

Halona Rd.

Puhuwai

**Maili Beach
Park**

④⑤

Mailiili Rd.
channel

❶

*T*he distinctive rounded hill at the *north west* end of **Maili Beach Park** called **Puu Mailiili** was formerly known by the Hawaiian name of **Kalaeokakao**, which means **Goat Point**. It was named for the large numbers of wild goats which freely grazed here during the 1800's, doing great damage to the environment. First brought to Hawaii by Captain Cook in 1778, the Hawaiians protected the goats under **kapu**, which meant it was forbidden to harm them. They multiplied so rampantly under this protection that they soon were invading cultivated food crops and causing erosion on hillsides by stripping them bare of watershed plants. Things got so bad that the herds had to be destroyed.

West of Mailiili Stream, below the head of this hill, begins the **undeveloped** shore known as **Lualualei Beach Park**. Its stretches from here to **Pokai Bay**. Its rocky shoreline makes it less than ideal for recreational swimming. There is also a litter problem which spoils the area's beauty. Sand dunes separate the beach from the highway, acting as a traffic noise buffer and offering privacy at the same time.

At **Lualualei Beach Park**'s most *western* point, near the border of Pokai Bay Beach Park and Kaneilio Point, there is a small grassy park with shade trees, picnic tables and a coconut palm-lined rocky shore that is a very nice picnic/sunset **viewing** spot. From FARRINGTON (93) HWY., *turn makai* onto POKAI BAY ROAD, which like Farrington Hwy. parallels the shore and ends at nearby **Pokai Bay Beach Park**. If instead you choose to bypass little POKAI BAY ROAD as you travel up FARRINGTON (93) HWY. at this point, continue ahead, *turn makai* when you reach the entrance of **Pokai Bay Beach Park**, and drive *straight ahead* and *toward the left*. This is **Kaneilio Point**, the southern border of the park, and the location of the sacred **Kuilioloa Heiau**.

The heiau is beautifully situated on the point, surrounded on three sides by water. This historic Hawaiian place of worship and ceremony is handsomely landscaped and dramatically placed. Local people can often be found here, as well as at other heiaus throughout the islands, who informally volunteer to instruct visitors unfamiliar with the purpose and meaning of these revered places. Visitors are rightfully asked to respect the grounds. But incongruously, this particular heiau, hidden and **unknown to most visitors** who pass by, is

often overrun with fast food litter and empty beer bottles and cans left behind by those who use it as a party spot.

Pokai Bay Beach Park itself is **protected by breakwaters** from high surf and has the distinction of being the only beach on the Leeward Shore that is **safe for swimming all year 'round**. The **view** from the breakwater at the heiau end of the park is **exceptional**, especially at the end of the day when the sun sidelights the corrugations of the distant pali. But please beware that the breakwater is in disrepair and footing on its rocks and broken concrete is **precarious**. The small boat harbor inside the breakwater is used by catamaran teams for winter rowing practice, as the waters behind the breakwall are protected from the seasonal heavy surf. During summer weekends, the harbor is quite alive with small pleasure craft and fishing activity. Pokai Bay Beach park has one lifeguard tower which is manned the year around on weekends and daily from June through August. The adjacent beach on the northwest end is the **Waianae Kai Military Reservation** beach. Its use is restricted to military personnel and their families.

Across the HWY. from the Pokai Bay entrance, WAIANAE VALLEY RD. leads deep into the valley where a number of modest agricultural enterprises, such as orchid farms, thrive.

Back to FARRINGTON (93) HWY, and still heading *northwest*, the highway crosses **Kaupuni Channel. Waianae Regional Park** then appears, with its big small boat harbor. Offering poor swimming possibilities and a comparatively unattractive environment, the park does have tennis courts and a softball field. Local men with their keiki (kids) fish from the long breakwater and exhibit the kind of touching paternal tenderness with their children that seems indigenous in Hawaii.

Mauna Lahilahi Beach Park is the next stretch of sand along this shore. **Mauna** *(Mountain)* **Lahilahi** *(Thin)* rises in all of its **231'**, knife-edged splendor at water's edge at **Lahilahi Point**, providing a distinctive landmark. The beach is a sandy and comparatively safe expanse that rarely has problems with strong backwashes or rip currents, but can be turbulent when surf is up. Check with the lifeguard or locals on the beach. During the winter here —as everywhere else in Hawaii— **when in doubt, stay out.**

TheBus
848-5555
Ask the driver for directions if unsure.

From Waikiki:
On the mauka side of Kuhio Ave., Saratoga Rd., Kalia Rd., or Ala Moana Blvd., board the #8 Ala Moana Center, the #19 Airport, #19 Airport-Hickam, or #20 Airport-Halawa Gate bus heading away from Diamond Head, to the Ala Moana Shopping Center on Ala Moana Blvd. Transfer there to the #51 Makaha bus, which visits all beaches along the Leeward Shore as far as Makaha, and ride it to the intersection of Farrington (93) HWY. and Waianae Valley Road in Waianae. To visit Waianae Valley, transfer to the #75 Shuttle with the windshield sign marked "NANAKULI-MAKAHA". Service runs only once an hour. Call ahead for time schedule.

Return:
In the opposite direction, board the #75 Shuttle bus back to Farrington (93) HWY. On the makai side of the HWY., transfer to the #51 Honolulu-Ala Moana Center and ride it to Kona St. in the Ala Moana Shopping Center.

Walk toward Waikiki (east) to the next bus stop marked for the #8 and #19 Waikiki-Beach and Hotels bus.

Photographs

1. An orchid farm in Waianae Valley uses shadecloth to protect the blooms from the harsh sun.

2. A sweeping view of Pokai Bay and the Waianae Mountains taken from the bay breakwall, late in the day.

3. Waianae Harbor.

4. Maili Beach is good puka shell territory.

5. Maili Beach Park's lawn area is clean and spacious, and a great place for an evening or sunset picnic.

6. Lualualei Beach Park is sandy for much of its length, but this area, adjacent to palm-shaded picnic tables along Pokai Bay Rd., has a rocky seashore.

All photos:
Kodachrome 64

❻

❸
❹
❺

Makaha

Every surfer's fantasy beach fronts a beautiful historic valley.

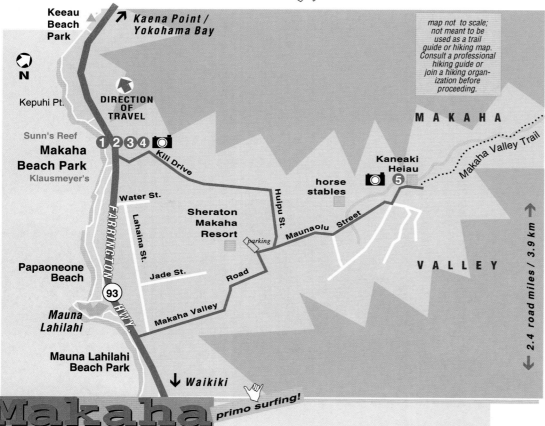

Keeau Beach Park

↗ *Kaena Point / Yokohama Bay*

N

DIRECTION OF TRAVEL

Kepuhi Pt.

Sunn's Reef

Makaha Beach Park

Klausmeyer's

① ② ③ ④ 📷

Kili Drive

Water St.

Lahaina St.

FARRINGTON HWY.

Jade St.

Sheraton Makaha Resort

parking

Huipu St.

Maunaolu Street

Road

Makaha Valley

93

Papaoneone Beach

Mauna Lahilahi

Mauna Lahilahi Beach Park

↓ *Waikiki*

M A K A H A

Makaha Valley Trail

Kaneaki Heiau

📷 ⑤

horse stables

V A L L E Y

2.4 road miles / 3.9 km

map not to scale; not meant to be used as a trail guide or hiking map. Consult a professional hiking guide or join a hiking organization before proceeding.

Makaha *primo surfing!*

❶ ❷

LEEWARD SHORE

---

*M*akaha Beach is 36 miles and one hour's drive from Waikiki. Makaha has been a mecca for surfers, boogie boarders and sun worshippers since their species have existed. Makaha's spectacular winter swells provide terrific board action and great photo opportunities. The beach is long and wide with deep sand. It has a steep slope down to the water with the usual resulting strong backwash in winter. Even at the height of seasonal erosion, Makaha is still very wide, but come summer the returning sands make it the widest strand on the Leeward Shore.

Due to its distance from Waikiki, tourists at Makaha are few and far between, despite the presence of the **Sheraton Makaha Resort** in Makaha Valley above. The beach attracts surfers and belly boarders, to be sure. But there is as eclectic a mix of beach goers as you'll find anywhere, including servicemen, local teens, retired people and a few visitors. Beach parking is roadside, with runoff from the outdoor shower often making things muddy on the southeast side of the comfort station. Swimming is safe during the summer and **wild in the winter**, when major waves, forceful backwash and a strong along-shore current demand swimmers' attention —but none of this seems to keep people out of the water. Most especially, keep eyes peeled for runaway surfboards washing ashore on incoming waves. The water is almost always wonderfully clear and the shore bottom sandy. And beach walking in the deep sand the length of Makaha Beach is great for the legs as well as a treat for the eyes. Especially beautiful and photogenic is the sight from the beach of surfers off **Kepuhi Point** catching swells as the fiery red ball of the sun sets behind them.

Across FARRINGTON (93) HWY from the beach, *turn right/mauka* onto KILI DR., which leads into lovely Makaha Valley past a bizarrely out of place condo highrise. *Turn right* at the highrise onto HUIPU DR., then *veer right* on ALA HOLO to reach the **Sheraton Makaha Resort**. Permission to visit the restored 18th century **Kaneaki Heiau** can be obtained at the **Sheraton's** front desk. The heiau is located toward the back of the valley and attracts flocks of displaying **peacocks** who come to feast on the papayas and other food offerings left at the heiau by the faithful. After leaving the Sheraton parking lot, *turn left* on ALA HOLO and in **0.1** mile, *turn right* on MAUNAOLU ST. Take it to the end. You will pass the **horse stables** on your left where you can book a guided ride into the valley. Also located on the left side of the street, across from the intersection of ALAHELE ST. (on your right) is the beginning of the **Makaha Valley Trail**. This trail passes along the west side of the Kaneaki Heiau and continues along **Makaha Stream** deep into beautiful Makaha Valley. To continue *northwest* along the coast, return to FARRINGTON (93) HWY via KILI DR., and *turn right* onto it. See **TheBus** information on previous page.

Photographs

1. The Lone Surfer.

2. Surfers squeeze in a last few rides before the sun disappears behind Kepuhi Point.

3. Young belly boarder goes airborn in backwash-created winter conditions.

4. A local catamaran team prepares for late day practice at Makaha Beach.

5. Wild peacocks feast on offerings of papaya left behind on the altar at the Kaneaki Heaiau in Makaha Valley.

All photos: Kodachrome 64

③ ④

⑤

Makaha to Yokohama Bay

Far from the maddening crowd.

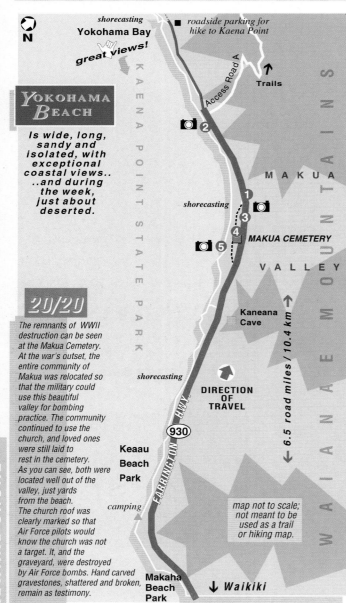

shorecasting
Yokohama Bay
great views!

N

Access Road A

Trails

roadside parking for hike to Kaena Point

KAENA POINT STATE PARK

YOKOHAMA BEACH

Is wide, long, sandy and isolated, with exceptional coastal views.. ..and during the week, just about deserted.

M A K U A

📷 2

shorecasting

1 📷
3
4
📷 5 **MAKUA CEMETERY**

V A L L E Y

Kaneana Cave

20/20

The remnants of WWII destruction can be seen at the Makua Cemetery. At the war's outset, the entire community of Makua was relocated so that the military could use this beautiful valley for bombing practice. The community continued to use the church, and loved ones were still laid to rest in the cemetery. As you can see, both were located well out of the valley, just yards from the beach. The church roof was clearly marked so that Air Force pilots would know the church was not a target. It, and the graveyard, were destroyed by Air Force bombs. Hand carved gravestones, shattered and broken, remain as testimony.

shorecasting

DIRECTION OF TRAVEL

← 6.5 road miles / 10.4 km →

camping

930
FARRINGTON HWY.

Keeau Beach Park

map not to scale; not meant to be used as a trail or hiking map.

Makaha Beach Park

↓ **Waikiki**

W A I A N A E   M O U N T A I N S

LEEWARD SHORE

Access road A at the entrance to Yokohama Bay leads up to the Kaena Point satellite tracking station and three popular hiking trails. Hiking permits required for use of the area are issued, along with free trail maps, by the Division of Forestry and Wildlife. All three trails pass through public hunting areas, so check with the DFW for current conditions. Better yet, join a Sierra Club or other organized hike.

Kuaokala Trail

The Kuaokala Trail follows the mountain ridge back toward Makua Valley for breathtaking ocean views, then descends the other side to intersect a road to the right that leads to the Mokuleia Forest Reserve. This trail is a circular route, if, every time you encounter an intersection, you continue left.

Kuaokala-Mokuleia Access Road

This road leads to the Mokuleia Forest Reserve and to the campgrounds at Peacock Flat.

Mokuleia Trail

The Mokuleia trail traverses the Mokuleia Forest Reserve for 2.5 miles, then continues onto private land.

*T*he beauty and solitude of this region is very seductive, and you may find yourself wanting to spend more time here than you originally thought. Just to be sure, stop at Makaha and pick up water and something to eat so that hunger and thirst don't cut your good time short. **There are no facilities north of Makaha.**

Drive *NW* on FARRINGTON (93) HWY. from Makaha Beach Park. You will find that **Keeau Beach Park** is not a good recreational swimming beach, as for most of its length the shore is made up of beach rock and both raised and submerged reef, causing problems for swimmers and surfers. Sharks have been a problem here as well, but when Keeau's gorgeous, perfect summer swells arrive, nothing will keep surfers out of the water. Discouraging swimming conditions like these, especially along such a lengthy span of isolated coastline, can be very attractive to those who are looking to be alone, or alone with someone special. Winter currents can be treacherous here, and the area is favored mostly by fishermen and picnickers. During calm summer days, snorkelers and scuba divers explore the underwater reef world. Keeau Beach Park has picnic tables, shade trees, a grassy area and restrooms, but no lifeguards.

About **2.0 miles** beyond Makaha you will see **Kaneana Cave** on the *mauka* side of the road. **Kaneana**, the Hawaiian **sharkman deity**, is supposed to have made his home here. The cave is hard to see as its opening faces traffic coming in the opposite direction. Kaneana Cave is huge and measures **450'** in length. But curiously in this proud and fiercely Hawaiian place, the sacred cave has been defaced extensively with spray-painted graffiti, much of it obviously local in origin. The beach along here is called **Ohikilolo**. It is made up of rock, and the only swimming possibilities are in a few shallow and protected tidal pools. It is undeveloped

---

❶

and has no facilities. Access to this shoreline is from a point below **Kaneana Cave**. This area marks the boundary of **Kaena Point State Park**.

After passing the cave, **Makua Valley** opens up on the *mauka* side of the road. Taken over by the military during World War II, the whole beautiful valley was used as a bombing range and the residents were forced to vacate their homes. Their little seaside **Protestant church**, despite being well out of the valley with its roof clearly marked so as not to be a target, was destroyed by Air Force bombs, along with many of the hand carved headstones in the adjoining graveyard. Today the **remnants** of the graveyard can be seen on the *makai* side of the highway opposite the gated road, about **0.1 mile** south of **Makua Stream**. Hiking into the valley should not be attempted due to the unknown whereabouts of **unexploded bombs** and the fact that it is still active military property.

Makua Beach, opposite the valley, is a beautiful, long sandy stretch that is safe for swimming when calm, but as with all leeward beaches, during the winter it can be treacherous. Notice the poignant memorial on the rocks at water's edge made by the distraught parents and grandparents of a little boy who was lost in the surf here. This area was used as a major location in the **1965 film** version of James Michener's novel **Hawai'i** starring Julie Andrews. After your visit, you may want to rent the film to compare what you've seen here to scenes in the movie. At Makua, winter waves crash on the beach, finding their way through openings in the rocky shoreline reefs. Especially at low tide, the receding waters form beautiful branching patterns in the sand in those places where they have removed the grains and pulled them back into the sea. This annual accretion of beach sand is responsible for exposing the rocky shoreline

❷

and diminishing the width of the beaches on the Leeward and North Shores during the winter. The sand is replaced with the coming of summer.

On weekdays this entire area can be all but deserted. There is real splendor in the open spaces and wild beauty of this shoreline, and to appreciate it fully, stop often, and look behind you as you go. Some of the best views will be at your back. The often empty road, along with the beautiful environment, imparts a feeling of solitude and discovery that many visitors hope to find in Hawaii. Needless to say, late in the day, when the sun is low on the horizon and illuminating this west-facing shore with golden light, the **views** along the coast back in the direction of Makaha are **vivid and lovely** to behold. And the further northwest along the Leeward Coast you travel, the truer this is.

Yokohama Beach is the last length of sandy beach along the Leeward Shore. Toward the center of the beach is a popular surfing spot — not for novices or those unfamiliar with the area due to a dangerous rocky sea bottom. Its always a good idea anywhere, but here especially, to **check with locals** on the beach before venturing into the water. Other winter hazards at Yokohama include sharks and a severe rip current and forceful backwash, not to mention runaway surfboards. The word is, don't go in the water if its not completely placid.

FARRINGTON (93) HWY. **ends** at Yokohama Bay. This is a **good spot for photographs**, as the surrounding area is flat and provides an unobstructed view back toward Makaha. The lava shoreline is pocked with hundreds of tiny tidepools. The wind blows fresh, saline, and clean after a thorough laundering by sun and spray over thousands of miles of open sea. The sun feels hot on unshaded skin, and except for the wind, there is only welcome silence.

From here, a trail closely follows the coastline for **2.5 miles** to **magnificent Kaena Point**. If you plan to take this hike, park your car out of the way of traffic —but not in the sand. There's no one for miles around to tow you out if you get stuck. Remove all items in the car from view before parking, but don't be seen putting anything in the trunk. If its solitude that you're after, this area is sparsely visited during the week, although its very popular with locals on weekends.

Photographs

1. Ghostly tree skeletons, victims of a brush fire, add to the mystery of lovely Makua Valley.

2. Ebony lava cliffs meet white sea foam at Pukano Point.

3. Trailing tail lights paint a pattern on the roadscape at Makua. This is a 30 second time exposure taken shortly after sunset. F16, 28mm lens.

4. Perfect little swells

5. Sharply sculpted lava along Yokohama Bay provides numberless tidepools for sea creatures, and just as many opportunities for those who hunt them.

race toward the deserted shore at Makua Beach.

All photos: Kodachrome 64

TheBus
848-5555

TheBus does not go beyond Makaha Beach. See bus information in the Waianae-Pokai Bay section, page 104.

❸
❹ ❺

The Kaena Point Leeward Shore Trail

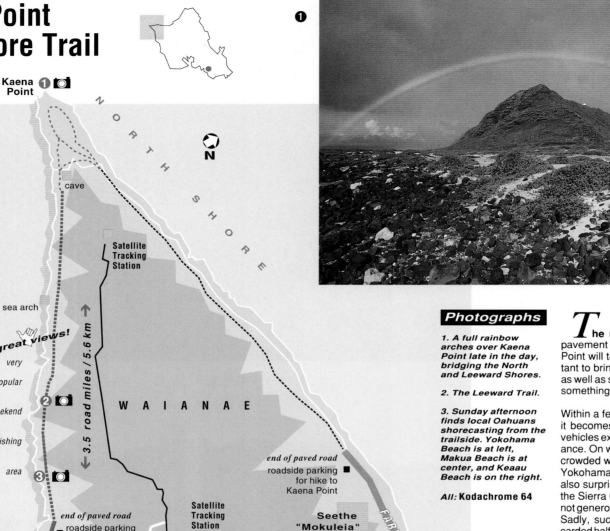

Its quite difficult on an island where uncommon beauty is commonplace, and where awe-inspiring vistas lie around every curve, to pronounce anything "the best".

However, considering the unique attributes of the Kaena Point Trails on both Leeward and North Shores, if any hike on Oahu deserves special acclaim, its this one. Actually more like a long amble than a hike, the only taxing part is carrying a full water bottle. The route follows a paved, level dirt jeep road that was originally the roadbed of the Oahu Railway. Even a ten or fifteen minute walk from road's end will be rewarding, exposing a matchless coastal vista on the Leeward side. For a complete experience, join a *Sierra Club* or *Hawaiian Trail and Mountain Club* hike.

Map labels

Kaena Point ❶ 📷

NORTH SHORE

cave

N

Satellite Tracking Station

sea arch

great views!

very popular weekend fishing area

❷ 📷

❸ 📷

← 3.5 road miles / 5.6 km →

WAIANAE

LEEWARD SHORE

end of paved road ■ roadside parking for hike to Kaena Point

Yokohama Beach

Satellite Tracking Station

end of paved road ■ roadside parking for hike to Kaena Point

See the "Mokuleia" section for details about the North Shore side of the trail.

YMCA Camp Erdman

FARRINGTON HWY.

930

MOUNTAINS

You will need a permit to hike, available from the Division of Forestry and Wildlife.

Access Road A

↑ Trails

↓ *Waikiki*

930

HAWAII

MALAMA KA AINA

map not to scale

Photographs

1. A full rainbow arches over Kaena Point late in the day, bridging the North and Leeward Shores.

2. The Leeward Trail.

3. Sunday afternoon finds local Oahuans shorecasting from the trailside. Yokohama Beach is at left, Makua Beach is at center, and Keaau Beach is on the right.

All: **Kodachrome 64**

The round trip trek from the end of the pavement at Yokohama Bay onward to Kaena Point will take about three hours. Its very important to bring water on this warm and thirsty hike, as well as sunscreen and body cover, and maybe something to eat.

Within a few yards of starting along the jeep trail it becomes evident that it is impassable for all vehicles except those with very high ground clearance. On weekends this area can be surprisingly crowded with local people enjoying the beach at Yokohama and the fine fishing beyond it. It will also surprise as extensively littered, especially if the Sierra Club or other public spirited entity has not generously volunteered recently to clean it up. Sadly, such items as fast food containers, discarded half-eaten plate lunches, empty beer cases and rusted cars are shamefully plentiful at the beginning of this otherwise exquisite trail.

The litter begins to thin out none too soon, and the hard packed, but at places deeply rutted, jeep road makes for easy walking. Old railroad ties from the dismantled Oahu Railway route are still evident at many places along the way. Short trails spur off the road, *makai*, leading the hiker to higher ground for **majestic unobstructed views** back along the Leeward Coast. This hike is especially wonderful late in the day when the accompanying photos were taken... the low angled sun paints the scene with a soft golden tint as it projects dramatic cloud and light patterns against

110

the deeply etched walls of the distant pali. Often, late afternoon showers festoon the scene with ethereal rainbows.

Mauka, the Waianae Mountains climb abruptly toward the sky, their lower flanks covered in golden grasses during the dry months, but turning emerald green with winter rains. *Makai*, you will encounter a sea arch, black smooth-bouldered beaches, snorkelers exploring the one or two shallow protected sea pools, and the eerie and primeval sound of air rushing through a blowhole. There are no sand beaches here and safe swimming opportunities are nonexistent, although the few protected tidepools *do* offer a shallow place to cool off. Close to Kaena Pt., notice the deep cave right below the path on the *mauka* side. Just past the cave, a prominent sign welcomes all to Kaena Point and outlines interesting facts and useful information.

The Kaena Point Natural Area Reserve was created in 1983, after the land had suffered decades of abuse by everything from the now dismantled Oahu Railway, which hauled sugarcane around the point from the leeward side to Waialua, to the more recent hordes of earth-chewing all-terrain vehicles. Kaena is one of the state's best examples of coastal lowland dune ecosystems.

Few of us realize the enormous impact we can have on an environment by simply being there, or by doing something as seemingly innocuous as walking on ground cover instead of a trail. Kaena Point may never fully recover as long as man is present, but by taking a few thoughtful precautions while we are there, we can help the comeback of flora and fauna alike.

In an area as wide open and exposed to the elements as Kaena Point is, healthy ground cover is critical for keeping surface sand and soil from blowing or washing away. In less than five years, more than **six feet** of sand **disappeared** from around the Kaena Point lighthouse due to ground cover destruction by jeep, motorbike, ATV and foot traffic. The closing off of Kaena to vehicular access is allowing dunes and native plants to begin recovering. We can all help this effort by not walking through plants or over the ground cover.

During **November**, the **Laysan Albatross** breeds here, and sandy areas in the Reserve are potential nesting sites. Enormous numbers of native Hawaiian plants have become extinct over the last two centuries, but Kaena's sand dunes and talus slope ecosystems cradle many native Hawaiian plant species. The reserve is also a refuge

for the very rare **Hawaiian monk seal**, and **green sea turtles** still crawl ashore as they have for eons to bury their eggs in the sand. Seabirds, including **Red-footed** and **Brown Boobies**, the **Wedge-tailed Shearwater** and **Brown Noddy** are common to the area. Humpback whales are seen breeching in the offshore waters during the winter breeding season.

Astonishing walls of water, commonly **40' in height**, and sometimes reaching an unbelievable **50'**, thunder toward the shore during the apogee of winter surf, making Kaena Point home to the consistently **largest waves in the world**. Surfers have long speculated on the possibility of

riding one of these monsters —and still living to tell the tale— but so far most have concluded it would be sheer suicide. Water conditions are very hazardous the year 'round, due to the confluence of currents around the point. Even on calm days

the **offshore currents are very powerful**. There are no sandy beaches anywhere near the point, and few places are protected enough even to get wet. Swimming is always dangerous.

The views from Kaena Point **late in the day** are wondrous, as they stretch forever into the distance along both the North and Leeward Shores. But if you plan to stay until sunset, bring a good flashlight or lantern so you can find your way back safely. See the **Mokuleia** section on page 94 for a rundown on what to expect on the North Shore side of the Kaena Point Trail.